URBAN HIGHLANDERS

URBAN HIGHLANDERS

Highland-Lowland Migration and Urban Gaelic Culture, 1700–1900

Charles W J Withers

TUCKWELL PRESS

First published in Great Britain in 1998 by
Tuckwell Press Ltd
Phantassie
East Linton
East Lothian EH40 3DG
Scotland

Copyright © Charles Withers 1998

ISBN 1 86232 040 3 (paperback)

British Library Cataloguing-in-Publication Data
A catalogue record for this book is available
from the British Library

Typeset by Hewer Text Limited, Edinburgh
Printed and bound by Cromwell Press, Trowbridge, Wiltshire

In memory of Hamish Hamilton

Contents

Figures

Figures

Tables

Tables

And did I not bid you remember, . . . that for each protagonist who once stepped onto the stage of so-called historical events, there were thousands, millions, who never entered the theatre – who never knew that the show was running – who got on with the donkey-work of coping with reality?

Graham Swift *Waterland* (1983)

Preface

Most work on Highland and Gaelic Scotland has focused upon the transformation of Highland society as the region and its population was subject, from the later seventeenth century onwards, to profound changes in economic and social relations. One of the consequences of these changes was the migration of people out of the Highlands or *Gaidhealtachd,* the Gaelic-speaking areas, in order to make a new life elsewhere. Many moved overseas, to the Americas or to Australia. But many did not leave Scotland, preferring, if they had any choice in the matter, to move to the urban Lowlands.

This book examines this group of people – urban Highlanders – in the eighteenth and nineteenth centuries in the main towns of Scotland: Glasgow, Edinburgh, Aberdeen, Dundee, Perth, Paisley, Stirling and Greenock. Two main sets of questions provide the basis to what follows. The first concentrates upon issues to do with the nature and extent of Highland-Lowland migration. Was this a mass and unstructured out-migration, for example, or something with a more precise geography? To which towns did Highlanders move? Did patterns of migration change over time? Was all such migration permanent? If not, can we recapture the rhythms of temporary migration and, even, document the mobility of those individuals for whom crofting in the Highlands demanded only a seasonal presence in the Lowlands? The second set of questions concerns the institutions of these urban Highlanders: Gaelic chapels, Highland societies, patterns of work and residence and issues to do with the use of Gaelic in urban settings. By the end of the nineteenth century, for example, there were sufficient Gaelic speakers in the urban Lowlands to justify the claim that Gaelic Scotland had two distinct geographies: one of decline within the *Gaidhealtachd* proper, and the other, a 'new' urban *Gaidhealtachd*, of growth since 1700. This book is concerned, then, to explore the processes of origin, the geography and the cultural characteristics constituting a unique chapter in the making of modern Scotland.

The book is structured in three parts. The first part, Chapters 1 and 2, examines the background to Highland migration by considering something of the wider context of population migration and migrant culture in Great Britain and Europe of which the experience of urban Highlanders

xiii

was part, and outlines in general terms the 'push' factors driving Highlanders to the cities. The second part, Chapters 3 and 4, discusses the nature of Highland-Lowland migration, both the geography of permanent movement and what can be determined of the seasonal and temporary circulation of Highland labour. Chapters 5, 6 and 7 make up the third part whose focus is upon the making of urban Gaelic life and culture. The sources available to document these issues are very variable, even within individual towns, and offer, indeed, a discontinuous insight into the questions to be explored. We know, for example, that there were permanently resident Gaelic-speaking Highlanders present in urban Scotland from the late seventeenth century and that temporary migration of Highlanders to the lowland harvests was by then well established. We can document in detail the foundation of Gaelic chapels from the later eighteenth century. But not until the 1851 Census of Scotland and the 'where born' evidence at parish level of lifetime migration can we systematically document how many Highland-born persons lived in each Lowland town, and from which Highland parish they had moved. And while we are able to record this geography of migration from the mid-nineteenth century, only from 1881, and, reliably, from 1891, can we connect evidence of Highland birthplace to ability in Gaelic within urban Scotland. In contrast, some of the documentary sources used here, notably parliamentary paper evidence, allow us to 'hear' the voices of ordinary Highlanders. For this reason, I have quoted at length from such sources to allow such people, so far as is possible, to 'speak for themselves'.

What follows does not claim to be a definitive account of this aspect of the historical geography of Scotland, or, more properly, of urban Highland Scotland. It is an attempt to synthesise a range of research by myself and others over the last fifteen years or so and, in so doing, to identify both gaps in our understanding and avenues for further work. It would be splendid to see this work built upon by others.

Charles Withers
Edinburgh
1998

Acknowledgements

My principal debt is to those researchers upon whose work I have drawn and to those colleagues and researchers who have helped in the analysis and discussion of sources. I am grateful to Tom Devine and William Sloan for their permission to draw from their work, to Anita Stevens for her examination of some of the 1891 Census material for Glasgow, and Bob Morris for comments on several of the chapters. Funds for the research were forthcoming from the British Academy via a Small Research Grant in the Humanities, the Institute of Historical Research 27 Foundation Award, the Nuffield Foundation and the University of Edinburgh, and I acknowledge this support with thanks. Research seminars on aspects of the material discussed here have been given to audiences in the universities of Aberdeen, Cambridge, Dundee, Edinburgh, Glasgow, Liverpool, London and Oxford and I am grateful for their comments. Ian MacDonald in Aberdeen has generously shared with me his detailed researches on the Gaelic community in that town even when our views on Gaelic church history have differed: his *Men and Ministers in the Aberdeen Gaelic Chapel* (privately printed, 1997) unfortunately arrived too late for its findings to be incorporated here.

I owe a great deal to those archivists and library staff who have patiently answered my many queries and advised upon source material: the Keeper of the Records and staff of the Scottish Record Office, the National Library of Scotland, and archive offices in Stirling, Dundee, the Sandeman Library, Perth, staff in the Mitchell Library in Glasgow, in the Central Library, Edinburgh, and in the libraries and special collections of the universities of Aberdeen, Edinburgh and Glasgow. The editors and publishers of journals and books in which some of the material presented has been previously published have been generous in allowing me to include parts of it here: I am grateful in this respect to the editors of *Northern Scotland*, of the *Scottish Geographical Magazine*, and *Scottish Gaelic Studies*, to Routledge Ltd. and the editors of *Social History*, Academic Press Ltd. and the editor of the *Journal of Historical Geography*, to Professor William Gillies and Edinburgh University Press to draw from material in *Gaelic and Scotland* (1989), and to Dr Alan Baker and Cambridge University Press to draw from work in my 1991 book, co-edited with Gerry Kearns, *Urbanising Britain: essays on class and com-*

munity in the nineteenth century. I also acknowledge the permission of Picador Publishers Ltd to quote from Graham Swift's *Waterland,* and that of the editor of the Abertay Historical Society to draw from my 1986 work on the Highland population in Dundee and in Perth. I am grateful to the Librarian of the University of Edinburgh for his permission to cite from Dr Robin Lobban's 1969 unpublished PhD thesis 'The migration of highlanders into lowland Scotland c.1750–1890, with particular reference to Greenock'. I have sought, through the University of Stirling's Library and Department of History, to contact Dr Jean Mackenzie in order to seek permission to cite from her 1987 unpublished PhD 'The highland community in Glasgow in the nineteenth century' and I hope my citing this work as I have pays due acknowledgement to her scholarship.

I am grateful to Julie Lawson, Sarah Stevenson and to Deborah Hunter of the National Galleries of Scotland for assistance in producing the cover illustration and I acknowledge with thanks the permission of the National Galleries of Scotland to reproduce as the cover illustration a detail from Thomas Annan's photograph, 'Close No. 29 Gallowgate'. Nicola Exley and Anona Lyons produced the maps and I am very grateful to Josie Priestley for typing and revising much of the manuscript. I owe a great deal to John Tuckwell for his patience as publisher and for his helpful comments. Finally, thanks to my wife and children who have had to live with me and with this book for too long.

PART ONE

The Background to Highland Migration

CHAPTER I

Introduction: Migration and Migrant Culture in Britain and Europe, 1700–1900

By the end of the nineteenth century, there were so many Highland-born persons in Glasgow that the *Oban Times* reckoned that city the 'Capital of the Highlands'. Some were the Glasgow-born children of Highland parents, a few others only temporarily resident. Many were first-generation migrants from the largely Gaelic-speaking rural north and west of Scotland. Like their counterparts in other towns across Scotland, they had left their native parishes as agricultural changes forced them off the land towards the opportunities and uncertainties of city life. This urban Gaelic diaspora was evident, too, in the foundation of specific migrant social institutions such as Gaelic chapels of worship and Highland societies. The circumstances of the urban Highlander in the eighteenth and nineteenth centuries – the subject of this book – are, however, one chapter in a much bigger story.

Population mobility has been a significant theme in the making of modern Britain and Europe. Migration in the pre-industrial European countryside was commonplace. Agricultural rhythms determined the seasonal re-location of labour; farm servants moved at the end of service, upon marriage and at re-employment through hiring fairs. Much of this movement was local and temporary in nature. Longer-distance movement also occurred, especially of apprentices to trades and skilled labour. From the later seventeenth century onwards, however, the principally local systems of migration and circular mobility that predominated throughout Europe were replaced by systems of longer-distance permanent population migration from countryside to town. These systems originated in changes in the nature and customary practices of rural society as well as the opportunities presented by growing urban economies. Such rural to urban movement was a crucial means to population increase for an urban Europe which, in general, did not either effect limitation upon high rates of urban mortality or control fertility until the later nineteenth century. More is known of the nature and extent of such migration for the countries of north-west Europe than elsewhere, particularly of England, France, Sweden and other countries bordering the North Sea, and our understanding of the bigger picture has been

complemented by numerous local studies. For Britain, work on population migration in the eighteenth and nineteenth centuries has concentrated upon the in-movement of rural labour to towns, and upon the
migration of Irish-born into urban England as well as upon the temporary
migration of rural labour.

What follows, then, in regard to the Highland-Lowland migration of
population from about 1700 and the creation of communities of urban
Highlanders in urban Scotland must, in general, be seen as part of the
transformation of 'old order' Europe, and, more specifically, should be
considered as part of the making of modern Scotland. A range of work on
the topic has already been done, by myself and others, and in one respect,
therefore, this book is a work of synthesis. It also extends such work,
however, by attempting to assess more precisely than hitherto both the
geography of movement and the nature of Highland migrant culture. This
chapter briefly outlines the wider context of which this specific study is
part, and examines Highland and migrant culture in relation to work on
culture and identity, including Gaelic and Highland Scotland.

MIGRATION, MOBILITY AND SOCIAL TRANSFORMATION: SCOTLAND AND EUROPE IN COMPARATIVE PERSPECTIVE, 1700–1900

Scotland moved rapidly from relative economic 'backwardness' to become urbanised and industrialised during the eighteenth and nineteenth
centuries, and experienced as it did so a pronounced redistribution of
population from the Highlands and, to a lesser extent, from the north-
east lowlands and its Borders region, to the cities of the central Lowlands.
Scotland had the fastest rate of urban growth in Europe between 1650 and
1850. By 1700, Scotland was more highly urbanised than Germany, by
1750 more than France and by 1850, with 32 per cent of its inhabitants in
towns of 10,000 or more people, was second only to England and Wales.[1]
This urban growth was fed not just by an influx of Highlanders but, and
chiefly, by large numbers of displaced Lowland peasants and rural
labourers and, from the 1790s, by the Irish who were always more
numerous than the urban Highland-born. It was urban growth largely
dependent upon permanent re-distribution of population. But two points
should be noted. First, such permanent migration marked a departure
from earlier existing trends of short-term short-distance migration
throughout Europe. Second, the terms conventionally used to document
migration – permanent, temporary, seasonal, stepped or step-wise – do
not always adequately describe the diversity of population mobility and
they are not at all useful in explaining cause of movement.

4

Broadly, permanent migration is used to describe those who make what must, from the administrative records available, be considered an intended definitive move. Often, because sources record only parish of birth and the place of enumeration, as in the Census records for Britain from 1851, such permanent migration is considered 'life-time migration' and conceived of as a direct move from one place to the other. Yet such migration was often made up of several shorter moves, often from countryside to village and from village to small town before location in the city, and such stepped migration may have taken longer than any direct move to the towns. Even then, when assessment of permanent migration may be presumed certain for those non-city-born people with urban employment and residence, the distinction between 'permanent' and 'temporary' migration is hard to determine for those visiting the city and perhaps only briefly resident. Temporary or seasonal migration is more easily understood, at least conceptually, and the terms 'circulation' and 'mobility' are often used to describe the regular movement of labour as part of established social and economic systems.[2]

With these working definitions in mind, the permanent re-location in towns and cities of Scotland's rural populations comes as a relatively late feature of the country's migration history.[3] Temporary migration within the countryside was a pervasive feature of Scottish life, the principal cause being service, either domestic or in husbandry. Hiring of servants for periods of six months or longer ('long hire') persisted in Scotland until well into the nineteenth century – long after it had been replaced in most of England, for example, by wage labour – maintaining a pattern of frequent, short-distance movement chiefly discernible from testimonials, certificates of religious and moral acceptability issued to movers from parish authorities.[4] Regional wage and price differentials were quite pronounced within different parts of the Lowlands, and still more so between the Highlands and the Lowlands.[5] Opportunities for migration between the two regions was also encouraged by social change in the rural Lowlands, notably by a reduction in the numbers of sub-tenants or cottars from 1780 which diminished the main reserve labour force, and by the demands for harvest labour. Poor Law restrictions which meant that the able-bodied poor were ineligible for relief would often mean that failure to secure a position as a farm servant led to a decision to move to the towns. For example, two questions in the 1844 Report of the Royal Commission on the Poor Law (Scotland) asked, 'Have any farm servants who have become unfit for hard work any difficulty in obtaining dwellings in your parish? And do you know any instance of such persons, who, on this account, have migrated to country towns or to the large towns?'. Approximately 30 per cent of the replies across Scotland stated that farm servants had difficulty in obtaining dwellings and that this was a determinant of migration within the countryside as well as of a smaller flow to the towns. The problem was most widespread in the Border counties, the southern Highlands and in the North East, including Angus and parts of east Highland Perthshire, where opportunities for employment in local textiles were also a cause of migration.[6] The mobility of Lowland farm labour was, in general, commonplace yet short-distance, a pattern that was widely recalled and still in operation in places as the system died out in the Lowlands in the first half of the twentieth century.[7]

The creation in Scotland of what Jones has termed a 'marginalised, seasonal labour reserve'[8] had different implications for the south and east farming Highlands than it did for the populations of the largely crofting parishes of the north and west Highlands. It was a characteristic, too, of much of western Europe. Seasonal migration from Alpine villages to the farming plains of northern Italy, for example, involved up to one-third of the mountainous districts' population during the later seventeenth century; the grain districts of northern Spain employed French and Spanish pastoralists from the Pyrenees, and, on a smaller scale, seasonal pasturing was commonplace between lowland and upland pastoral economies.[9]

The other type of temporary movement common until the eighteenth century was that of apprentices indentured between the ages of approximately 12 and 16 years to urban craftsmen and tradesmen for periods of between three and seven years. Scottish evidence broadly parallels that of England: longer-distance apprentice movement to the capital declining in importance over time; persistent regional migration source areas to smaller centres of population. Casual mobility for work was pronounced among groups such as drovers, chapmen and masons: the equivalent of itinerant specialists such as *colporteurs* and *Wanderbuschen* on mainland Europe.[10] Likewise, what is known of vagrant mobility in late seventeenth- and eighteenth-century Scotland suggests a predominance of younger single males similar to English patterns: movement of whole families was unusual except in periods of severe dearth. There is for Scotland, as for Germany, Norway and Ireland, much evidence of temporary movement to alleviate hunger following bad harvests: in the 1620s, 1690s, 1741, 1782 and 1799, for example.[11] It is clear in that respect that the schemes of forced labour mobility used to relieve hardship following the Highland potato famine of 1847–1856 would not have been entirely unfamilar to Highland populations used, if only on local or even familial scales, to seeing the Lowlands as a means to seek respite from straitened circumstances at home. There is some evidence, for example, that beggars moved as groups within the northern Highlands to central Tayside and that others moved as groups from Lowland parishes to the towns, but it is not possible either to identify numbers or chart their movement exactly.[12]

The circulation of labour mobility is better understood (because better documented) in the nineteenth century. Lucassen, for example, has concentrated upon temporary migration in the 'North Sea System', principally in the Netherlands and in adjoining areas. Important 'pull areas' for labour in north-west Europe about 1800 were the Paris basin and East Anglia in England, while comparable areas in the south were Castile, the Catalonian coast, Languedoc, Provence, the Po valley and central Italy. Such systems did not develop in eastern Europe until the 1830s and 1840s. Although the numbers involved and the specific nature and duration of seasonal employment varied within these major systems, they share a number of features. Most movement was for harvest work, a feature apparent in Britain in the large numbers of Irish-born from the later eighteenth century and in Scotland with the Irish and Highlanders. Migrant labour in the Paris basin and to Castile in the early nineteenth century also centred on the harvest with a variety of other non-agricultural pursuits. Castile was served by large numbers of labourers from pastoral Galicia. Migrant labour was an economic necessity for both Castilian and Galician peasants, and in terms of such dependency as well as in the seasonal nature of movement, there are close parallels with Highland Scotland and with parts of the Lowlands where arable farming was less common. Indeed, within each of these European systems, migrant labour commonly came from mountainous regions with a predominantly pastoral economy to grain-growing lowland districts and was prompted by income needs rather than by direct population pressure. There are some exceptions to this. In Ireland in the 1820s and in parts of Germany in the 1830s, for example, as well as in Highland Scotland, there is evidence of increased seasonal migration as a response to numbers growing beyond the capacity of the local subsistence economy. And not all such movement was of rural labour. In the North Sea system, seasonal urban employment seems to have been relatively unimportant excepting the movement of Finnish labour to help build St Petersburg and of Swedes from Dalecarlia to Stockholm in the eighteenth and nineteenth centuries. In contrast, large cities within most other other west European migratory labour systems – those centring upon Paris, Madrid and northern Italian towns, for example – drew in large numbers of construction and service workers.[13]

By its very nature, temporary migration is hard to quantify. Knowing precisely the numbers involved, for Highland Scotland or anywhere else, is perhaps less important than understanding that such mobility was not a consequence of the break-up of rural society but rather a means to maintain it in the face of change. For the Highlands, the persistence of seasonal labour circulation was both the result of what Jones has called 'the abrupt impact of capitalist influences . . . on a primitive clan-based mode of production' and of what Devine considers 'a vivid demonstration of the strength and resilience of an old-established peasant society'.[14] Through such migration, rural regions throughout Europe were closely connected with neighbouring urban economies. Referring to the Hebrides in general at the start of the nineteenth century, one commentator noted how 'the population is so thinly scattered, and the means of subsistence so limited . . . that regular and stated employment cannot always be procured: and accordingly the young men run to canal and road-making in other districts, and the young women go as maid-servants to Inverness, Greenock and Glasgow, and thus deprive their own islands of their most active and most useful hands for a series of years'.[15] For several reasons, therefore, we should not straightforwardly equate temporary migration with ignominious poverty and rural isolation. Temporary movement was an important means of monetary income and familiarised many with social customs beyond their native parishes. Throughout Europe, such migration had an impact upon age at marriage and proportions marrying and, thus, upon marital fertility and overall population totals, even if the exact nature of the impact cannot always be determined. The picture we must hold of rural Europe in this period is, then, one both of considerable rural movement rather than that enduring but now discredited image of a 'static' countryside, and of regional economies connected one to another through such population movement. It is likely, then – and these are issues explored further in what follows – that those permanently resident migrant Highlander communities that we can identify in urban Scotland by the later eighteenth century were underlain by circuits of temporary mobility. Further, the category 'permanent' migrant, of Highlanders and others, would certainly have embraced a variety of circumstance and meaning for those resident in the city, including the possibility of return migration.

Accurate quantification of permanent population relocation within Scotland becomes possible only from 1851. Osborne and others have shown accelerating net movements from northern and southern Scotland into the urban-industrial Lowlands: net in-movement to the western counties of Dumbarton, Renfrew and Lanark totalled 81,512 persons in 1851, for example, with a further 28,524 persons as net-movers into the Lothians. The principal areas of supply were the Highland counties (Argyll, Ross and Cromarty, Inverness-shire and Sutherland) which together shed 48,787 persons, and the south-west of Scotland. By 1901, net in-migration to the western Central Lowlands totalled 168,383 persons, with 63,709 moving into the Lothians. In contrast to mid-century, net migration from the counties of north-east Scotland was much greater: 52,825 as opposed to

2,066 in 1851. This increased level of permanent migration, the result of farm enlargement and a shift in parts of the north-east toward capitalised diarying and grazing, occurred alongside increased emigration from the region.[16] In understanding the facts of Highland migration and knowing the numbers of urban Highland-born in Lowland towns – two important matters in what follows – we must recognise that such movement was part of a much bigger picture. Conversely, the study in detail of Highland-Lowland migration can offer insight into these wider issues. Permanent migration within nineteenth-century Britain was chiefly towards urban centres, dramatically so in the case of movement within England and Wales towards London, which drew in one degree or another from all parts of the British Isles, but such movement was notable, too, in migration to Liverpool, Manchester, the south Wales coalfields, and, in a series of numerically smaller and shorter distance flows of labour, in movement to Sheffield, the textile towns of Lancashire and the industrial towns of north-east England. In France, Paris similarly dominated permanent migration in the nineteenth century. Many of these migration patterns, notably to the capital cities, have been shown to be remarkably persistent over time.[17]

We should not forget, however, that such migration is not simply a 'fact' to be enumerated and inspected by later researchers. Migration, especially if permanent, was a harsh and unwelcome reality for many. If it is true that most such migration involved individuals, usually young persons, at least in the initial movement, and families only later and that it was for many an economic necessity, it is still the case that such move-ment took people away from their family, families from their commu-nities, and, in the case of overseas migration and Highland-Lowland migration, communities away from their home and country. It is not always possible to capture that experience, however, to 'hear' as it were the voices of real individuals caught up in those processes later unemo-tionally termed 'rural change and urban growth'. A range of recent work using emigrants' letters, notably of the Irish in nineteenth-century Aus-tralia, has documented something of the emigrant experience: of longing for home and family, the strange and harsh nature of the new environ-ment, the requests for money or the despatch home of hard-won sums, the fear of dying in a foreign land.[18] There is some comparable evidence for the Highlander overseas. In the work of James Hunter and David Craig, for example, the voices of the descendants of Highlanders forced to leave have been used to articulate a powerful collective memory of the facts of departure, the separation from friends, the 'lament' at loss of home.[19] It is also clear that, in an important sense, the *idea* of the *Gaidhealtachd* as a Gaelic culture region was enlarged through this experience, however unwelcome such forced migration was, and that there was, for many, a new Highlands being made overseas that was connected with the old through correspondence and by returning emigrants.[20] One of the issues explored here is whether there is anything similar for the Highlander in urban Scotland. Given that many may be presumed to have been familiar with the Lowland economy and to have maintained connections with fellow Highlanders in the city and with their native parishes, it is reasonable to suppose that some sort of tie would be apparent in migrant letters or personal recollections. For the very same reason, however, perhaps we should not expect this to be, if some urban Highlanders intended returning home and if the distances between those resident in the urban Lowlands and the Highlands were not that large, however great the difference in way of life.

What is important to recognise is that the personal circumstances of the vast majority of urban Highlanders are not documented – either in family letters or in official records – and must, therefore, remain uncertain. A range of sources has been explored here in examining the migration and migrant culture of urban Highlanders: published and unpublished census material, manuscript records from a variety of institutions and official papers. In most instances the picture we are given is an aggregate one, not of individuals or groups of persons in detail. It is just that lack of individual clarity that is symbolised in the photograph by Thomas Annan which forms the cover illustration of the book. An unknown man and woman, he wearing a Highland bonnet and she a tartan shawl, stare out at the camera. They are, momentarily, fixed and visible in lives of movement otherwise hidden from us. The children, restless at being asked to hold a pose, have moved and are blurred in consequence. There were many Highland-born in Glasgow's Gallowgate in the 1840s but they, like the people Annan photographed, either remain unknown to us or are at best, like the children here, captured only in fuzzy outline as flitting shadows in the wynds and lanes of Scotland's towns. Iain Crichton Smith, the Gaelic poet, noting that 'The past's an experience that we cannot share', has written of just this vestigial presence in his poem 'You Lived in Glasgow':

> I left you, Glasgow, at the age of two
> and so you are my birthplace just the same.
> Divided city of the green and blue
> I look for her in you, my constant aim
> to find a ghost within a close who speaks
> in Highland Gaelic.[21]

Just how many 'ghosts in Highland closes' did speak Gaelic is discussed towards the end of the book, using the 1891 Census records.

The question of language and of being able to 'hear' urban Highlanders' voices extends also to that language of official scrutiny and
enumeration which provides the source material for much of this book.
The urban Highland presence was not entirely silent and ghostly. In the
course of numerous investigations into the social and religious condition
of the Scottish population in the nineteenth century, we are afforded some
insight into the lives of ordinary Highlanders or of those acting on their
behalf, both as they gave testimony to Poor Law commissioners or to
religious authorities, for example, or, more commonly, as such authorities recorded their opinions about Highlanders and others in the city. I
have drawn upon such material here in order to record something of the
Highlanders' voice and have sought where possible to place such commentary in its wider context. Specifically, this has the purpose of adding,
where possible, an individuality to the general character of migration and
migrant culture and of letting Highlanders speak for themselves. More
generally, however, we must be alert to the fact that such enquiries were
directed at all persons in Scotland and were begun from moral and
political concerns about the state of the nation, not just of a particular
migrant group. Even with such personal testimony as we have here, it is
not always easy to capture the meanings that migration had in the past, to
know exactly how Highlanders were regarded by others, or to understand
how one's identity in the urban Lowlands – as a Harris man, as a shipyard
labourer or domestic servant, as a Gaelic chapelgoer or in other ways –
was made and negotiated in everyday life.

URBAN MIGRANT CULTURE AND HIGHLAND IDENTITY

A range of work has discussed, with regard to British and European cities
and especially for the nineteenth century, the existence and persistence of
urban migrant populations.[22] The migrant urban Irish figure centrally in
these accounts, partly because of their distinctiveness and partly because
their place of origin is so easily defined. We are told, for example, of the
Irish in London that they possessed a 'cohesive way of life' based upon the
extended family, common use of particular institutions, residential concentration in certain districts and shared occupational characteristics.
Most Irish lived, it has been claimed, 'outside and below the social
organisation of the communities in which they lived'.[23] The Irish dom-
ination of particular occupations or levels of employment – what the 1836
Report on the State of Irish Poor termed 'the lowest dependents of
manual labour' – is confirmed in most studies, a fact which some have
seen as part of an ethnic division of labour in the development of urban
capitalist society.[24] If Irish migrant distinctiveness was made in part

through occupation, so, too, it was apparent in religion: 'In direct contrast to the English workers, . . . the Irish avidly pursued their religion, providing them with a source of unity and an emotional escape from the deprivation of their ghettos'.[25] And the presence in many English industrial cities of what contemporaries referred to as 'Irish town' or 'Little Ireland' was considered a further source of Irish distinctiveness. Questions of residence, employment and institutional affiliation have been considered significant in the study of other urban migrant groups. In contrast to the Liverpool Irish-born, for example, the Welsh-born there were considered by their hosts 'industrious', 'enterprising' and a 'steady and sober race', for whom, as in London, the chapel was of central importance.[26]

The extent to which these migrant groups saw themselves as distinct and acted in various ways to maintain that distinctiveness was matched by the ways in which they were perceived by their hosts as 'Other'. Blacks in nineteenth-century urban Britain were viewed as an almost subhuman underclass in the context of prevalent racial theories, for example, and the Irish were seen by many contemporary commentators as racially inferior: part of a wider belief in this period in the intrinsic superiority of the white over the coloured skin, the Anglo-Saxon over the Celt, the imperialising 'West' over the colonised 'Rest'.[27] Such racialised notions and the claims of those ethnological 'sciences' that underpinned them (like craniometry: attributing intellectual capacity and social development to skull shape and size so as to suppose the white man the 'most developed'), are alone insufficient, of course, to explain that general sense of 'outcastness' with which the migrant Irish (and others) were viewed. But taken together, issues of occupational class, nationality, religion and race tended to identify the Irish migrant in the minds of the English and especially in the minds of moralising social commentators of the nineteenth century as 'a people set apart and everywhere rejected and despised'.[28]

In general terms, this book shares something of this tradition of enquiry: the sources used are similar, there is a shared interest in the nature of Highland migrant culture, and attention is paid to particular institutions, notably to Gaelic chapels, and the extent to which they offered a means to migrant distinctiveness. But for several reasons, this book also differs from and extends such work. Firstly, it is clear that whilst migrant groups may have been distinct in language, religion or occupation from others in the city, migrant populations were also themselves split along lines of class and status. How true was this of the Highland populations in Scotland's cities in the past? How far can we trace kin or parish loyalties amongst urban Highlanders? Did such issues affect migration flows? Given the largely clan-based and familial nature of Highland society, it is reasonable to ask such questions in relation to migrant groups not just moving from different parts of the Highlands but with varying social mix and with some persons perhaps having prior experience of urban life or expectation of support from kin already established in the Lowlands. Allowing for such differences *within* the migrant populations is important: without it we may be condemned to a simple relativism – 'hosts' (Same) and 'migrants' (Others) – far removed from the more complex circumstances of migrant identity and city life.

Secondly, it is possible to admit that migrant identity meant more to individuals or particular groups of people than simply having, or not having, certain attributes: being from Skye, speaking Gaelic, going to Gaelic religious services, living in Glasgow's Gallowgate with other Highlanders, and so on. Such issues are sometimes neglected in studies where migrant 'culture' or 'identity', even 'migrant community', are terms used to describe presumed shared interests consequent upon birth-place or a commonly understood language. One overview of the Irish in nineteenth-century Britain, for example, has referred to 'their reluctance to integrate and the host society's reluctance to accept' as functions of a 'cultural distance' between the two groups, a distance evident in language and institutions as 'the simple manifestations of group identity not uncommon among many immigrant groups in many lands'.[29] Yet people integrate with others or separate themselves from others for reasons that may have nothing to do with being a migrant. Migrant identity can be seen, then, not as fixed or as something that one loses as, for example, one drops one's language and becomes 'assimilated'. It may be possible to consider migrant identity as *relative* rather than absolute, as dependent upon circumstance and upon how some persons might seek solidarity with others like them (as fellow Gael or as Lewis-man or as Dundonian), yet distance themselves from other Highland-born persons not in similar jobs or in the same congregation.

In what follows, then, I do not see migrant culture as something shared, uniform and 'traditional', nor would I wish to see migration as a simple means of cultural 'assimiliation' into a society wholly different. Rather, the question of migrant culture is treated not as a rigid social 'thing' that migrants and others either had or did not have, but as a dynamic and mediating mechanism between a largely Gaelic speaking and rural social system being transformed in a variety of ways, and an urbanising society itself subject to great change. Migrant culture is conceived of here as being continually made and re-made, as something differently lived and expressed according to the social status of migrants, the beliefs they brought to the cities and the alliances they made there. Whichever particular Highland institutions were established or cultural traits practised should be seen not as essential characteristics of a displaced people, but as attempts at making sense of the world urban Highlanders lived in. For some, this might mean a sustained attachment to cultural beliefs they brought with them to the cities, as for others it might mean a wholesale and conscious rejection of their background, or support by non-Highlanders. Consider, as a brief illustration, the examples of Alexander Campbell of Hallyards and Angus Mackay, both members of the Gaelic Club of Gentlemen, begun in Glasgow in 1780. Of Campbell, we are told that he, 'like many others of the same name who have "come out of the Highlands"', was the architect of his own fortune; having, through unwearied activity, high probity, and great mercantile ability, raised himself to the head of one of those leading West India houses which were at that period in the ascendant in Glasgow'. Mackay, in contrast, was elected to the position of piper in the Club in 1798. As the summary history of the Club noted, Mackay appears to have required 'other *considerations* on taking office than the mere salary and Highland toggery formerly given'. Simply, 'the married men present promised to recommend him to their ladies as a good grocer!'[30] (original emphasis). A shared identity in being Glasgow businessmen 'come out of the Highlands' was, we may speculate, reinforced by this common institutional bond. Campbell was a merchant of some standing, whilst Mackay owed what commercial success he had to a wider network of Highland wives. Both men were urban Highlanders but their lives were shaped by circumstances quite other than being migrants. We must admit, too, that migrant bodies themselves made for differences within the urban Highland population. This is clear in the several associations reflecting origins in different parts of the Highlands that were set up in the later nineteenth century. The Mull and Iona Association, established in 1866, can be used to make this more general point:

> The objects of the Association shall be, to afford natives of Mull and Iona, resident in Glasgow, an opportunity of meeting frequently together, to cherish their native attachments, and to give mutual assistance in advancing each other's interest in the city and elsewhere; the collecting and preserving of the literature [of] those Islands; and to render assistance in special cases of distress to natives, whenever the Association considers itself in a position to do so.[31]

In one sense, this Association was actively constituting a very precise Highland identity. In another, it will be shown to be one of dozens of such bodies each constructing its own idea of Highland culture in Glasgow. This book attempts to discern how much urban Highlanders 'made themselves' in these complex ways as well as being made by the nature of city life.

This intrinsic diversity within the idea of Highland culture finds support not just in that work which sees terms such as 'community' and 'identity' as complex and nuanced rather than absolute categories,[32] but in recent work that has examined both Gaelic identity and what may be called the 'New' Highlanders. Macdonald's discussion of contemporary Gaelic culture in the Highlands is a matter of local anthropology: 'an ethnographic study of cultural identity in a community which I call Carnan . . . on the Isle of Skye . . . I look at ways in which local people express their senses of belonging, and in particular at their responses to Gaelic language policies'.[33] Her work is also concerned with the position of Gaelic in Scotland more generally, with that contemporary Gaelic 'renaissance' evident in Gaelic pre-school play groups, new policy statements for the language and increased awareness of Gaelic's place in Scottish culture. The book has a yet wider purpose in considering how the Highlands and the Highlander have been historically 'imagined' and are now being 're-imagined' as part of this renaissance. Gaelic culture or aspects of it have for long been considered 'authentic' and 'traditional' in writings about the Highlands in the past, and, in turn, 'In the Gaelic renaissance the Scottish Highlands are cast – not for the first time – as a repository of 'real' Scottish identity'. As Macdonald notes:

> Highlanders are regarded as having the right ingredients of 'a people': that is, a history, a culture, a community and a language. At the same time, however, 'real life' Highlanders are often thought to be somehow alienated from their true identity and out of touch with what ought to be their authentic way of life. Moreover, they may also find themselves assumed to be ill-educated rural rustics, bogged down in their own primitive culture.[34]

Like Macdonald, I am not claiming here that migrants brought with them an 'essential' Highland culture or Gaelic identity, or even arguing that there is or has been such a thing. As I hope to show, migrants came from a region and economy with a long record of connections with 'the outside world' and were members of a culture that was never internally cohesive, however much the mythic construction of Highland Scotland as clannish, Gaelic-speaking and isolated has been allowed to determine otherwise in people's minds.[35]

Jedrej and Nuttall have also shown the question of identity to be a matter of considerable and contested significance in the modern Highlands. One of the most notable features of life in contemporary rural Scotland is a reversal of the population loss through migration that has characterised Scotland since the later eighteenth century. This rural repopulation is not everywhere the same in either extent or effect: the rural Borders continue to shed population, for example. But in some parts of the western Highlands, such as Skye and Kyle of Lochalsh District, the 1980s and 1990s have witnessed one of the highest population growth rates in the United Kingdom. The recent incoming in large numbers of 'white settlers', usually but not always affluent people from England (or perceived as such), has been accompanied by debates about loss of 'native identity' and the debasement of 'traditional' Highland culture. It is interesting in this respect how the rhetorical force of the term 'white settlers', used of many incomers into the Highlands, is clearly dependent upon a self-image (albeit unstated) as 'black native', a colonial position-ing that supposes an ethnic purity that is simply denied in any proper understanding of the region's history. As Jedrej and Nuttall note, who is a 'local'? What do we mean by terms like 'incomer' and 'native'? What, exactly, is the 'local community'? These terms cannot, they claim, be given straightforward analytic meanings: rather, 'the vocabulary of 'locals' and 'incomers' is a complex and deeply-embedded metaphor providing the terms through which people express and give meaning to the experiences which constitute their lives'.[36]

For just these reasons, I have tried where possible to avoid the use of terms like 'mainstream culture' or 'host culture'. I have used more general, even slightly 'loose' terms like 'migrant population' and 'migrant group' in describing the urban Highlanders' experience rather than arguing for a precision in relation to 'migrant community' and 'migrant culture' which the facts do not support. In one important regard, however, I have been very precise: the definition of the Highlands as a source area for migration. Eighteenth- and nineteenth-century com-mentators understood the Highlands to be that region where Gaelic was prevalent or commonly spoken and, in those terms, the *Gaidhealtachd* embraced the north-west mainland and islands parishes, western Caith-ness, parts of upland Aberdeenshire, Nairn, Banff and Morayshire and north and west Perthshire, and was separated from 'English-speaking' Scotland by the 'Highland Line'.[37] But the definition of the Highlands as the Gaelic-speaking region of Scotland, although linguistically and his-torically correct, is of no value as a definition in terms of migration since the *Gaidhealtachd* declined between 1700 and 1900, and one cannot consistently measure migration and its change over time from a region that changed its extent in the same period. In administrative terms, the Highlands are conventionally taken as the pre-1974 counties of Ross and Cromarty, Sutherland, Inverness and Argyll (that is, the nineteenth-century counties before regional re-organisation in 1974), and this usage has been adopted in much of the work to date upon Highland migration. But this definition ignores those Gaelic speakers in parts of Highland Perthshire and the north-east central Highlands present until at least the

1950s. The Highlands have been defined here as the pre-1974 counties of Argyll, Bute, Inverness, Ross and Cromarty and Sutherland together with those parishes elsewhere in Scotland where, by 1891, Gaelic was spoken by more than 25 per cent of the parish population: a definition which has the effect of including in the Highlands some parishes in western Caithness, Nairn and Morayshire, and, notably, parts of north-west Perthshire (see Figure 1.1). This definition has been used elsewhere in work on Highland-Lowland migration and has the benefit of providing a consistent definition of the Highlands as a migration region based on linguistic grounds that contemporaries would have recognised.

In contrast to the focus of those working to explain the 'new' Highlands, this book is centrally concerned to understand the creation of an earlier 'new' Gaidhealtachd as a particular chapter in Highland and Scottish cultural and historical geography. The structure may be seen, in general terms, as reflecting the stages that Highland migrants themselves experienced: social change, migration, a Gaelic culture in the urban Lowlands. Part One, background to Highland migration, considers the transformation of Highland society and economy from the early eighteenth century in which migrants were caught up. In Part Two, the nature of Highland-Lowland migration, the detailed definition of the Highlands used here has allowed the preparation of sequences of maps which show, for individual source parishes and given Lowland towns, the numbers of persons moving south in given periods. As will also be made clear, however, these maps, although summarising a wealth of information, should be seen as static 'moments' in dynamic processes of population movement which, often, were far from as simple as a direct move from Highlands to Lowlands. Part Three considers the making of urban Gaelic culture and, in relation to Gaelic language use, occupational circumstances and the role of the Gaelic chapels, raises questions about the nature of urban Highland life.

Figure 1.1 *The Highland parishes*

KEY TO NUMBERED HIGHLAND PARISHES:

1 Edderton	34 Abernethy and Kincardine
2 Tain	35 Kingussie
3 Tarbet	36 Kirkmichael
4 Fearn	37 Moulin
5 Nigg	38 Logierait
6 Logie Easter	39 Little Dunkeld
7 Kilmuir Easter	40 Weem
8 Rosskeen	41 Glenorchy and Inishail
9 Alness	42 Ardchattan
10 Kiltearn	43 Muckairn
11 Dingwall	44 Kilmore and Kilbride
12 Fodderty	45 Kilninver and Kilmelfort
13 Urray	46 Kilbrandon and Kilchattan
14 Lochcarron	47 Craignish
15 Lochalsh	48 Kilmartin
16 Urquhart and Logie Wester	49 Kilchrennan and Dalavich
17 Resolis	50 Inverarary
18 Cromarty	51 Lochgoilhead and Kilmorich
19 Rosemarkie	52 Strachur
20 Avoch	53 Kilmichael Glassary
21 Knockbain	54 North Knapdale
22 Killearnan	55 Stralachlan
23 Kiltarlity and Convinth	56 Kilfinan
24 Urquhart and Glenmoriston	57 Kilmodan
25 Kirkhill	58 Inverchaolain
26 Inverness and Bona	59 Dunoon and Kilmun
27 Dores	60 Kingarth
28 Daviot and Dunlichty	61 Rothesay
29 Petty	62 North Bute
30 Ardersier	63 Kilcalmonell
31 Croy	64 Saddell and Skipness
32 Moy and Dalarossie	65 Killean and Kilchenzie
33 Duthil and Rothiemurchus	66 Gigha and Cara

NOTES

1. M. W. Flinn, *The European Demographic System, 1500–1820* (London, 1981); J. De Vries, *European Urbanisation, 1500–1800* (London, 1984), p.39; E. A. Wrigley, 'Urban growth and agricultural change: England and the continent in the early-modern period', *Journal of Interdisciplinary History* 15, 1985, pp.683–728; T. M. Devine, *The Great Highland Famine* (Edinburgh, 1988), pp.28–29; R. A. Houston and I. D. Whyte (eds.), *Scottish Society 1500–1800* (Cambridge,1989), p.6.

2. A reasonable summary of Census analysis and of migration terminology is to be found in the several essays in R. W. Lawton (ed.), *The Census and Social Structure: an interpretative guide to the nineteenth century census for England and Wales* (London, 1978); E. A. Wrigley (ed.), *Nineteenth-Century Society: essays in the use of quantitative data* (Cambridge, 1972); D. Mills and C. Pearce (eds.), *People and Places in the Victorian Census* (Cheltenham, 1989).

3. H. Jones, 'Evolution of Scottish migration patterns: a social-relations-of-production', *Scottish Geographical Magazine* 102, 1986, pp.151–164; an overall attempt to model the development of migration patterns in relation to societal development is W. Zelinsky, 'The hypothesis of the mobility transition', *Geographical Review* 61, 1971, pp.219–249.

4. A. Kussmaul, *Servants in Husbandry in Early Modern England* (Cambridge, 1981); T. M. Devine (ed.), *Farm Servants and Labour in Lowland Scotland, 1770–1914* (Edinburgh, 1984); R. A. Houston, 'Geographical mobility in Scotland, 1652–1811', *Journal of Historical Geography* 11, 1985, pp.379–394; *idem*, '"Frequent Flitting": geographical mobility in mid-nineteenth century Greenlaw, Berwickshire', *Scottish Studies* 19, 1985, pp.31–47; D. Tidswell, 'Mobility from place of birth in early nineteenth-century Scotland', in A. H. Dawson, H. R. Jones, A. Small and J. A. Soulsby (eds.), *Scottish Geographical Studies* (St. Andrews, 1993), pp.176–185.

5. L. M. Cullen, 'Incomes, social classes and economic growth in Ireland and Scotland, 1600–1900', in T. M. Devine and D. Dickson (eds.), *Ireland and Scotland, 1600–1850* (Edinburgh, 1983), pp.248–260; A. J. S. Gibson and T. C. Smout, *Prices, Foods and Wages in Scotland, 1550–1780* (Cambridge, 1995).

6. I. Levitt and T. C. Smout, *The State of the Scottish Working Class in 1843* (Edinburgh, 1979), pp.224–225.

7. See R. Anthony, *Herds and Hinds: Farm Labour in Lowland Scotland, 1900–1939* (East Linton, 1997), pp.197–219.

8. Jones, 'Evolution of Scottish migration patterns', p.155.

9. Good summary surveys of the nature of European migration are to be found in J. Lucassen, *Migrant labour in Europe, 1600–1900: the drift to the North Seas* (London, 1987); L. P. Moch, *Moving Europeans: migration in western Europe since 1650* (Bloomington, Indiana, 1992); D. Hoerder and L. P. Moch (eds.), *European Migrants: new perspectives* (Boston, 1996).

10. Lucassen, *Migrant Labour in Europe*, pp.3–4; P. Clark and D. Souden (eds.), *Migration and Society in Early Modern England* (London, 1987); I. D. Whyte and K. A. Whyte, 'Patterns of migration of apprentices to Aberdeen and Inverness during the seventeenth and eighteenth centuries', *Scottish Geographical Magazine* 102, 1986, pp.81–91.

11. M. W. Flinn *et al*, *Scottish Population History* (Cambridge, 1977), pp.223–224;

M. Anderson, *Population Change in north-western Europe, 1750–1850* (London, 1987), pp. 52, 57–59.

12. I. D. Whyte, 'Population mobility in early modern Scotland', in R. A. Houston and I. D. Whyte (eds.), *Scottish Society* (Cambridge, 1989), pp.56–57; I. D. Whyte and K. A. Whyte, 'The geographical mobility of women in early modern Scotland', in L. Leneman (ed.), *Perspectives in Scottish Social History* (Aberdeen, 1989), pp. 40–43.

13. Lucassen, *Migrant Labour in Europe*, pp.105–111; D. Baines, *Migration in a Mature Economy: emigration and internal migration in England and Wales, 1861–1900* (Cambridge, 1985); Moch, *Moving Europeans, passim; idem, Paths to the City: regional migration in nineteenth-century France* (London, 1983).

14. Jones, 'Evolution of Scottish migration patterns', p.152; T. M. Devine, 'Temporary migration and the Scottish Highlands in the nineteenth century', *Economic History Review* 32, 1979, p.359.

15. J. Macdonald, *General View of the Agriculture of the Hebrides* (Edinburgh, 1811), p.544.

16. R. H. Osborne, 'The movements of people in Scotland, 1851–1951', *Scottish Studies* 2, 1958, pp.1–46; see also I. Carter, *Farm Life in Northeast Scotland 1840–1914* (Edinburgh, 1979); M. Gray, 'The social impact of agrarian change in the rural Lowlands', in T. M. Devine and R. Mitchison (eds.), *People and Society in Scotland Volume 1, 1760–1830* (Edinburgh, 1988), pp.53–69; M. Harper, *Emigration from North-East Scotland* (Aberdeen, 1988).

17. Moch, *Paths to the City*; Baines, *Migration in a Mature Economy*; C. Pooley and J. Turnbull, 'Long-run migration trends in British rural areas from the eighteenth to the twentieth centuries', *International Journal of Population Geography* 2, 1996, pp.12–31.

18. See D. Fitzpatrick, *Oceans of Consolation: personal accounts of Irish migration to Australia* (Melbourne, 1995); and M. Rose, *Australia, Britain and Migration, 1915–1940: a study of desperate hopes* (Cambridge, 1995). The utility of fiction in examining the contemporary experience of migration is discussed by R. King, J. Connell and P. White (eds.), *Writing Across Worlds: literature and migration* (London, 1995).

19. J. Hunter, *A Dance Called America* (Edinburgh, 1994); *idem, Glencoe and the Indians* (Edinburgh, 1997); D. Craig, *On the Crofters' Trail: in search of the Clearance Highlanders* (London, 1990).

20. This point is made well by Marion Maclean in her study of the Glengarry Highlanders of Upper Canada in the early nineteenth century: *The People of Glengarry: Highlanders in Transition, 1745–1820* (Montreal and London, 1991).

21. Quoted in H. Whyte, *Noise and Smoky Breath: an illustrated anthology of Glasgow poems, 1900–1983* (Glasgow, 1983), p.98.

22. This material is reviewed in C. W. J. Withers, 'Class, culture and migrant identity: Gaelic Highlanders in urban Scotland', in G. Kearns and C. W. J. Withers (eds.), *Urbanising Britain: essays on class and community in the nineteenth century* (Cambridge, 1991), pp.55–79; and in M. Engman, F. Carter, A. Hepburn and C. Pooley (eds.), *Ethnic Identity in Urban Europe* (Dartmouth, 1992).

23. L. H. Lees, 'Patterns of lower-class life: Irish slum communities in nineteenth-century London', in S. Thernstrom and R. Sennett (eds.), *Nineteenth-century Cities* (London, 1976), p.360.

24. British Parliamentary Papers (hereafter BPP), *Report on the State of the Irish Poor in Great Britain*, 1836, XXIV, p.427; J. G. Williamson, 'The impact of the Irish on British labour markets during the Industrial Revolution', *Journal of Economic History* 46, 1986, pp.693–720; R. Swift and S. Gilley (eds.), *The Irish in the Victorian City* (London, 1985).

25. J. M. Werly, 'The Irish in Manchester, 1832–1849', *Irish Historical Studies* 18, 1973, p.350; L. H. Lees, *Exiles of Erin: Irish migrants in Victorian London* (Manchester, 1979).

26. G. Jones, 'The Welsh in London in the nineteenth century', *Cambria* 12, 1985, pp.149–169; C. Pooley, 'Welsh migration to England in the mid-nineteenth century', *Journal of Historical Geography* 9, 1983, pp.364–382.

27. N. File and C. Power, *Black Settlers in Britain, 1555–1958* (London, 1981); G. Stocking, *Bones, Bodies, Behaviour: essays on biological anthropology* (Madison, WI, 1988).

28. Swift and Gilley, *The Irish in the Victorian City*, p.9; S. Gilley, 'English attitudes to the Irish in England, 1798–1900', in C. Holmes (ed.), *Immigrants and Minorities in British Society* (London, 1978), pp.81–110.

29. M. A. G. O'Tuathaigh, 'The Irish in nineteenth-century Britain: problems of integration', in R. Swift and S. Gilley (eds.), *The Irish in the Victorian City*, pp.23–24.

30. J. Strang, *Glasgow and its Clubs* (Glasgow, 1856), pp.137–138.

31. *Constitution and Rules of the Mull and Iona Association* (Glasgow, 1867).

32. I think here for example, amongst a wide-ranging and complex literature, of B. Anderson, *Imagined Communities* (London, 1991 edition); Z. Bauman, *Modernity and Difference* (Oxford, 1991); A. P. Cohen (ed.), *Belonging, Identity and Social Organisation in British Rural Cultures* (Manchester, 1982); *idem, The Symbolic Construction of Community* (Chichester and London, 1985); *idem,* 'Owning the nation, and the personal nature of nationalism: locality and the rhetoric of nationhood in Scotland', in V. Amit-Talai and C. Knowles (eds.), *Re-situating identities: the politics of race, ethnicity and culture* (Peterborough, Ontario, 1992), pp.267–282; J. Friedmann, *Cultural Identity and Global Process* (London, 1994); M. McDonald, 'The construction of difference: an anthropological approach to stereotypes', in S. Macdonald (ed.), *Inside European Identities: ethnography in Western Europe* (Oxford, 1993), pp.219–236; J. Nadel-Klein, 'Reweaving the fringe: localism, tradition and representation in British ethnography', *American Ethnologist* 18, 1991, pp.500–517.

33. S. Macdonald, *Reimagining Culture: historians, identities and the Gaelic renaissance* (Oxford, 1997), p.xv.

34. *Ibid*, p.99.

35. C. W. J. Withers, 'The creation of the Scottish Highlands', in I. Donnachie and C. Whatley (eds.), *The Manufacture of Scottish History* (Edinburgh, 1992), pp.143–156; J. Agnew, 'Liminal travellers: Hebrideans at home and away', *Scotlands* 3, 1996, pp.32–41.

36. C. Jedrej and M. Nuttall, *White Settlers: the impact of rural repopulation on Scotland* (Luxembourg, 1996), p.12.

37. The changing boundary of the *Gaidhealtachd* is discussed in C. W. J. Withers, *Gaelic in Scotland, 1698–1981: the geographical history of a language* (Edinburgh, 1984). 'English speaking' is here used to describe Scots English and its variations as well as Standard English.

CHAPTER 2

The Transformation of Highland Life, 1650–1900

The movement of Highlanders to the cities of Lowland Scotland was the result both of the real and imagined opportunities offered by those urban economies and of profound changes in Highland society itself. This chapter examines the principal changes in the economic and social foundations of Highland life and considers the material transformation of Highland life as background to the emergence of urban Highland migrant communities.

When, in 1796, one anonymous commentator considered that 'The influence of regular government and sound policy has been experienced by the inhabitants of the highlands of Scotland within a very short period of time so that it may be said that they have but lately emerged from a state of barbarity',[1] he was not only reflecting contemporary opinion on the Highlanders' supposed backwardness: he also saw the Jacobite Rebellion and its ending at Culloden in April 1746 as a turning point in Highland history. This view of the mid-eighteenth century as a critical moment between 'barbarity' and the benefits of 'civilised society' has had an enduring place in the historiography of the Highlands. The '45 and the 'improvements' that came in its wake have been seen in relation to the region much as the 1707 Act of Union has been seen, by some, in relation to Scotland as a whole: the end of the old backwardness and the beginnings of 'enlightenment'.[2] That this view has been so persistent is largely the result of eighteenth- and nineteenth-century improvers' own view of their civilising mission – whether focused on language, education, agriculture, or industry – and their self-legitimating beliefs in the rightness of their actions.

It is an interpretation to be resisted for several reasons. Firstly, it supposes a separateness between Highlands and Lowlands that did not exist. In economic relations, in tenurial practices, in marriage patterns, and in the routines of seasonal migration, the Highlands and Lowlands were closely connected.[3] Secondly, the Highlands had been subject to the ideology and practical consequences of improvement long before the mid-eighteenth century. Both Macinnes and Dodgshon amongst others have shown that the policies of civilisation as an anglicising process linked to the commercial incorporation of the clan elite into the Lowland market economy date from the late 1500s and early 1600s.[4] Thirdly, the Highlands are not a uniform region. The north and west 'crofting Highlands' differ from the 'farming Highlands' of the south and east in the basis of their agrarian economy, in the nature of their population experiences and in their capacity to shed labour on a temporary or permanent basis to the Lowlands. Lastly, we should not suppose the Highland 'way of life' to be a timeless 'traditional' means of existence whose transformation was everywhere immediate and wholesale. Highland society from the clan chiefs and the middle ranks of tacksmen to the tenantry and sub-tenants was based upon principles of loyalty and mutually understood systems of social obligation over the holding of land, the management of cattle, and the working and marketing of arable products. However much it is the case that land in the Highlands was, simultaneously, laid out to ensure effectiveness within the agricultural economy and to stabilise a recognised class structure, it is also true that there was 'constant conflict between the demands of productive efficiency and the old obligations of class to class'.[5]

Changes are first apparent in the attitudes of the clan élite to the commercial opportunities bound up in land, and are initially concentrated in the central and south-west Highlands.[6] But the capitalisation of Highland agriculture, changes in the established practices of holding and working land, and the processes of class formation within Highland rural society all took time and had particular geographies. There was, too, considerable opposition from within the Highland tenantry, notably from the later eighteenth century, to the sweeping away of customary systems. The related failure of the Highland economy to industrialise, despite the several attempts of those who equated industry and the qualities of industriousness with civic virtue and the social improvement of the 'barbarian' Highlander, lent shifts in the agricultural sector added emphasis. Linked with these changes, and crucially important in shaping their geographical expression within the Highlands and in establishing the patterns of population movement from the Highlands to the Lowlands, are the facts of demographic change.

POPULATION CHANGE IN THE HIGHLANDS, C.1755–1901

There is no source before Webster's 1755 Census by which we may estimate Highland population totals, and not until the 1850s can we accurately measure net migration between Highlands and Lowlands. We know something of population totals within parts of the Highlands from late seventeenth-century poll tax and hearth tax records, and there is evidence that crises due to famine in the Highlands in 1604, in the 1650s, the 1680s and notably in the 'Seven Ill Years' from 1696 prompted Highlanders to migrate to the Lowlands to seek relief.[7] But the fact that the first source by which to know overall totals and to infer something of the differing geography of Highland population dates only from the mid-eighteenth century means we cannot be certain of longer-term trends in Highland demography.

Total numbers and the geography of population change, 1755–1901
Webster's 1755 Census gives a total population for Scotland of 1,265,380 persons, a figure revised in later re-examination to a total of 1,269,390. The four principal Highland counties of Argyll, Ross and Cromarty, Inverness, and Sutherland together had a population of 194,707 persons (15.4 per cent of the national total). Mitchison's re-assessment of Webster's enumerations has suggested that rapid population growth in the Highlands, conspicuous by the 1790s, may have started relatively late in the century.[8] By 1801, the Highland population was 233,384 persons (14.5 per cent of Scotland's total). The region continued to increase in population until 1841, from which point the region underwent a progressive but geographically variable decline in population: Argyll reached its maximum population in 1831, Inverness in 1841, Ross and Cromarty and Sutherland in 1851 (Table 2.1). Flinn has considered that

> It is not possible to set a precise date or even a decade to the moment when the pressure of Highland and Hebridean populations began to press against the limits of the capacity of their usable resources of land. But evidence, principally in the form of substantial emigration, begins to suggest that these limits were being approached after the middle of the eighteenth century.[9]

Assessment of net rates of intercensal population changes reveals that the population of the Highlands increased by 19.9 per cent between 1755 and 1801, much lower than Scotland as a whole (Table 2.1b). From 1801, there is a much lower rate of population increase in the region until, between 1841 and 1851, the region begins a decline in numbers evident into the early 1900s.

Gray has identified east-west regional differences in the geography of Highland population growth, differences in which the north and west parishes had markedly higher rates of growth than the south and east Highlands.[10] In the second half of the eighteenth century many parishes in the north and west, notably in the Outer Isles and on the coast, had a population increase in excess of 50 per cent. In the eastern Highlands in contrast, population totals declined in the same period. Some southern parishes increased their population between 1801 and 1851, but the far

Table 2.1

POPULATION TOTALS AND INTERCENSAL POPULATION CHANGE (PERCENTAGE CHANGES), HIGHLAND COUNTIES, 1755–1891*

(a) Population totals

					Dates						
Counties	1755	1801	1811	1821	1831	1841	1851	1861	1871	1881	1891
HIGHLANDS	194,707	233,384	248,694	279,879	296,108	298,637	294,298	275,264	268,482	268,839	264,026
Argyll	66,286	81,277	86,541	97,316	100,973	97,371	89,298	79,724	75,679	76,468	75,003
Inverness	59,563	72,672	77,671	89,961	94,797	97,799	96,500	88,888	87,531	90,454	89,317
Ross & Cromarty	48,084	556,318	60,853	68,762	74,820	78,685	82,707	81,406	80,955	78,547	77,810
Sutherland	20,774	23,117	23,629	23,840	25,518	24,782	25,793	25,246	24,317	23,370	21,896
[SCOTLAND]	[1,265,380]	[1,608,420]	[1,805,864]	[2,091,521]	[2,364,386]	[2,620,184]	[2,888,742]	[3,062,294]	[3,360,018]	[3,735,573]	[4,025,647]

(b) Intercensal population change

					Periods					
Counties	1755–1801	1801–11	1811–21	1821–31	1831–41	1841–51	1851–61	1861–71	1871–81	1881–91
HIGHLANDS	19.86	6.56	12.53	5.79	0.85	–1.45	–6.46	–2.46	0.13	–1.79
Argyll	22.61	6.47	12.45	3.75	–3.56	–8.29	–10.72	–5.07	1.04	–1.91
Inverness	22.01	6.87	5.82	5.37	3.16	–1.32	–7.88	–1.52	3.33	–1.25
Ross & Cromarty	17.12	8.05	12.99	8.81	5.16	5.09	–1.57	–0.55	–2.97	–0.93
Sutherland	11.27	2.21	0.89	5.78	–2.88	4.07	–2.12	–3.67	–3.89	–6.30
[SCOTLAND]	[27.10]	[12.27]	[15.81]	[13.04]	[10.81]	[10.24]	[6.00]	[9.72]	[11.17]	[7.76]

*Based on Webster 1755 in Kyd (1952), and *Census of Scotland*.

north and west exhibited a continued disproportionate increase in population which saw some parishes treble their population from 1755 to 1851. Yet by the second half of the nineteenth century, with the exception of a few parishes, the population of virtually the whole region was declining. This regional and local variation is of great importance in understanding the geography of Highland population growth and as a background to the differential patterns of Highland-Lowland migration. Walker's review in 1808 of population changes in the Highlands notes both this fact of east-west variation and hints at its causes:

> Their real increase in population has, no doubt, been much greater during these forty years, but in this period, these countries have, in different ways, been severely drained of their inhabitants. The ordinary egress to the low countries has been considerable. Great numbers of men have been drawn-out to the army and navy, and many have emigrated to America. But the most depopulating effects have proceeded from the enlargement of sheep farms, and especially those for the pasture of sheep. This unfavourable alteration has chiefly prevailed in the parishes next adjacent to the low-lands, in many of which the number of people has been deplorably diminished; but in the more remote parishes not affected by this depopulating cause, the people have increased one-third and upwards in the course of the above forty years.[11]

It is also clear that Highland population totals were the result of more strictly demographic indices, including changing crude birth and death rates, age-specific marital fertility, age at marriage and proportions marrying, and issues of age-and sex-structure as well as mortality. Unfortunately, assessment of the crude birth (CBR) and crude death rate (CDR) is only possible from 1855. During the second half of the nineteenth century, the Highlands had a lower CBR and CDR than Scotland as a whole, and an illegitimacy ratio lower than the national average (Table 2.2). The extent to which the data for this period are informative of the important decades at the end of the eighteenth century is difficult to know. The evidence of sex ratios for the mid- and later nineteenth century provides some help. The sex ratio in the reproductive age range (15–49 years) and in the 'marrying' age group of 25–29 was 76.2 in 1861: one woman in four or five would have been unable to find a mate of her own age, even if all the males married. The result was a relatively high mean age at first marriage *and* low nuptuality. In 1861, for example, 42 per cent of Highland women aged 25–29 were married: the national figure for the same age cohort was 54 per cent. Since both illegitimacy and age-specific marital fertility were generally low in comparison with

Table 2.2

CRUDE BIRTH RATES, CRUDE DEATH RATES, AND ILLEGITIMACY RATIOS BY HIGHLAND COUNTIES, 1855–1895*

	Periods							
	1855–60	1861–65	1866–70	1871–75	1876–80	1881–85	1886–90	1891–95
(a) *Crude Birth Rates*[1]								
Argyll	26.4	26.9	27.0	25.7	26.1	25.6	24.5	22.4
Inverness	25.3	27.4	27.8	26.5	26.8	25.7	24.5	23.9
Ross and Cromarty	27.9	27.7	26.5	25.1	25.0	26.1	24.9	24.3
Sutherland	24.0	22.9	17.6	22.1	23.6	23.0	22.4	21.9
[Scotland]	[34.1]	[35.1]	[34.9]	[35.0]	[34.8]	[33.3]	[31.4]	[30.5]
(b) *Crude Death Rates*[2]								
Argyll	16.3	18.5	17.9	19.2	19.0	17.1	16.6	17.3
Inverness	14.9	18.0	17.7	18.0	17.0	16.8	15.7	17.6
Ross and Cromarty	15.5	17.4	15.6	16.8	16.0	15.7	15.9	17.2
Sutherland	13.7	15.4	12.0	16.2	16.5	16.0	16.2	17.3
[Scotland]	[20.8]	[22.1]	[22.0]	[22.7]	[20.6]	[19.6]	[18.8]	[19.0]
(c) *Illegitimacy Ratios*[3]								
Argyll	6.62	6.91	7.84	7.77	7.81	7.35	7.62	7.97
Inverness	7.57	7.96	8.01	8.40	8.16	7.59	8.13	7.42
Ross and Cromarty	3.84	4.24	4.86	4.57	4.54	4.78	5.08	4.79
Sutherland	3.78	5.23	6.07	6.90	6.58	7.36	6.53	5.72
[Scotland]	[8.74]	[9.79]	[9.85]	[9.09]	[8.49]	[8.27]	[8.04]	[7.41]

* From *Detailed Annual Report* of the Registrar-General for Scotland quoted, with permission, from M.W. Flinn, *Scottish Population History from the 17th century to the 1930s* (Cambridge, 1977), pp.339–340; 350–1; 380–1: Tables 5.3.1, 5.4.1, 5.5.5.

[1] Live births per 1000 living, averages of five-year periods.

[2] Annual average deaths per 1000 living, averages of five-year periods.

[3] Number of illegitimate births per 100 live births, averages of five-year periods.

national rates, it is possible that low crude birth rates in the Highlands after 1855 were the result of late marriages and low marriage rates. These facts were themselves the result of imbalances in the sex- and age-structure of the population given differential patterns of out-migration.

For the later eighteenth century, we know only that age at marriage was 'early in life'.[12] If we may presume for the later 1700s that illegitimate fertility was then as low as it was for the nineteenth-century Highlands, it is probable that one principal means of population increase between 1755 and 1801 was a higher age-specific marital fertility rate in the younger marrying ages especially, given both the suggested prevalence of 'early' marriage and what commentators like Walker perceived as the 'obvious cause, . . . a greater frequency of marriage'.[13] This is also to suggest that the observed greater rate of population increase in the north and west Highlands was due to a higher proportion of early marriages than in the south and east Highlands. This proportion reflected the continued residence of the younger marriable sections of the population, especially males, for whom migration to the Lowlands, which altered the age- and sex-structures, was, as Walker hinted, not as commonly practised as by their southern counterparts.

Figures on mortality in the Highlands are uncertain before 1855. We know of plague in mid-seventeenth-century Argyll and that there may have been periodic mortality crises associated with harvest failure as well as epidemic disease elsewhere and at other times in the 1600s. There is unlikely to have been any marked rise in mortality related to the poor Highland harvests of 1740, 1756, 1782–83, and 1799. The potato famine of the 1830s and 1840s prompted migration rather than increased mortality.[14] Inoculation against smallpox suggests control of that disease from the mid-eighteenth century was significant in reducing mortality. Most of the western isles, for example, had smallpox outbreaks during the eighteenth century, with severe if localised incidents in 1784 and 1792.[15] But inoculation, particularly of children, was not always widely adopted after its introduction: as Sinclair noted, 'Before the scruples respecting inoculation were got over, many of these little innocents fell victims to stupidity and superstition'.[16] In Lewis in the 1820s, distrust of inoculation meant smallpox mortality was very high amongst infants. The principal source of mortality through infectious disease in the nineteenth-century Highlands was tuberculosis. There is some evidence to suggest for that disease in the later nineteenth century, and for periodic increases in death by cholera and typhus in the 1830s and 1840s, that mortality within the Highlands was increased by returning migrants transmitting what locals called 'low country diseases'.[17] This term was also occasionally applied to reported outbreaks of gonorrhoea amongst returning female Highland domestic servants.[18]

In reviewing the changing numbers and differing geography of Highland population change, the evidence for the later eighteenth century would suggest that a high CBR, a high rate of age-specific marital fertility within the 20–29 age ranges, low illegitimacy rates and an early age at marriage were important trends, perhaps particularly in the north and west. Later decline in that region was due to delay in marriage resulting from imbalances in the age- and sex-structures following migration. In the farming Highlands, population expansion was accommodated both by related changes in the agricultural economy and by population displacement to the lowlands.

Migration, emigration and population change
In considering the numbers and geography of migration between the Highlands and the rest of Scotland, we are hindered by a lack of firm statistics before 1851. The evidence of Table 2.3 shows clearly the loss of overall numbers from the Highland counties (and the Borders and northeast Scotland in the mid-nineteenth century) and the corresponding gain in the central Lowlands. These totals, prompted by changes in Highland agriculture, landlord policy, and influenced by patterns of temporary migration, will be shown in what follows to have considerable variation over time and space. Added to the known totals of internal net migration are the less precise facts for emigration from the Highlands.

We know from several sources of the emigration of Highlanders to Ulster, Sweden, Russia and the Americas in the seventeenth century, and it has been suggested that two-thirds of the 20,000 Scots who left for the colonies between 1768 and 1775 were Highlanders.[19] Bailyn has shown a high proportion of negative circumstances to have motivated the eighteenth-century Highland emigrant: high rent increases, poverty, unemployment, landlord oppression.[20] Boswell, having witnessed emigrants leaving Skye in 1773, spoke of a 'rage for emigration', a view shared by some other contemporaries. We know something of the local geography of Highland emigration: 831 persons from Ross and Cromarty, 288 from Bute and Argyll, and 735 from Sutherland in 1772–73; 50 persons from Glenorchy and 77 from Appin in 1775 bound for North Carolina, for example.[21] It is difficult to know total numbers and assess the demographic consequences of such out-movement. Sinclair (1825) recognised connections between the nature of Highland agriculture, early marriages, and emigration in his remarks on Skye:

> Thus the population of Skye have been constantly increasing for eighty years, the inhabitants had so much multiplied, that between August 1771, and October 1790, no less than eight large transports sailed from that island

Table 2.3

NET MIGRATION, BY COUNTIES, SCOTLAND 1851–1901*

County	1851		1901	
	Nos.	Rate	Nos.	Rate
Aberdeen	+ 5,451	+ 2.7	23,815	7.4
Angus	+ 12,704	+ 8.0	+ 2,359	+ 0.9
Argyll	24,099	21.7	16,969	19.3
Ayr	11,522	6.5	34,485	12.7
Banff	4,103	7.1	17,363	22.3
Berwick	7,415	17.7	9,564	25.2
Bute	+ 560	+ 3.7	+ 1,671	+ 10.5
Caithness	3,003	7.3	11,537	25.7
Clackmannan	+ 2,139	+ 10.9	2,613	7.9
Dumfries	6,494	8.2	13,207	16.5
Dunbarton	+ 844	+ 2.2	+ 15,881	+ 19.0
East Lothian	5,919	14.7	9,157	20.2
Fife	8,776	5.6	7,769	3.6
Inverness	9,078	8.7	13,257	13.2
Kincardine	4,110	10.8	5,685	12.6
Kinross	792	8.2	2,062	23.2
Kircudbright	803	2.0	3,082	7.7
Lanark	+ 80,495	+ 23.2	+ 152,398	+ 15.3
Midlothian	+ 37,982	+ 19.7	+ 77,226	+ 21.1
Moray	652	1.7	5,722	11.6
Nairn	+ 1,348	+ 15.9	240	2.6
Orkney*	2,630	4.1	4,840	14.6
Peebles	2,995	22.6	1,103	7.2
Perth	25,225	15.8	21,253	15.3
Renfrew	+ 173	+ 0.1	+ 104	+ 0.0
Ross & Cromarty	7,648	8.5	15,502	17.1
Roxburgh	+ 531	+ 1.1	8,029	15.0
Selkirk	+ 377	+ 4.2	+ 867	+ 4.0
Stirling	7,278	8.4	528	0.4
Sutherland	2,329	8.3	4,296	16.9
West Lothian	3,539	11.6	4,360	6.9
Wigtown	4,194	10.5	10,622	25.7
Zetland*			3,446	11.1

*From *Census of Scotland*.

with 2400 emigrants, to seek settlements in America, and carried with them £24,000 Sterling, ship freights included. In the small island of Eigg, also, containing only 399 souls, no less than 176 persons emigrated between 1788 and 1790; the principal cause of which, we are told, was, the country being so *overstocked with people*, that the lands were unable to supply them sufficiently with the necessaries of life. This was greatly owing to the practice which prevailed of a parent dividing his farm, however small, with his son, when he married, there being no other means of industry or occupation, than the culture of the earth. The prospect of this division, however, promoted early marriages; but by such continued subdivisions, the occupiers were ultimately reduced to a state of extreme misery.[22]

Much emigration at this time was of whole families and communities, and was often influenced in its destination and in its communal nature by the decision to emigrate of the tacksman, who, as a mediating figure in the allocation of land within clan society, had considerable bearing upon the fortunes of tenants and kin relations. What McLean has shown about the claim of emigrants from western Inverness-shire in the 1780s that the 'McDonalds . . . hope to found in the new land a new Glengarry' is likely to have been evident for other Highland migrant groups.[23] The idea of emigration providing a geographically-enlarged sense of Highland community – a wider Gaidhealtachd beyond both Highlands and Scotland – has important bearings on the cultural geography of Highlanders in the urban Lowlands. It is also the case, however, that migration and emigration sundered the connections between Highland people and their land and marked a profound psychological as well as geographical distancing. Hugh MacCorkindale's '*Oran Le Seann Ileach*' (Song of an Islayman), of uncertain age but probably dating from the early 1800s, noted:

> It is now more than twenty years
> since I left my ancestral glens;
> it was useless to remain there
> for employment was scarce in the land.
> I took a trip to the Lowlands
> where I had promise of small earnings;
> I didn't like things at all,
> and prospects were not attractive.
>
> They did not appeal to me at all,
> and I left the townspeople behind.
> Then I came over to Canada,
> a place twice as good for me.[24]

There are several other instances of internal migration being precedent and prompt to emigration, and it is likely that international seasonal harvest migration was also a prelude to emigration flows.[25]

Richards has argued that 'The main peaks of Highland emigration appear to coincide with special plans for recruitment or subsidisation, for example by Highland tacksmen to the American colonies in the 1770s, by Canadian and American emigration agents in 1801–1803, by Lord Selkirk for the Red River colony in 1813–114, and by Australian bodies in 1837–41 and 1852–54'.[26] As he and others have shown, the nineteenth century witnessed the deliberate clearance of Highland farms and lands by landlords for whom a resident but increasingly pauperised tenantry, even if kin, was no source of rent and a barrier to agricultural innovation. Richards and others have discussed the trauma of the 'Clearances' in some detail:[27] notwithstanding their undoubted effect on Highland *mentalité*, and the fact that perhaps 250,000 people left the Highlands between 1800 and 1860 (leaving aside seasonal patterns of movement to the Lowlands), the demographic effect was, as shown, insufficient to achieve an absolute population reduction across the Highlands before 1841–1851.[28]

Emigration following the Highland potato famine was more from the north-west crofting Highlands than the farming Highlands. Many of the 16,553 Highlanders who emigrated over the famine period did so directly from the Highlands and with the assistance of landowners and the Highland and Island Emigration Society, with more travelling to Australia via the Colonial Land and Emigration Commission. The fact that many of the 1,681 persons from South Uist who arrived in Quebec on 15 September 1851 were 'totally impoverished and without adequate clothing'[29] was a problem for the receiving authorities in Canada as well as the Highlanders. Even by the 1920s, the last great wave of Highland emigration, many of the young from Lewis who responded to requests like that from the Canadian Pacific Railway Company to become domestic servants, as well as less clearly-identified emigrants, were quitting a society whose economic and cultural base had changed dramatically even in the course of their own lifetimes.[30]

HIGHLAND RURAL ECONOMY AND SOCIETY, 1650–1900

Local variations in population change as well as in physical environment mean we should be cautious about seeing the transformation of Highland agrarian society as a sequence of neat stages or Highland life to have been at once and everywhere the same. Similarly, the views of contemporaries on Highland 'backwardness' and the lack of improvement (both actual and potential) reveal more about attitudes to the region than they do about the facts of real life there.

The central unit of Highland life, certainly in the farming Highlands, was the joint farm whose essential elements were the clachan (a small group of dwellings and farm buildings), arable land divided into infield and outfield, and common grazing. Arable holdings were disposed over infield and outfield in parcels or rigs. Arable crops were chiefly oats or barley. This system did allow expansion of the cultivable margins – but once the limits to efficient production had been reached and given, too, the facts of inheritance – almost the only means of flexibility was sub-division of holdings. Continued sub-division produced population pressure on usable resources and, as Sinclair noted of Skye, often stimulated emigration. Tenants paid rent, in a mixture of money and kind, to the tacksman or directly to the landlord. Cattle everywhere provided cash income for rentals or the purchase of imported luxuries. On the Highland margins with easier access to Lowland markets and grainstuffs, the practices of this subsidence economy were replaced by more externally-oriented farming systems in which movement of goods and people across the 'Highland Line' was common.

The coincidence of interest and customary obligations between landlord and tenant that underlay this system was repeated between tacksman, tenants, and sub-tenants. The tacksman, usually but not always a collateral relation of the chief, leased land from the chief, sub-let it to the majority of the population and lived off the difference. As a social system, the clan comprised three groupings: the *clan* itself (from the Gaelic, *clann*, meaning children), the *sliochd* or major descendants, and those of lesser generational depth, the *cloinne*. The *clan* was a patrilineal structure of extended families in which military and other service to the chief was expected. In return, clan chiefs protected their *clan* as a whole from outside threat and were arbiters of disputes between *clann* or *sliochdan*.[31] As an agricultural system, there were few, if any, legal bonds to connect the several kin groups. Territorially, men of minor *clann* usually possessed conjoint rights to usufruct within the joint farm. But no laws recognised the collective *duthchas* of the tenants or other customary rights such as the *oigreachd*, or individual heritage.[32] Threats to these notions invoked the principles of 'ancient possession', and claims to ancestral holdings were without formal foundation in law. The ties binding the subordinate adherents to the land were likewise without a recognised legality and varied in practice. Least firmly attached were cottars, who worked a small amount of arable and provided labour in return for a cow's grazing. Crofters also worked a patch of arable but usually held their land directly from the landowner. The growth of the crofting systems in the north and west Highlands from the later eighteenth century tied tenants to the land but also demanded periods of out-migration or the development of by-employments, given the generally small size of holdings and the facts of holding sub-division. If, then, there were established systems of allocating and managing land, Highland rural society should not be seen as without internal friction or external involvement. Changes to the system involved the adoption of new

methods of farming and working the land and the increased incorporation of existing trends within Highland life into more thoroughly
capitalised external economies.

Prices, rents and money income in Highland agriculture, 1650–1850
There is considerable evidence of upward pressure upon rentals and the
adoption of formal leases in the seventeenth-century Highlands, and
enough to suggest important geographical variations in these trends.
Shaw notes that, where evidence survives, it shows that tacks granted by
proprietors in the more southerly islands of the Hebrides were for much
shorter terms than those granted by proprietors further north. Short tacks
encouraged tenants to work land efficiently, since there was no automatic
longer-term tenancy, and provided landlords with more frequent opportunity to raise rents and ensure loyalty through eviction of disloyal
tenants. By contrast, 'The longer tacks of the more northerly isles
reflected a society where security and clan loyalties were still felt to
matter more than increasing the monetary yield of the estate, and where
the more commercial land policies of the Lowlands had not yet filtered
through'.[33] This claim is borne out by what we know of estates in
Glenorchy, in Kintyre, in parts of eastern Ross and Cromarty and in
central Perthshire by the later seventeenth century.[34]

In the absence of firm evidence from different locations, it is difficult to
know the extent to which differences in length of lease or the existence of
formal leases were always transmitted to the smaller tenantry. Rentals
examined for Gairloch from 1660–70, for the MacLeod estates on Skye in
1678, and for Breadalbane in 1769, reveal great variation in landholding
but no clear distinctions in terms of the prevalence either of tacksmen or
tenants holding land directly of landowners.[35] Rental payments in
parishes on the Highland margins were usually in money with a few
cattle: in the north and west, the reverse obtained. By the later seventeenth century and for a variety of places – the McLeod estates on Harris
after 1680, Lismore from 1660, Skye by the 1670s, and Breadalbane in
1692 – there is considerable stress on an increasing cash proportion within
rental payments.[36] Such changes reflected the increasingly commercial
outlook of many clan elite and also marked the beginning of the end for
the tacksman. These changes were more apparent in the southern Highlands. But even in Lewis by the 1750s, the McKenzies were considered
'Remarkably disposed to grow rich. They have screwed their rents to an
extravagant Height'.[37]

Richards has distinguished three phases in the connections between
prices, rents, and money income after 1750: an expansive phase from 1750
to 1815, a period of decline and monetary collapse from 1815 to 1850, and

a period of relative rise in rents and prices between 1850 and 1882.[38] The period 1750 to 1815 was characterised by increased rents and prices from the sale of livestock and the increased profits to be gained by turning ancestral arable holdings into sheep runs under the management of Lowland graziers. Livestock prices were artificially inflated in the later eighteenth and early nineteenth centuries, however, by restrictions on foreign imports during the Napoleonic Wars. After 1815, prices for Highland goods dropped dramatically and did so at a time of rising population, holding sub-division, and growing dependence by the majority of the population upon the potato as a staple. The fall in prices was not accompanied by a fall in rentals. From the second decade of the nineteenth century, landlords were dependent upon rent from an increasingly pauperised tenantry and on lower returns from sheep and cattle. Arrears of rental meant capital depletion amongst landlords. For tenants, the build-up of debt was felt chiefly by those with small regularised holdings and little, if any, livestock or fixed capital reserves – the crofting classes: 'In terms of the distribution of income, it seems likely that, from 1815 to about 1850, the crofter class suffered not only an absolute decline in welfare . . . but also a deprivation disproportionate to the rest of the Highland community'.[39] There is certainly evidence of a more marked rise in arrears in the north and west than in the south and east in the later eighteenth and early nineteenth centuries.[40] Anderson (1831) saw connections between regional geographies, high rents, and the decline of customary social ties:

> The pressure of high rents has already done away, in a great measure, with the hereditary notions of obedience and devotedness to the chief, on the part of the dependent, in Argyllshire; but in the secluded parts of the counties of Ross and Inverness, we may yet see the interesting spectacle of a people preserving the habits of former times, and affected by the relations of feudal and patriarchal attachment.[41]

Yet even in eastern Ross and Cromarty, with that region's close connections with the lowlands, rents rose in the later eighteenth century because of increased arable acreage. Native tenants were unable to purchase lands and farms due to lack of capital. Impoverishment and consequent out-migration to the Lowlands took place not because of any sudden cutting of 'patriarchal attachments' but because of the combined and drawn-out effects of increased monetary hardship allied to changes in land use and incoming Lowland graziers, and because changes in tenurial systems could be coped with, with relative ease, by leaving the land and the area altogether. In the north and west by the 1830s and 1840s, rental arrears in some parishes exceeded the year's rent: only small sums were deemed 'recoverable' by landlords.[42] Temporary migration was an important means to cash income within the crofting tenantry, but the depressed financial condition of many led to permanent migration.

Changing practices of land use, c.1750–1850

For many commentators of the later eighteenth century, changes in the ways land was worked and managed in the Highlands demanded both material and intellectual transformation.

> In the cultivated parts of the country, the farmers are well acquainted with the most profitable methods of culture, and will not fail to prosecute them, for their own advantage . . . but the case is widely different in the uncultivated parts of the north: There, the labourers of the soil are unacquainted with the improvements that would be most beneficial to themselves and their country. Their knowledge is confined.[43]

Changes in arable agriculture took four principal forms: the abolition of the runrig infield-outfield system; the engrossing and enclosing of holdings (facts crucial to the emergence of the crofting system); the introduction of turnips, artificial grasses and new rotations; and, of great importance, a move away from oats and barley to a dependence upon the potato. Changes in the pastoral sector took the form of the replacement of small-scale sheep management by large-scale sheep farms, and the extension of commercial cattle ranching.

The break-up of the runrig system was greatly motivated by what Gray has termed 'the singularly unanimous abhorrence which the articulate thinkers of the eighteenth century held for anything but individual and permanent tenure of land'.[44] But it was not everywhere equal either in the extent or the consequences of its destruction. Estates in Argyll and in Breadalbane were consolidating arable holdings by the third quarter of the eighteenth century. Change in the north and west Highlands was generally later. Gray has claimed that as compact holdings replaced fragmented runrig and enclosure followed, the whole frontier of change moved north and west so that by 1850, the old system was virtually extinct. But even in the 'advanced' areas of agrarian rationalisation – the Argyll estates and the south-west and central Highlands generally – changes in runrig and in enclosing were not undertaken by all. Smith, writing of Argyll in 1805, noted that 'Good enclosures are the foundations of all improvements', but also that 'In this country, enclosures, as yet, are chiefly confined to the possessions of proprietors; many of whom have sufficiently enclosed and subdivided the farms in their own hands. . . . But the general appearance of the country is still naked and open; and must remain so, if landlords will not enclose them, or give their tenants longer leases'.[45] Of Ross and Cromarty in 1810, we know that 'native farmers have an aversion to inclosures'.[46] In the crofting Highlands more generally, runrig was certainly displaced over time and enclosing became more accepted, but in those regions consolidation of the arable left lotted holdings too small to sustain a livelihood without by-employment or migration. And much arable land was simply replaced by sheep farming. Lastly, practices of land use in the north and west were particularly affected by the impact, demographic and economic, of the potato.

The potato was introduced into the Hebrides in the 1690s, but not until the 1740s was it more widely cultivated throughout the Highlands. The potato was only one of a number of new crops introduced during this period, but it was the single most important. It became a major item in the food supply of the Highland population by the end of the eighteenth century. Its advantages were principally threefold: it could be grown on poor-quality land unable to support grain crops; it could sustain population on smaller acreages per family or holding than was required for a principally grain diet; and, in being a subsistence crop, it allowed population to expand very largely irrespective of external markets. By 1755, the tenantry of Morvern were said to 'find this Root of such Singular Service that it is planted in great quantitys on the side of the Hills that were formerly uncultivated'.[47] Elsewhere, we are told how 'Before the Introduction of Potatoes, no Care was taken to reclaim any untillaged Earth, but now a great deal of waste land is yearly broke-up.[48] Potato cultivation was aided by the Highlanders' available technology: the foot plough or *cas chrom* could break up rough ground the horse-drawn plough could not. Seaware was common as a manure, and the practice of 'lazy beds', *feannagan taomaidh*, also allowed maximum use to be made of poor ground. Some observers appreciated the appropriateness of these practices to the Highland environment:

> In a cultivated country, it is contrary to the interest of the tenant, of the landlord, and of the public, to raise potatoes any other way than with the plough. But where there is much land that can be profitably reclaimed, by the potato crop, and with spade culture, the case is different. In this case, the interest of the landlord, the progressive improvement of the country, and indeed the interest of the tenant, if he has a lease of any considerable length, are all deeply concerned in the efforts of the spade.

But if, as Walker also noted, 'by the lazy-bed culture, much arable ground has also been acquired; and that by the same practice, a great addition may be annually made to the cultivated land in the Highlands',[49] we may clearly see how the potato was one main cause of Highland population increase. As one contemporary recognised of potato cultivation, 'it had already done more, and is able, by having the cultivation of it farther extended, to do more to keep our people from emigrating, than any other expedient, which has been hitherto devised'.[50] MacDonald (1811) reckoned that potatoes constituted four-fifths of nourishment of the Hebrides' population and that 'the produce of potatoes . . . promises, by tolerable management, to triple the numbers of inhabitants every 75 years without ever burdening the country'.[51] Population increase was due to factors other than the demographic effect of the potato. But potato crop failure was a prompt behind both temporary and permanent migration (see below, pages 68–75). And the effects of the potato were made more severe by related changes in the region's pastoral economy.

Before about 1750, livestock and pastoral agriculture were largely synonymous with black cattle. All pasture lands were communally managed by 'souming and rouming', that is, by allocating the number of head individual tenants might graze on common pasture, and by agreed timings for the movement of stock to summer pastures and sheilings.[52] Cattle sales provided much of the money element of the rent. There is evidence of increased attention to more commercially-oriented cattle rearing in the early 1700s, a positive response first evident amongst estate owners and landlords in Argyll. New levels of stocking required the engrossment of holdings and the extinction of runrig, if not the wholesale replacement of arable by the extension of grazing grounds. This provided some opportunity for employment as a Highland drover. There are many accounts of temporary migration connected with such seasonal migration beyond the Highlands. But these changes also demanded the replacement of customary practices. The coming of commercial sheep farming accelerated these trends.

The geography and chronology of the coming of Lowland sheep to replace the smaller Highland sheep which was used almost alone within the domestic economy is well understood. The movement begins about 1752 with the introduction of Lowland Blackface in Argyll around Lochgoilhead and Kilmorich. By 1763, sheep and shepherds from 'the south Country' (the Borders and Ayrshire) were common on the Balnagown estates in eastern Ross and Cromarty. Cheviot sheep (later to replace the Blackface throughout the Highlands) were introduced into Caithness in 1791–92, and large-scale sheep farming begins in Sutherland in 1806 with the leasing to Lowland graziers of lands in Lairg and Strathnaver owned by then by the Marquis of Stafford.[53] The main effects of the commercialisation of sheep farming are also understood, by contemporaries and modern scholars alike. Singer (1807) provides a useful summary: rise in rents; supply of wool on unprecedented scales; reduction in numbers of black cattle; reduction 'in the extent of cultivated grounds'; depopulation are all identified as the major effects. The last mentioned was, in turn, the result of four factors: the management of sheep flocks on large scales was unknown to the established tenantry; landowners faced difficulties in finding 'new methods of subsistence for their people' since 'the people dissatisfied with the change, and irritated in their minds, were generally averse from engaging in any new occupation on their native soil'; the pull of America; and the activities of departing tacksmen and middling tenants in inducing sub-tenants and lesser kin to quit estates.[54] Early clearances of population for sheep in the south and central Highlands followed quite closely population displacement occasioned by commercial cattle raising, rental increase and arable re-organisation. In the north and west, the coming of *na caoraich mora*, the 'Big' or Lowland sheep, was more sudden and dramatic and migration more of a psychological trauma:

> The introduction of sheep . . . affected, everywhere in the Highlands, a complete revolution in the condition of the population. It snapped the tie which bound the occupant to the owner of the soil . . . the anticipated result followed. Vast tracts of our straths and valleys, of our moors and mountains, exchanged stock and occupants . . . One or other of three alternatives was adopted by the unfortunate mountaineer, – that of removing to some of the manufacturing towns of the south, – of emigrating to America, – or of contenting himself with a small patch of land, with the keep of a few cows, in some assigned locality in his native strath or valley.[55]

Class formation and changes in Highland rural society

Management of agriculture and tenantry was an indirect affair for most Highland landowners. Before about 1770, authority in agrarian management was vested in the tacksman. Whilst we must allow for variety of outlook and type between individuals, the description of Johnson in 1773 highlights the main features of this class and their place as agricultural agents within and between *clan*, *sliochdan* and *cloinne*:

> Next in dignity to the Laird is the Tacksman; a large taker or lease-holder of land, of which he keeps part, as a domain in his own hand, and lets part to under tenants. The Tacksman is necessarily a man capable of securing to the Laird the whole rent, and is commonly a collateral relation. These tacks, or subordinate possessions, were long considered as hereditary, and the occupant was distinguished by the name of the place at which he resided. He held a middle station, by which the highest and lowest orders were connected. He paid rent and reverence to the Laird, and received them from the tenants. This tenure still subsists, with its original operation, but not with the primitive stability.[56]

40

Many contemporaries saw the role of the tacksman and the facts of sub-letting as obstacles to agrarian improvement: '. . . immoderate and unreasonable Profits acquired by these Tacksmen without any Industry, makes them careless about any Improvement'.[57] Direct leasing was not the only cause of the going of the tacksmen, but it was an important influence. The decline of their military role was also important. Hunter has also considered that commercial attitudes to land and the waning of customary beliefs in the hereditary *duthchas* of holdings motivated the tacksman class to go. It is a view echoed by contemporary observers: '. . . they found themselves uneasy at home, by alteration in the state of property to which they had not been accustomed, and to which their minds and views could not correspond'.[58]

Given that many tacksmen took with them kin groups as they emigrated and that the system to which they were central was often recreated in the new farms and émigré communities of Canada, we ought not to see the tacksman as of necessity a barrier to the transformation of Highland rural society. Since they were often replaced by estate agents or factors, we should not see in the departure of the tacksman a polarisation of Highland society into the two classes of chiefs-cum-landowners and tenantry bound more and more by capital and less and less by custom to their commercialising chiefs. The going of the tacksman left a void filled by Lowland land agents or estate factors. The growth of the crofting community in particular was accompanied by stratification within the tenantry: between crofters, cottars, and squatters. Although all shared in the increasing landlessness of the tenantry in the north and west High-lands from the later eighteenth and early nineteenth centuries (the last-named the most), there are important differences between them. They have their origins (and their continued problems) in sub-division of holdings. The cottar was an inhabitant of dwellings built on holdings whose officially-recognised occupants were usually close relatives. The cottar commonly cultivated a part of that croft and paid a proportion of the rent. The squatter lived on the margins of the common grazings, paid no rent, and was without any fixity of tenure. If it is true that 'Crofting occupied a half-way house between the status of an independent pea-santry and that of a totally dispossessed proletariat',[59] we should not lose sight either of the social and tenurial gradations encompassed in the term or of the fact that, through the growth of a rentier economy, through contact with Lowland sheep farmers or in the rhythms of seasonal labour mobility, Highlanders of all social positions were closely connected with economic and social issues beyond their immediate locale.

'Highland climacteric': the effect of the Great Highland Famine, 1836–1856

The view of Flinn *et al* in 1977 was that 'The potato famine, starting in 1846, constituted the climacteric of the social history of the Hebrides and western Highlands in modern times':

> For almost a century, but above all in the half-century before 1846, the potato effectively held back the tide of emigration. But it allowed the population to build up to the point at which the sheer weight of numbers finally broke the dam, releasing the flood-waters of renewed migration. The dam was not re-built, and the outflow of Highlanders, the only known safety valve in the Highland socio-economic system, continued unabated.[60]

More recent analyses would not dissent from this overall view of the potato famine as a crucial moment in Highland history, but they have provided a more detailed anatomy of the famine, and clear insight into the differing geography of its consequences.[61] One such outcome was a heightened out-migration of Highlanders to Lowland cities and an increase in numbers of temporary Highland migrants, (see below, pp. 68–75). What is considered here are the essential facts of the famine and the relationship between the famine and those other agencies acting to transform Highland life.

Subsistence crises were no stranger to the Highlander. Shortage of foodstuffs, chiefly in consequence of climatic impact upon grain and harvest returns, was known in 1740–41, 1751, 1756, 1763–64, 1771, 1782–83, 1806–08, 1811 and 1816–17: 1783 is remembered as *Bliadhna na peasrach*, the year of pease-meal, government aid being given in that form then. The food shortage of 1782 is held by Richards to have accelerated the replacement of arable practices by sheep farming,[62] and it is possible that similar changes in land use and outlook accompanied scarcity in 1806–1808, 1812–3, and 1816–7. What is clear from our understanding of the potato famines for the twenty years from the mid-1830s is how much the native population was by then dependent upon the potato and how the failure of the potato acted to accelerate other changes in Highland life yet varied in its geographical impact.

We are told in March 1837 that there were by then, in consequence of potato blight, from 50–80,000 persons in the areas from Argyll to Sutherland including Skye and the Hebrides 'who would require a very extensive supply of food . . . there is the greatest want in the entire extent of the above named districts, of seed barley, oat, and potatoes'.[63] Local evidence confirms this picture: in parts of Stornoway parish, about 45 per cent of all families were 'totally destitute of all supplies of food'; in Portree, 30 per cent of the parish population were 'wholly without provisions' in 1837.[64] In the Outer Isles, shortage was made worse by the earlier processes of agrarian change and the degree of dependence upon the potato. On North Uist in 1837, 'it is notorious, that there are no less than 390 families not paying rents, but living chiefly on the produce of small spots of potato ground given them by some of their neighbours and relatives'.[65] The totals and the variation are repeated in the destitution following the crop failure of 1846. Devine suggests the numbers of inhabitants then 'seriously at risk' to have been 66,705 (about 28 per cent of the Highland population), with the great part of this total concentrated in the western mainland parishes of Ross and Cromarty and Inverness, and in the Hebrides, increasingly the 'epicentre of destitution' by the early 1850s.[66] The farming districts were not unaffected, but the scale of food shortage was much less severe. And what further weakened the crofting Highlands in particular was the effect upon cash income, either from the relative levels of money brought through temporary migration, or the decline in income from cattle which had been used to buy grain: 'This was almost as great a disaster as the failure of the potatoes'.[67]

Geographical differences were accompanied by social variations within the crofting tenantry. Three groups in particular were most vulnerable – widows with families, elderly spinsters, and the cottar class – and much of the explanation for this rests in the failure of the Poor Law in the Highlands. Relief measures sought not to re-align any class divisions or to improve tenurial positions within the destitute populations. The Central Board of Management of the Fund for the Relief of the Destitute Inhabitants of the Highlands considered that relief, either as employment schemes or as distribution of meal, should be undertaken 'to make it conducive to increased exertion', but also to preserve the tenurial and social *status quo*: 'The destitute population were relieved in a mode which left them in their natural position and there was no interference whatever with the ordinary relations of society'.[68] The proportion of cottars was lower in the south and east Highlands, a fact which was seen both as a matter of societal order as well as partial explanation of the varying geography of destitution: 'The population of these districts was in an entirely different position from that of the Western Districts. The different classes of society were in their proper place . . . there were all the appliances of an advanced society, in which purchased food forms a principal feature of the subsistence of the people'.[69] The famine highlighted the weakening connections apparent within the crofting community between people and land. Population migration, either within the estate, overseas, or on a permanent or seasonal basis to the lowlands, was for some a consequence of heightened awareness amongst landlords of the need for what they considered estate rationalisation. As Hunter has argued, 'the famine of the 1840s served only to intensify Highland proprietors' hostility to the crofting system and to make "redundance of population" an even more "prominent topic of lamentation" in land-owning circles'.[70] The clearances and emigrations of the famine and immediately post-famine years have been detailed elsewhere: important instances should be noted in Glencalvie in Ross and Cromarty in 1845, throughout Strathconan in Easter Ross in the 1840s, at Sollas on North Uist in 1849, Strathaird on south-west Skye in 1850 and Suishnish on Skye in 1849, 1852 and 1853, Coigach in 1852–3, Greenyards in Strathcarron in 1854, and, notable for their thoroughness, on South Uist, Barra, and Benbecula in 1848–51.[71] Neither clearance nor agrarian transformation were without opposition. But they did most directly affect a crofting population by then drained of any financial capacity to resist. It was this monetary insecurity as well as the break in customary attachments to land and kin that underlay movement to the Lowland cities.

Recovery and Legislation: Highland agriculture and rural society,
c.1856–1900
Richards has considered the period 1850 to 1882 'in many ways the most interesting and the most enigmatic for the social and economic history of the highlands'.[72] The trends in prices favoured producers: wool rose in price by one-third between 1850 and 1880, cattle prices twofold. Crofters' rents did not rise in any significant way. In consequence of rises in price, the size of sheep flocks increased and prosperity for the sheep farmer was maintained despite parallel increases in rents. What these circumstances do not indicate, however, is the profound transformation in patterns of Highland landownership.

Changes in estate- and land-ownership in the Highlands before about 1830 were principally between Highland proprietors. From that date, no significant land purchase was undertaken by a Highland resident with hereditary connections with the region. The shift from clan chief or major kin relation to commercially-conscious landowner was sometimes attended from within the tenantry by what has been termed 'residual deference' to the old customs of kin loyalty as well as to long-established practices of holding and working land.[73] But by 1850, the patterns of landownership in the western Highlands and Islands had been transformed 'by the large-scale and rapid penetration of a new breed of proprietors from outside the region'.[74] The alienation of Highland land from Highland people continued throughout the later nineteenth century but was not, as is too readily assumed, apparent only within the land-working populations.

Highland sheep farming suffered a relative decline from the 1870s, the result of stock loss in severe winters in 1878–9 and 1882–3, the importation of cheap frozen mutton from New Zealand and Australia, and the better profits to be gained from working the land as deer forest or as hunting grounds. There was a dramatic rise in the number of deer forests from 1850: a total of 155 being formed, chiefly in the north and west mainlands, between 1850 and 1900 in comparison with the 45 laid out before 1850.[75] Deer forests were a response both to the need for financial gains other than from a pauperised tenantry or sheep and to the increasing commercialisation of the Highlands as a sporting arena. Increased acreage of deer forest compensated for falling wool prices and prompted rental rise. For Inverness-shire, for example, the total rental of the county in 1845 was about £200,000, rising to £296,353 by 1871–2: 'Inverness-shire has its grouse shootings and deer forests in a considerable degree to thank for swelling its rent-roll'.[76] Rents had also been increased for arable farmers at the expiry of their leases with the twin effect of stimulating greater production on lands already worked and of bringing waste ground into cultivation. Arable acreage in Inverness-shire increased by 88 per cent between 1854 and 1870; in Sutherland by 34 per cent between 1853 and 1879.[77] However, those changes took place in farming districts anyway, and largely amongst the larger tentantry. Expansion of the arable margins was not possible for crofters and cottars. And here we have something of a paradox for the crofting population.

By the 1850s and 1860s, rental arrears ensured continued dependence by crofters upon their lands, even recognising that their holdings were often subdivided for and occupied by kin or others as cottars or squatters. Being in arrears, or having been cleared altogether, the tenantry were not seen as major contributors to estate finances. They could not expand their holdings both because of their intrinsic poverty and the relative price of sheep grazings or deer forests. In combination, the effect was to make the crofting tenantry more secure than before, albeit under-capitalised and on marginal land, to perpetuate the crowding and to hinder attempts at improvement from within, but to leave them alone. If, then, the 1860s and 1870s were, relatively, a period of stability and prosperity for crofting tenants, it is also the case that much of their well-being was rooted in connections with the wider world. Temporary migration to the fishing or to Lowland harvests was a crucial source of cash. Yet such sources of income were at the mercy of changing wage levels, fluctuations in job opportunities, and externally-derived price levels. It was prosperity without security: security against the vagaries of return from marginal land; security undermined by any fall in wage levels or decline in cash income if the herring did not appear or if rental arrears built up; and security against eviction that they might both legally retain possession and the right to improve the land. All these issues are apparent in the evidence of the Napier Commission. Tremendously valuable as a social document of Highland life, the Napier Commission's Report identified the root causes of the crofters' problem as the small size of holdings, insecurity of holdings, high rents, and the virtual absence of a proper economic infrastructure. What it also exposed was chronic land shortage, occasioned both by other land uses and by subdivision of holdings amongst crofters, cottars, and 'landless' squatters. The 1886 Crofters' Act gave crofters an unprecedented security of tenure and recognised their rights to some grazing ground as well as providing a statutory means to redress of grievance through the Crofters' Commission. But it did not give crofters the material means to adapt and improve their system. Land shortage together with intrinsic restrictions upon crofters' rights to improve their own lot was a source of conflict and concern until the 1930s, despite the work of the Board of Agriculture and the Congested Districts Board.[78]

Opposition to transformation: rural social protest in the Highlands, c.1780–1930
The main features of the chronology and geography of rural protest in the Highlands have been reviewed elsewhere and need not be detailed here.[79] In summary, a tradition of protest that begins in the early 1780s in opposition to the advance of commercial pastoralism has been shown to extend through the nineteenth century, with a concentration in the Land Wars of the 1880s, into the 1930s. The principal cause of rural protest was a concern about loss of land and claims to the customary holding of 'ancestral lands'. The belief expressed even by land raiders of the 1920s in the inalienability of their right to land presents powerful testimony of the Highlanders' attachment to land.

What is important is that many of the protests against clearance or against enclosure, and particularly many of the events making up the Land Wars in the late nineteenth century, were influenced in their frequency by patterns of Highland-Lowland seasonal migration and by wider political connections between the Highlands and the rest of Britain, connections made in a number of ways through migrant Highlander organisations. The relative economic prosperity of crofters ended in 1881 with a bad harvest in the north and west, compounded by poor returns from fishing. Whilst these events intensified hardship, they also prompted further protest since the failure of the fishing meant that men who might otherwise have left the area did not. There is also evidence that protest depended upon connections with Ireland, then experiencing its own Land Wars and rural unrest. As one commentator on the lawlessness of Skye in 1882 noted, 'I am confident that all is quiet till winter when the men will return from the Irish fishings – what will be done then I consider depends on the state of Ireland'.[80] And we are told elsewhere how 'Ireland was certainly the origin of the Skye agitation'. The return of the fishermen from Kinsale immediately preceded the first note of discontent in the Braes, near Portree.[81] Protest was likewise seasonal because of the temporary absence of crofters at Lowland harvests or fishing, even by the early twentieth century: twenty-one of the thirty-five principal land raids enumerated in the Outer Isles between 1913 and 1922 took place between November and March, for example, upon the return of male activists.[82]

The politicisation of crofter unrest from within the Highlands was aided by outside newspaper coverage of protest and, crucially, by the involvement of Highland societies in the Lowlands and by radical societies there and further afield. The Glasgow Argyllshire Society, founded in 1851, the Islay Association, the Sutherland Association (1860), the Skye Association (1865), the Tiree Association (1870), the Lewis Association (1876), the Mull and Iona Association, the Ross-shire Association, the Lochaber Society, the Appin Society, the Coll Society, and the Ardnamurchan, Morvern and Sunart Association were all Highland migrant bodies in the Lowlands involved in political support for the crofters.[83] The fact that opposition to transformation of Highland rural society was voiced amongst émigré Highlanders in Canada and in Australia is further testimony to the notion of a migrant Gaelic cultural consciousness beyond the Gaidhealtachd itself.[84]

HIGHLAND TRANSFORMATION AND THE FAILURE TO INDUSTRIALISE

Small-scale domestic industry was a minor but integral part of Highland life. The extension of what contemporary commentators in the eighteenth and nineteenth centuries saw as industry should be seen both as the commercialisation of production, the extension of a regulated division of labour, and a more industrious way of Highland life. 'Manufactures' as both process and products depended upon the extension of 'a spirit of industry' amongst Highlanders, although some commentators regarded Highlanders as almost innately incapable, morally and physically, of being industrious.[85]

The development of commercially-oriented industry and manufactures in the Highlands before about 1900 is principally the story of kelp, fishing, and textiles. Each industry had important connections with the processes affecting rural society, notably in the rates and geography of population change, the economic bases to Highland life and in the circumstances prompting out-migration.

Kelp-making involved burning seaweed to make a calcined ash useful in the manufacture of glass, soap, and iodine. It was, before the adoption of chemical substitutes from the 1820s, an important component of the economy of the north and west Highlands. Kelping had been introduced in the northern isles by the 1720s, but was not widespread in the Hebrides until the 1760s when it became a principal means of cash income until its decline as an industry in the 1830s. The income from kelp was unequally distributed. Almost all went to the landlords. But because there was some benefit to tenants, rental levels were often increased, a fact which represented simply a surrogate means of benefiting landlords. Kelping was seasonal (for roughly eight weeks from early June). As an industry, it demanded the temporary coastal relocation of tenants as labourers. An important effect of the industry was to ensure dependence upon agricultural production but, simultaneously, to remove tenants from their land and yet to encourage sub-division of holdings in response to the retention of population. Kelping was an important means of capital accumulation for the landlord class, but a limited short-term gain, ultimately restrictive of agricultural development, for the labouring classes. As MacDonald noted of the Hebrides in 1811, 'On kelp estates the land is almost entirely sacrificed to that manufacture and is at best, with regards to its agriculture, in a stationary condition'.[86] The collapse of kelping after 1830 had several effects on the crofting economy. For landlords, a vital source of cash income was removed. This was an important prompt to the sales of estates at this time. For tenants, rental arrears increased steeply. The fact that no regular division of labour had accompanied kelp production and that the raw materials were local meant there was no industrial infrastructure. The relocation of population to the coastal margins acted only to make worse the facts of land shortage caused by conversion of arable lands to sheep grazings.

The gathering together of the region's population was, in the eyes of some contemporaries, greatly to be welcomed in regard to the region's social and economic transformation since it permitted the establishment of villages, and, in turn, manufactures: 'Our only means of making the natives industrious, is to make them depend on each other for many of the necessaries of life, and this can only be done by collecting them in towns'.[87] The establishment of villages in the Highlands was difficult, however, given the natives' self-sufficiency: '. . . almost every person executes most of the mechanic arts that are necessary for their own accommodation. This renders the formation of a Highland village

48

peculiarly difficult'.[88] Beyond fishing in a few coastal settlements in the north and west, manufacturing was chiefly evident in the development of textile villages in the central and south-eastern farming Highlands. In Highland Perthshire and around eastern Inverness-shire and Ross and Cromarty, there is evidence from the later eighteenth century of the involvement of Lowland merchants and urban entrepreneurs in marketing Highland textiles in ways that paralleled the involvement of the agrarian economy in externally-oriented circuits of capital.[89] Within the Highlands, the creation of textile villages drew in sections of the population rendered surplus to the needs of more efficient farming systems. Movement to these planned villages was principally short distance, although the movement of Highland labour to the hemp factory in Cromarty represents one example of longer-distance migration.[90] For some commentators, creating poor houses in which textile manufacture might be undertaken as a means of encouraging qualities of industriousness was, simultaneously, a means of retaining Highland labour and skills otherwise lost through migration to the Lowlands:

> I think Argyllshire as fit for carrying out of manufactures of Spinning yarn, making linnine, and course woolan cloaths, as any country in Scotland; we have great numbers of poor in it, and consequently labour must be cheap. Our poor goe in great shoals to the low Country for two or three months in the harvest, to reap the corns there, and immediately return, with what they have sav'd, commonly very little, to be a burden for the other nine or ten months of the year on their country: to prevent this practice, make the poor happy and usefull to the Country, I humbly think two houses for them after the example of Glasgow and Edinburgh might be erected, one att Inverarae, the other att Campbeltown, under the direction of the Justices of the Peace.[91]

Localised textile manufacturing in the farming Highlands effectively ended by the 1830s, and attempts at establishing small-scale manufacturing villages in the north and west Highlands failed earlier, more from a combination of mismanagement and distance from Lowland markets than from any inability amongst Highlanders. The region simply could not lend itself to accommodate these technical changes and the centralisation of labour crucial to the success of the factory system of production. Textile manufacturing never provided the means to establish a division of labour or a more general 'spirit of industry' and, crucially, did not draw people away from working the land.

The fishing industry in the Highlands shares a number of general features with textiles: essentially small-scale systems of production; limited expansion under the aegis of outside agencies rather than through harnessing local domestic markets; development that did not free population entirely from dependence upon the land. These circumstances are apparent in their different ways in the three regional geographies of the Highland fishing industry: the Lochs of Argyll and the Clyde estuary; the north-west coastal mainland and Outer Isles; and the north-east Highland coast of Sutherland and Caithness. The first was generally successful because of its proximity to the Lowlands and its thorough-going commercial organisation. The second area was much less successful. Distance from the Lowlands, the lack of capital, involvement with agriculture, and no tradition of fishing for commercial gain must all be cited as reasons: 'it is no easy task', noted one commentator in 1825, 'to teach men, habituated from infancy to tend herds on the hillside, to drag for subsistence in the deep sea'.[92] The efforts of the British Society for Extending the Fisheries and Improving the Sea Coasts of the Kingdom (the British Fisheries Society), begun in 1786, in establishing fishing villages in the north-west Highlands were limited to partial success at Ullapool and Tobermory.[93] Related changes in agrarian society served only to hinder the localised development of fishing despite the clearance of population to the coastal fringes. An excess population on marginal land with holding sizes too small to permit productive agriculture and with neither experience of fishing nor the capital with which to undertake it was bound not to make fishing a success.

On the east coast of the Highlands, however, the development of fishing and commercial fishing villages was successful. Lowland capitalists were drawn to the Sutherland and Caithness fisheries not as exploitative outsiders but as partners in an indigenous industry. A further cause of the area's success was that, in Sutherland particularly, new villages and holdings had been purposefully designed for fishermen as the intended end result of estate rationalisation. From the 1840s, the larger boats of the east coast began systematically to fish northern and western waters. This marked the integration of two regional economies and also brought to the north-west fisheries an organisational structure above and beyond the capacity of the individual crofter-fisherman. The involvement of larger, better-organised fleets and curing practices provided wider employment opportunities – jobs in curing and drying for women, for example – but restricted family-unit fishing. Increased catches provided employment but the boats and the capital were of east-coast origin. The wages derived from seasonal employment in gutting, drying and curing the fish were crucial to the crofting economy, and many Highland women would return with the fleets to the eastern coasts for the summer fishing there. Such seasonal migration as curers and as labourers in the fishing industry grew rapidly in the second half of the nineteenth century.

The failure of the Highlands to industrialise, in the eighteenth and nineteenth centuries especially, is, generally, to be explained by the dependence of the population upon returns from the land, lack of capital, and an inability to generate a distinct division of labour between employment sectors as well as to maintain one between the occupations of individuals within a traditionally subsistent rural economy. The Highlands were not without the capacity for industry. Localised centres of textiles in Highland Perthshire; fishing on the north-east coast; slate quarrying at Easdale; coal mining at Brora; and distilling all provided some industrial base. But the facts of comparative geographical advantage weighed heavily against the Highlands.

CONCLUSION

The transformation of Highland society in the period under review is best seen as the gradual resolution of a conflict between two ways of life. This resolution had different consequences both over time and socially in terms of the land-owning and the land-working classes, and, crucially, had varying outcomes in the north and west crofting Highlands and in the south and east farming Highlands. The transformation of customary rural practices may be measured in the material indices of rent levels, changes in land use, and in the sales of estates. It should also be understood as an ideological matter in which the alienation of Highlanders from their land produced varied reactions: social protest in various forms; what some have seen as pyschological trauma at the facts of emigration; a view of the new Highland settlements created in Upper Canada or in Australia as part of a wider Gaidhealtachd. Highland population change must not be interpreted as a matter of numbers only.

The transformation of the Highlands had local geographies, dependent upon the rate and the degree of social and economic change. At the regional level, the difference between the farming Highlands and the north-west crofting Highlands was crucial. In the former, population change from the 1750s was generally less rapid than in the latter, with several parishes experiencing net population loss from 1755. Out-migration provided a 'safety valve'. Parts of the central and south-east Highlands were, by the end of the eighteenth century, worked by tenants holding land directly of landlords. In this region, the moves to improvement in rental systems, in arable farming, and in the commercialisation of the pastoral economy were all accommodated earlier than in the crofting Highlands and with less disruption.

In the north and west, population increase was rapid from 1775, if not before, and population was pressing against usable resources by the end of the eighteenth century. Out-movement took the form of direct emigration, of re-location to the urban Lowlands, and, as an integral part of the crofting economy, of seasonal migration. The same processes of social and economic change that had brought about the growth of a farming population in the central and southern Highlands led to the formation of a crofting peasantry in the north and west. Gradations within the crofting tenantry were the result of established if weakening familial relations, and, from the later 1700s, land shortages were felt most severely by cottars and squatters.

Selkirk, writing in 1806, argued that

> Accustomed to possess land, to derive from it all the comforts they enjoy, they naturally consider it as indispensable, and can form no idea of happiness without such a possession. No prospect of an accommodation of this kind can enter into the views of any one who seeks for employment as a day-labourer, still less of those who resort to a manufacturing town.[94]

This chapter has outlined the principal agencies behind the transformation of Highland society and has suggested how migration from the region to the manufacturing towns has to be seen as following from structural alterations in the Highland way of life.

NOTES

1. National Library of Scotland (hereafter NLS), MS 1034, Observations on the North of Scotland, 1796, ff.104–105.
2. On this point, see I. Carter, 'Economic models and the recent history of the Highlands', *Scottish Studies*, 15, 1971, pp. 99–120; Charles Withers, 'The historical creation of the Scottish Highlands' in I. Donnachie and C. Whatley (eds.), *The Manufacture of Scottish History* (Edinburgh, 1992), pp. 143–156.
3. The pioneering work of Eric Cregeen is important in this context: E. Cregeen, 'The tacksmen and their successors: a study of tenurial reorganisation in Mull, Morvern, and Tiree in the early eighteenth century', *Scottish Studies*, 13, 1969, pp. 93–114; *idem*, 'The changing role of the House of Argyll in the Scottish Highlands' in N. T. Phillipson and R. Mitchison (eds.), *Scotland in the Age of Improvement* (Edinburgh, 1970), pp. 5–23; R. A. Dodgshon, *Land and Society in Early Scotland* (Oxford, 1981); M. H. B. Sanderson, *Scottish Rural Society in the 16th Century* (Edinburgh, 1982).
4. R. A. Dodgshon, ' "Pretense of Blude" and "Place of Thair Dwelling": the nature of Scottish clans, 1500–1745', in R. A. Houston and I. D. Whyte (eds.), *Scottish Society 1500–1800* (Cambridge, 1989), pp. 169–198; *idem*, 'West Highland Chiefdoms, 1500–1745: a study in redistributive exchange' in R. Mitchison and P. Roebuck (eds.), *Economy and Society in Scotland and Ireland 1500–1939* (Edinburgh, 1988), pp. 27–37; A. Macinnes, 'The Impact of the civil wars and interregnum: political disruption and social change within Scottish Gaeldom' in R. Mitchison and P. Roebuck (eds.), *ibid*, pp. 58–69; *idem*, 'Crown,

Clans and Fine: the 'civilizing' of Scottish Gaeldom, 1587–1638', *Northern Scotland*, 13, 1993, pp. 31–56; D. Stevenson, *Alasdair MacColla and the Highland problem in the seventeenth century* (Edinburgh, 1980).

5. M. Gray, *The Highland Economy 1750–1850* (Edinburgh, 1957), pp. 23–24.
6. Macinnes and Dodgshon (n.5 above); R. A. Gailey, 'Settlement and population in Kintyre, 1750–1890', *Scottish Geographical Magazine*, 76, 1960, pp. 99–107; A. McKerral, 'The Tacksman and his holding in the south-west Highlands', *Scottish Historical Review*, 26, 1947, pp. 10–25.
7. M Flinn *et al* (eds.), *Scottish Population History* (Cambridge, 1977), pp. 51–57; I. D. Whyte, *Agriculture and Society in Seventeenth Century Scotland* (Edinburgh, 1979), pp. 11, 12, 40, 240–251.
8. R. Mitchison, 'Webster Revisited: a re-examination of the 1755 'census' of Scotland', in T. M. Devine (ed.), *Improvement and Enlightenment* (Edinburgh, 1989), pp. 62–77.
9. Flinn, *op. cit.*, p. 30.
10. Gray, *Highland Economy*, pp. 59, 60–61.
11. J. Walker, *An Economical History of the Hebrides and Highlands of Scotland* (Edinburgh, 1808), I, p. 30.
12. Walker, *op. cit.*, p. 32; T. Pennant, *A Tour in Scotland and Voyages to the Hebrides* (London, 1790), II, p. 314; *Old Statistical Account* (OSA), VIII, 1793, p. 368; X, 1794, p. 384; XI, 1794, p 425; XVII, 1795, p 279; J. Sinclair, *Analysis of the Statistical Account of Scotland* (Edinburgh, 1826), p. 147.
13. Walker, *op. cit.*, p. 56.
14. Flinn, *op. cit.*, pp. 209–240; T. M. Devine, *The Great Highland Famine* (Edinburgh, 1988), pp. 57–82.
15. *OSA*, VI, 1793, p. 190; XI, 1794, p. 425.
16. Sinclair, *op. cit.*, p. 167.
17. Scottish Record Office (hereafter SRO), E.783/68(1)/(2); E.788/11, ff.1–4; E.783/87; E.728/57/1, ff.1–20; E.727/63 (1) – (5); GD 46/1/526, f.13.
18. *OSA*, VIII, 1793, p. 409 (Kilmallie); SRO, E.783/68/(1)/(2); E.728/57/1. ff. 1–4.
19. M. W. Flinn, *The European Demographic System, 1500–1820* (London, 1981), p. 71; T. C. Smout, *A History of the Scottish People 1560–1830* (Glasgow, 1972), pp. 144, 154–155; M. Perceval-Maxwell, *The Scottish Migration to Ulster in the reign of James I* (London, 1973).
20. B. Bailyn, *Voyagers to the West: Emigration from Britain to America on the eve of the Revolution* (London, 1987).
21. J. Boswell, *Journal of a Tour of the Hebrides* (Oxford, 1970 edn.), pp. 129, 141, 192; *Calendar of Home Office Papers, 1773–1775*, No. 585; M. Flinn, 'Malthus, emigration and potatoes in the Scottish north-west, 1770–1870' in L. M. Cullen and T. C. Smout (eds.), *Comparative Aspects of Scottish and Irish Economic and Social History* (Edinburgh, 1977), pp. 47–64.
22. Sinclair, *op. cit.*, p. 147.
23. M. McLean, *The People of Glengarry: Highlanders in transition, 1745–1820* (Montreal and London, 1991), quoted on p. 97.
24. M. MacDonell, *The Emigrant Experience: songs of Highland emigrants in North America* (Toronto, 1982), pp. 140–141.
25. MacDonnell, *op. cit.*; D. Baines, *Migration in a mature economy: emigration and internal migration in England and Wales, 1861–1900* (Cambridge, 1985); Devine, *Great Highland Famine*, pp. 117–118.

26. E. Richards, 'Varieties of Scottish emigration in the nineteenth century', *Historical Studies*, 21, 1985, p. 476.

27. Richards' two volume history of the clearances is likely to remain the major interpretation for some while: E. Richards, *A History of the Highland Clearances Volume 1: agrarian transformation and the evictions* (London, 1982) and *A History of the Highland Clearances Volume 2: emigration, protest, reasons* (London, 1985). Also important is Devine's *Great Highland Famine*. The issues of the psychological trauma of emigration are explored best in Richards' 1985 article (n.26 above).

28. Devine, *op. cit.*, pp. 192–211.

29. BPP., 1852, XXXIII, *Papers relative to Emigration to the North American Colonies* p. 567.

30. Good surveys of personalised memories of emigration are provided in D. Craig's *On the Crofters' Trail: in search of the Clearance Highlanders* (London, 1990) and J. Hunter *A Dance called America* (Edinburgh, 1994).

31. See, on this topic, the useful work of Rosemary Ommer: R. Ommer, 'Highland Scots migration to southwestern Newfoundland: a study of kinship' in J. J. Mannion (ed.), *The Peopling of Newfoundland: essays in historical geography* (St Johns, 1977), pp. 212–233; *idem*, 'Primitive accumulation and the Scottish *clann* in the old world and the new', *Journal of Historical Geography* 12, 1986, pp. 121–141.

32. *Duthchas* does not permit of easy translation, but in tenurial terms means the collective heritage of a holding in which it was believed that any holding or plot, having been held and continuously worked by a family group over four generations, belonged by customary right to those tenants. The *oigreachd* of a holding translates as 'inheritance', 'possession', or even 'freehold', but is essentially of an individual. For some discussion on these terms and their importance in tenurial protest, see Charles Withers, 'Give us Land and Plenty of it': the ideological basis to land and landscape in the Scottish Highlands', *Landscape History*, 12, 1990, pp. 45–54.

33. F. Shaw, *The Northern and Western Islands of Scotland: their economy and society in the seventeenth century* (Edinburgh, 1980), pp. 50, 56.

34. McKerral, 'The tacksman and his holding . . .', p. 10–14; Mowat, *op.cit.*; see also Macinnes and Dodgshon (n.5 above).

35. Dodgshon, *Land and Society in Early Scotland*, *op.cit.*, pp. 276–277.

36. SRO, GD 112/9/3. 12, 15, 18, 21, 23–24, 26, 33.

37. C. Innes, (ed.), *The Black Book of Taymouth* (Edinburgh, 1885), pp. 352–356.

38. Richards, *Highland Clearances Volume 2*, *op. cit.*, pp. 424–441.

39. *Ibid.*, pp. 480, 482.

40. R. C. Macleod (ed.), *The Book of Dunvegan 1340–1920* (Aberdeen, 1938), II, pp. 79 *et seq.*; SRO, GD 112/9/33, GD 112/9/49, 112/9/67; GD 174, ff.1, 7, 10, 838 (4); GD 221/2/20; GD 84/2/50, f.14.

41. J. Anderson, 'Essay on the present state of the Highlands and Islands of Scotland', *Transactions, Highland and Agricultural Society of Scotland*, II, 1831, p. 22.

42. Gray, *Highland Economy*, pp. 182–183; SRO, GD 84/2/50, f.14; GD 221/38/43; GD 46/13/199, f.1; GD 221/90/2 (Rentals on Lord MacDonald's estate in Skye, Whitsun 1823 – Whitsun 1824).

43. Walker, *op. cit.*, I, pp. 66–67.

44. Gray, *Highland Economy*, p. 66.

45. J. Smith, *General View of the Agriculture of the County of Argyle* (London, 1805), pp. 66–67.
46. G. MacKenzie, *A General Survey of the Counties of Ross and Cromarty* (London, 1810), p. 184.
47. EUL, La. II. 623, f.11.
48. M. McKay, *The Rev Dr John Walker's Report on the Hebrides of 1764 and 1771* (Edinburgh, 1980), p. 210.
49. Walker, *op. cit.*, I, pp. 252–253.
50. J. Robertson, *General View of the Agriculture of the Southern Districts of the County of Perth* (London, 1794), pp. 39–40.
51. J. MacDonald, *General View of the Agriculture of the Hebrides* (Edinburgh, 1811), p.17.
52. R. W. Munro, *Taming the Rough Bounds: Knoydart 1745–1784* (Coll, 1984); A. Bil, *The Highland Sheiling* (Edinburgh, 1988).
53. Gray, *Highland Economy*, *op. cit.*, pp. 87–88; D. S. MacLagan, 'Stock rearing in the Highlands, 1720–1820', *Transactions of the Royal Highland and Agricultural Society*, 6th Series, II, 1958, pp. 63–71; M. L. Ryder, 'Sheep and the Clearances in the Scottish Highlands: a Biologist's view', *Agricultural History Review*, 16, 1968, pp. 155–158; MacKenzie, *General View . . .*, pp. 128–129, 130–131; J. Henderson, *General View of the Agriculture of the County of Sutherland* (London, 1812), p. 103; McKay, *op.cit.*, p. 129.
54. W. Singer, 'On the introduction of sheep farming into the Highlands; and on the plan of husbandry adapted to the soil and climate, and to the general and solid interests of that country', *Transactions of the Highland and Agricultural Society of Scotland*, III, 1807, pp. 544–545.
55. NSA, VII, 1845, p. 93 (The parish being described here is Glenorchy and Inishail, Argyllshire).
56. S. Johnson, *A Journey to the Western Isles of Scotland* (London, 1775), p. 78.
57. Walker, *op. cit.*, I, pp. 53–55; McKay (ed), *op. cit.*, p. 101; MacDonald, *op. cit.*, 74–75.
58. Hunter, *op. cit.*, p. 120; Walker, *op. cit.*, I, p. 406.
59. Richards, *Highland Clearances Volume 2*, *op. cit.*, p. 356.
60. Flinn, *Scottish Population History*, *op. cit.*, p. 438.
61. Devine, *The Great Highland Famine*, *op. cit.*, *passim* and Richards' two-volume work on the Highland Clearances.
62. Richards, *Highland Clearances Volume 1*, *op. cit.*, p. 183.
63. SRO, GD 46/13/199, f.1. Letter of J. A. Stewart MacKenzie to Lord John Russell.
64. SRO, GD 46/13/199, f.3; GD 46/13/213; GD 46,13/215, (1)-(6).
65. NSA, 14, 1837, p. 181.
66. Devine, *Great Highland Famine*, *op. cit.*, p. 46; ('Seriously at risk' is defined by Devine as having up to one third of their populations on the relief lists at any point between 1847 and 1850).
67. *Ibid.*, p. 37.
68. SRO, HD 16/95, (Memorandum regarding the mode of relieving destitution by Co-operative arrangements with Proprietors of Estates upon which there is a destitute population).
69. Destitution Papers, Second Report by the Committee of Management to the Edinburgh Section for 1850, p. 11 (Quoted in Devine, *Great Highland Famine*, *op. cit.*, p. 43).

70. Hunter, *Making of the Crofting Community*, *op. cit.*, p. 73.
71. *Ibid.*, pp. 85–87; Richards, *Highland Clearances, passim.*
72. Richards, *op. cit.*, Volume 2, p. 485.
73. Hunter, *op. cit.*, pp. 13–14.
74. T. M. Devine, 'The emergence of the new elite in the western Highlands and Islands, 1800–1860' in *idem*, (ed.), *Improvement and Enlightenment* (Edinburgh, 1989) pp. 108–142.
75. W. Orr, *Deer Forests, Landlords and Crofters* (Edinburgh, 1982), pp. 168–181.
76. W. MacDonald, 'On the Agriculture of Inverness-shire', *Transactions of the Highland and Agricultural Society of Scotland*, 4th Series, IV, 1872, pp. 2, 17, 22.
77. J. Macdonald, 'On the Agriculture of the County of Sutherland', *Transactions of the Highland and Agricultural Society of Scotland*, 4th Series, XII, 1880, p. 49.
78. These agencies are discussed in more detail in Hunter and Richards; see also A. M. McCleery, 'The role of the Highland Development Agency, with particular reference to the work of the Congested Districts Board 1897–1912', (unpublished PhD thesis, University of Glasgow 1984).
79. Hunter, *op. cit.*; Richards *Highland Clearances, op. cit. passim*; Withers, 'Give us Land and Plenty of it', *op. cit.*, n.42; *idem, Gaelic Scotland: the transformation of a culture region* (London, 1988), pp. 327–401; I. Robertson, 'The historical geography of rural social protest in Highland Scotland 1919–1939' (unpublished PhD thesis, University of Bristol, 1995);
80. SRO, GD 1/36/1, 21 May 1882; GD 1/36/1/12. f.25; on these links, see Charles Withers, 'Rural protest in the Highlands of Scotland and in Ireland, 1850–1930' in S. J. Connolly, R. J. Morris, and R. A. Houston (eds.), *Conflict, Identity, and Economic Development: Ireland and Scotland 1600–1939* (Lancaster, 1995), pp. 172–187.
81. SRO, GD 40/16/32. f. 3, M. McNeill, Confidential Report to the Secretary of State for Scotland on the Condition of the Western Highlands and Islands', October 1886.
82. See Withers, 'Rural Protest in the Highlands of Scotland and in ireland', *op. cit.*; SRO, AF 67/61–65, 143–154, 157–160, 292, 299, 324, 325, 326, 328, 329, 331, 345, 348, 370–371, 389.
83. 'Directory of Highland and Celtic Societies', *The Celtic Magazine*, IV, 1879, pp. 35–38.
84. E. Richards, 'How tame were the Highlanders during the Clearances?', *Scottish Studies*, 17, 1973, p. 46.
85. See, for example, J. Millar, *The Origins of the Distinctions of Ranks* (London, 1779), p. 276.
86. MacDonald, *General View of the Agriculture of the Hebrides*, *op. cit.*, pp. 119–120.
87. G. S. MacKenzie, *Letters to the Proprietors of Land in Ross-shire* (Edinburgh, 1803), p. 17.
88. Walker, *An Economical History . . .*, *op. cit.*, II, pp. 152–153.
89. I. D. Whyte, 'Proto-industrialisation in Scotland' in P. Hudson (ed), *Regions and Industries* (London, 1988), pp. 228–251.
90. R. A. Houston 'Geographical mobility in Scotland 1652–1811: the evidence of testimonials', *Journal of Historical Geography*, 11, 1985, pp. 379–394; D. G. Lockhart, 'Patterns of migration and movement of labour to the planned villages of north-east Scotland', *Scottish Geographical Magazine*, 98, 1982, pp. 35–49;

idem, 'Migration to planned villages in Scotland between 1725 and 1850', *Scottish Geographical Magazine* 102, 1986, pp. 165–180; Charles Withers, *Gaelic in Scotland 1698–1981: the geographical history of a language* (Edinburgh, 1984), pp. 199–200.

91. SRO, GD 14/17, 10 February 1744, f.5 Anent Improvements in Argyll.
92. A. Sutherland, *A Summer Ramble in the North Highlands* (Edinburgh, 1825), p. 103.
93. J. Dunlop, *The British Fisheries Society 1786–1893* (Edinburgh, 1978); M. Gray, *The Fishing Industries of Scotland 1790–1914: a study in regional adaptation* (Aberdeen, 1978).
94. Selkirk, Earl of, *Observations on the Present State of the Highlands of Scotland with a view of the Causes and Probable Consequences of Emigration* (Edinburgh, 1806), p. 50.

PART TWO

The Nature of Highland-Lowland Migration

CHAPTER 3

Seasonal and Temporary Highland-Lowland Migration, c.1680–1900

Urban Gaelic migrant communities in the Lowlands depended upon the settlement of Highlanders for whom the move south was permanent. Such permanent migration was underlain from at least the late seventeenth century by the seasonal and temporary migration of Highland labour, chiefly to harvest and other agricultural employment in the Lowlands, to the fisheries or construction work, or, for women, by periods in domestic service. The nature and causes of such movement are quite well understood, though more is known about its economic importance to the crofting regions and cottar populations within the Highlands, the varying geography of the flow and the cultural effects than about the exact numbers involved. Recent research has also documented the stepped or stage-by-stage patterns of migration adopted by Highlanders in moving to the cities. Far from moving directly citywards or doing so relatively quickly, many migrants moved either within the Highlands or from clachan and village to town to larger town and across different parts of Scotland over a number of years before settling in the urban Lowlands. Experience of urban Scotland did not depend upon residence in it. It is with these issues that this chapter is concerned.

Making a distinction between temporary (including seasonal) and permanent migration poses problems. Firstly, we cannot always be sure that any Highlander recorded as resident in the Lowlands did not intend to return to his or her native parish. Secondly, while the distinction may be one based upon length of residence, it is clear that many Highland women took periods of domestic service in the urban Lowlands for a year or more before returning. Many men and women did more than one job and visited more than one place before moving home. Many harvest labourers had regular patterns of labour mobility which, whilst seasonal in nature, were regarded by them and their Lowland hosts as a regular feature of the agricultural year. Thirdly, both seasonal and temporary migration was paralleled by long-distance rurally-based movement within the Highlands – often undertaken in a series of steps – as well as by shorter-distance permanent relocation within individual estates. Macpherson's work on Laggan parish in Inverness-shire has demonstrated continuity in the migration patterns associated with marriage from before

1750 to the later eighteenth and nineteenth centuries. Marriage patterns within the Highlands before about 1750 were used to maintain clan authority over territory, and the movement of partners was usually short-distance. Distances of over 25 miles were, however, not uncommon even for predominantly agnatic and endogamous marriages in the period 1775–1854.[1] Labour mobility within the Highlands was commonplace on a variety of scales. Gailey's study of the Inverneil estate in Ross and Cromarty has shown how considerable mobility amongst the tenantry declined with the reduction of multiple tenant holdings as people left the land altogether.[2] Because, in general, Highland districts possessed abundant grazing, and arable districts in the southern and eastern Highlands had a surplus of grainstuffs, seasonal exchanges of cattle and transactions in meal determined persisting patterns of population across the Highland-Lowland border, notably in eastern Inverness-shire, in Easter Ross, Sutherland and throughout Perthshire.[3] The seasonal and temporary movement of Highlanders also took place against the permanent redistribution of population within estate boundaries, especially from the 1820s, as cash crises occasioned by falls in rent, the failure of kelp, and falls in livestock prices led landlords to clear their tenantry to marginal areas, or remove them from the land altogether. Such movement has been identified for Lewis in the 1850s, east Sutherland in the 1820s, for movement into Tobermory in the 1790s, and for the southern Highlands in the 'Census of the Inhabitants of Blair Drummond Moss, 1814' which shows movement into the newly-drained lands principally from Balquhidder and Callander parishes with only a few persons moving from any distance.[4] Notwithstanding these typological and other difficulties, seasonal and temporary migration was a crucial fact of life for many within and beyond the Highlands.

THE NATURE AND PATTERNS OF SEASONAL AND TEMPORARY MIGRATION

The seasonal circulation of labour from predominantly pastoral to chiefly arable districts, the movement of domestic servants, and of specialised trades like masons and shoemakers, was as we have seen a common feature throughout Europe.[5] Such circulation of population was an established part of local custom – what Moch has called 'long-standing migration itineraries'[6] – as well as a source of labour and cash income for the receiving and source areas. For Moch and others, most such migration before about 1815 was on regional scales and to long-established patterns: only in the later nineteenth century did these practices begin to decline. Lucassen's emphasis on migrant labour in north-west Europe from 1600 concentrates upon labour movement within the Netherlands and adjoining areas but, additionally, identifies several other regional systems involving a minimum of 20,000 migrants, Lucassen's criterion of a major migratory system.[7] If we accept Lucassen's criterion of an annual displacement of 20,000 persons as the basis of a 'major migratory system', it is difficult to know if Highland-Lowland temporary and seasonal migration should be so termed. Devine has estimated that by the early 1800s virtually every family in the southern and eastern Highlands had at least one member involved in temporary or seasonal migration and that this mobility was even more important to the populations and economy of the north and west crofting Highlands.[8] But it is impossible to be certain of numbers. Reports from Lowland parishes in the late eighteenth century indicating 'great numbers of Highlanders . . . who come into the country for the purpose of harvest' (of Cockburnspath in Berwickshire in 1794), or from the many Highland parishes which simply note the then common place seasonal departure of population, do not allow firm totals to be calculated.[9] The totals for persons recorded as 'temporarily absent' from numerous Highland parishes in the Census records for 1841, 1851, and 1861 give, respectively, totals of 3,204, 3,310, and 3,912 persons. But such migration was occurring for other parishes for which there is no numerical total of those 'temporarily absent', and in many other cases, we are told only of 'a considerable number at work in the south country'.[10] The census records only a moment in what was a dynamic process embedded in the cultural practices of Highland life and the demands of a wider economy. If, in general terms, such short-lived movement for whatever purpose was of a 'marginalised seasonal labour force',[11] it is likely it numbered several thousand each year by the later 1700s and for much of the following century. Although precise numbers are uncertain, it is, however, possible to be more precise about the principal characteristics of this movement.

Harvest migration
Highlanders were regularly moving south in search of harvest work from the later seventeenth century. Sir Robert Sibbald, the Geographer Royal, recorded Highland migration to the lowland 'hairst' in his accounts of Scotland in 1698, and the practice probably predates his evidence.[12] On occasion, local food shortage or harvest failure within the Highlands prompted seasonal migration or an increase in the numbers involved. Highlanders were more numerous in Stirling and Perth in 1623, for example, and again in the 1680s, because of destitution in their native parishes.[13] From about 1752 until the end of the century, the Gaelic community in Edinburgh was inflated by the presence of destitute

shearers and agricultural labourers from the Highlands, who, in the 1700s, drew upon the limited poor funds of the Gaelic chapel there in order to return home.[14] Much more common from the mid-eighteenth century was the seasonal migration of Highlanders to the Lowland harvest, a reflection both of changes within the Highland economy and of the need for labour within the Lowlands. Initially, such movement was of cottars and small farmers, and mainly the younger generations. Later, it involved crofters and older age groups.

Hiring fairs throughout the Lowlands and on the edges of the High-lands at places like Doune, Gartmore and Drymen directed the flow. Regular systems of 'south country' migration for harvest and other agricultural work were in existence from Mull in the 1780s, from parts of Sutherland by a decade later, and throughout Argyll.[15] So widespread was this seasonal out-movement that we must suppose that Highlanders moving south to take up residence in the urban Lowlands would have known what to expect. Familiarity with wage labour, with regulated work practices, some knowledge of where to go in the cities to meet with fellow Highlanders and, perhaps, either to worship in Gaelic or to receive assistance, were facts determined as much by the regularities of the harvest year as they were by the urban economy. Furthermore, it is clear that migration to the harvest was not always an individual decision, and that it was not an unstructured outpouring. Estate organisation within the Highlands was used to marshal and direct seasonal labour: in Sutherland in 1808, for example, the Marchioness of Sutherland 'dis-patched 108 of those least wanted at home' to a farmer in Dumfriesshire for six weeks.[16] The 'many hundreds' who annually went south to harvest from Tiree and Coll in the 1830s, many of them young unmarried women, treated such migration as a cultural event in its own right, something shared with others and important for the cash and the experiences of Lowland life that it would bring.[17] The droving of cattle from the Highlands had similar customary traditions and a familiarity with the urban market economy associated with it.[18]

It has been argued that seasonal employment opportunities for High-landers in Lowland agriculture declined from the 1820s in consequence of the influx of a seasonal Irish labour force which was prepared to accept lower wages, to work harder, and was able to get to the hiring fairs in the south and central Lowlands more easily than Highlanders.[19] This view has been revised for several reasons. It is now acknowledged that there was a *partial* displacement of Highland female harvest labour in the west central-Lowlands and in the Lothians but that that trend was not evident in major ways elsewhere, and that numbers moving south from the Highlands continued despite competition from the Irish. The major impact of the Irish was to reduce wage levels rather than to monopolise employment, and although the Irish scythe-hook did over time displace the Highlanders' toothed sickle in the central Lowlands, it also increased the need for hired hands at harvest time. From the 1830s on, there emerged a regional division of labour: the Irish predominated in the western Lowlands and in Lothian, the Highlanders in that broad sweep of arable land from Fife and Tayside to Caithness, excepting Aberdeen and Banff. As Devine has shown, much of this arable region had '. . . a virtual monopoly of Highland seasonal migrants until the mechanization of the harvest reached its climax in the 1890s with the widespread adoption of the mechanical reaper-binder'.[20]

Much of this movement was of young unmarried women. Women were involved in seasonal and temporary circulation of labour from the earliest period, and recent research has shown that, as for men, movement was bound up in complex ways with the localised and frequently repeated moves of domestic labour and farm servants and with longer-distance mobility to towns as servants or as vagrants.[21] The temporary migration of women as harvest labour was commonplace throughout Britain in this period. O'Dowd's analysis of the *spalpini* (temporary migrants, usually female and involved in agriculture) and 'tatti hoker' tradition of migratory labour from Ireland shows female labour to have been a crucial element, and also to have had its own culture, aside from the menfolk. Partly, this was a culture evident in tales and songs from the young women themselves. Oral tradition survives with regard to such migration, the memory of home and of encounters with society further afield.[22] Partly, too, there is evidence relating to female migration which is expressed as a moral judgement of the young women by external (largely male) authorities. Comments were made on the (supposed) licentiousness of roving bands of young women, on their habits and dress, and so on. And the reverse obtained in terms of Highland commentators who spoke of how Highland girls had been 'demoralised' during their time spent in the Lowlands.[23] The same is true for those Welsh girls, the *Merched y Gerddi* (the 'Garden Girls'), who took up seasonal jobs in horticulture in London in this period.[24]

The important point here is that female harvest migration in particular was not just a matter of population displacement. More so than for males, there was a moral dimension. In the north-east Lowlands, where the 'bothy' system was widespread and where Highland female labour was so important, illegitimate fertility was the highest in rural Scotland in the later nineteenth century and customary practices like 'bundling' (permitting sexual intercourse between unmarried partners on the understanding it would lead to marriage) certainly involved Highland girls.[25] In the Highlands, high levels of female migration created an imbalanced sex ratio which lead to a rising age at first marriage, decreasing nuptuality, and higher rates of age-specific marital fertility.[26] What is also clear is that these factors were complicated by increased proportions of older adults, women included, engaging in seasonal migration by the second half of the nineteenth century, and by the rise, from about mid-century, of other opportunities for temporary migration.

Migration to the fisheries, domestic service, and the construction industry

From the second half of the nineteenth century, alternative employment opportunities were growing as seasonal and temporary migration assumed crucial importance for the Highland economy. Part-time employment in fisheries, around the Clyde coast and notably in eastern Caithness and Sutherland, was the single most powerful influence upon such migration from the crofting Highlands and western islands from about 1855. Highlanders were employed for short periods on many of the herring boats trading from Greenock and the west coast from the mid-1700s, but numbers were few and movement was principally from Argyll and the south-west Highlands.[27] By the 1870s and 1880s, about 5,000 people, men and predominantly young women, were moving annually to the east-coast fishing villages principally from the north and west Highlands. One report for the 1880s noted the seasonal movement of about 10,000 Highland migrants into towns like Wick and Peterhead. Rates of pay – £4 was being paid for six weeks' work to 'the lads from the West Highlands engaged for the herring season' at Petty near Nairn in 1841[28] – provided a vital supplement to agricultural income. Indeed, over the period 1850–1880, seasonal fishing earnings were the main source of income on Skye, and, for the north-west mainland parishes, there is some evidence to suggest that employment on the east coast was the only means by which the croft could be maintained and the rent paid. For women especially, the end of the fishing season in August allowed them to take up harvest work, an occupational shift which often determined further mobility within the Lowlands. Periods of absence were as short as two months, but often the intended short-term move lasted a year or more. As Neil Macpherson of Braes noted in May 1883, speaking of the many migrants leaving Skye for the Lowland fishing and harvest, 'It is by their work in the south country that they are making a living . . . [Some] stay away till the next spring season comes. . . . I myself have been in the habit of being away a whole year, ever since I have been able to work'.[29] The regional economies of the north-west and of the north-east had a mutual dependence upon the fishing industry. The former provided a ready supply of labour and maritime skills, the latter a source of cash income that was vital to the crofting sector. Population movement was seasonal, often long-distance, and in stages. Many Lewismen, once the Stornoway season had ended, moved to the east coast and then to East Anglia, where, in Great Yarmouth in the 1870s, a Gaelic-speaking catechist ministered to their spiritual needs.[30] But this dependence upon income earned beyond the home parish brought undue hardship when the fishing failed: lower catches in 1886 and 1887, for example, 'caused . . . the return penniless from the east Coast of hundreds – nay thousands – of able-bodied men whose position but a few years ago was one of affluence'.[31] This decline in real income and the fall in expectations that it signalled was a major contributor to the rise of rural social protest within the north and west Highlands from about 1886–1887 onwards. Other factors should be noted – the effects of the sub-division of land holdings and land shortage, and the conversion of ancestral lands to deer forests and shooting estates – but the seasonal absence and return of male migrants especially often determined the timing of protest (see above, pp. 46–47).

Domestic service for Highland women was commonplace from the later eighteenth century. For some, it involved both occupational and residential mobility within the Lowlands as they sought better positions. Such temporary migration was not necessarily seasonally determined, although there is evidence that Highland domestic servant girls would return home in the winter to help manage the holding. Some Highlanders employed in Glasgow's gasworks in the early 1900s returned home or followed the fishing in the summer.[32] Movement to railway work was important by the early 1840s, and grew in importance in the construction 'mania' of 1846–47. More than half the 2,100 men employed in railway construction in the Lothians in the 1840s were Highlanders, and there were large numbers working on railways elsewhere.[33] Donald McLeod, killed in an accident whilst working on the Scottish Central Railway near Lecropt in Stirlingshire in September 1847, had been labouring only a few days there 'he had previously been employed on another railway which he had left and gone to the harvest in Lothian, whence he had come to this neighbourhood to join his brother'.[34] Work on the railways was an important means of relief from poverty in the north and west Highlands during the Highland potato famine.

In truth, a whole variety of tasks in the urban economy was seasonal, prompting short-term circulation of labour from the Highlands: construction work, dock labouring, textile manufacture. Proximity to the Lowland centres of industry, ease of communication, and varying agricultural demands in the native parishes and in the Lowlands all influenced the direction of temporary migration and the duration of stay. The main patterns of seasonal and temporary migration between about 1680 and 1900 (see Figure 3.1) should be interpreted neither as a formal distancing from the Highlands by migrants, nor as a permanent experiencing of the Lowlands. Such population movement embraced a variety of needs and motivations and had well-established geographical features. Indeed it was undertaken by many precisely to maintain the culture and society of the Highlands. Highland migrants resident only for a period were also a customary feature of Lowland life, in town and country. Much of the complexity of this type of migration, and the connections it forged between the two regions, is evident from the following quote from McNeill's report of 1851:

> For twenty successive years, one of the crofters had worked for the summer six months in East Lothian with the same master, from whom he had a certificate of character and conduct, such as any man in his position might be proud of. At the commencement of each winter, he returned to the small croft in Waternish, at the northern extremity of Skye, on which his family resided, and for which he paid a rent of £5 a year from the wages he earned with Mr Dudgeon, of Easter Broomhouse, near Dunbar. When short of meal or seed-corn in the spring, he applied to Mr Dudgeon, who kindly furnished him with what he required, on the credit of his next summer's work. Here, then, was an intelligent, enterprising, industrious man, who had lived for one-half of the last twenty years in East Lothian, where he established an excellent character, and found a kind employer, to whom he was attached and grateful, yet the idea of permanently removing appeared never to have occurred to him. He must have been nearly as familiar with life in East Lothian as with life in Skye: but the attractions of his croft in Waternish continued to be irresistible. He travelled about six hundred miles, separated himself from his family, and worked hard for six months every year, that he might continue to enjoy his croft and comparative idleness for the other half-year in Waternish.[35]

Against this general picture must be placed the particular connections between the Highland potato famine and temporary migration.

TEMPORARY MIGRATION, URBAN HIGHLAND COMMUNITIES AND THE HIGHLAND POTATO FAMINE, 1837–1855

The Great Highland Famine of the mid-nineteenth century was the last great subsistence crisis on the British mainland.[36] It is likely, as shown of Edinburgh in the 1750s, that earlier periodic subsistence crises – in 1771–72, 1772–3, 1795–6, 1806–7, 1816–17, and 1825 – prompted larger number

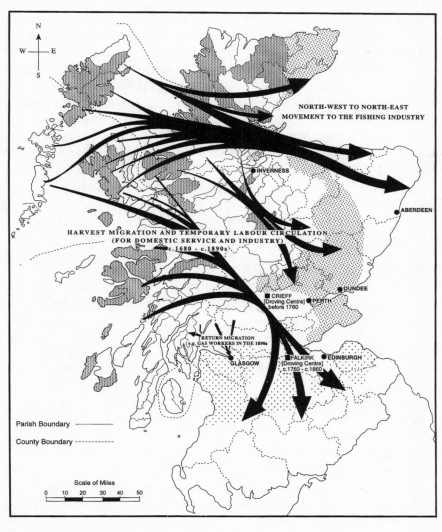

Figure 3.1 *Principal patterns of seasonal and temporary Highland–Lowland migration, c.1680–1900*

of Highlanders to move south. Shortfalls in returns from kelp production, or in returns from local fishing, likewise pushed people south. As John Bowie stated in evidence to the 1841 Select Committee on Emigration, the diminishing returns from kelp in the north-west Highlands meant that the 'redundant population' had been increasingly 'in the habit of going away at the time of harvest to seek for work in other parts'.[37] This helped reduce poverty in the area. But nothing rivalled the effect of the potato famine. As Devine long ago noted, 'the famine seems to have been a watershed in the evolution of temporary migration'. Because of the shock it administered, more people than ever before were eager to seek work outside the Highland zone rather than depend on the slender and uncertain returns from monoculture'.[38] More recent work by that author and by others has documented the extent of the famine and the directed labour mobility consequent upon it.

Dependence upon the potato was greatest in the crofting Highlands where, in places, it constituted four-fifths of all nourishment by the early 1800s. Potato blight appeared first in Argyll in 1833 but was not the cause of widespread crop failure until 1836–37. Crop returns document districts with two-thirds and upwards of potato crops 'utterly spoilt'; incessant rains rotted grainstuffs and the resultant meal produced dysentery; and most tenants had 'neither money, credit, or employment'. Nearly half a million people in the crofting areas were said to 'have before them the prospect of absolute want'.[39] That this total, or even a fraction of it, did not starve had much to do with temporary migration and the relief funds gathered in the Lowlands.

There is abundant evidence to point to a very substantial increase in temporary migration during the potato famine. 'Vast numbers' were recorded as leaving the west Highlands during 1846 and 1847, to the extent that one government official feared the distress and absence of people in Skye would undermine the future economy of the region. Devine has documented three characteristics of this increase in temporary migration.[40] Firstly, there was an alteration in the age and social composition of migrant groups, with an increased proportion of crofters and older age groups involved, including a higher proportion of heads of household than previously. Secondly, there was considerable movement from parishes which had little experience of substantial temporary migration, such as the Outer Hebrides. Forty men from Harris, for example, a parish whose population were 'always singularly averse to this migration and have never practised it in harvest time like the other Highlanders', made the move south late in 1846.[41] Thirdly, the period of absence became longer, both because of shifting patterns of occupation whilst away – from the fishing to railway work rather than returning home – and because the labour market in the Lowlands was very buoyant. Three formal agencies also did much to facilitate and direct this movement to the Lowlands: landowners, the Free Church of Scotland, and the Central Board of Management of the Fund for the Relief of the Destitute Inhabitants of the Highlands. This last body operated through a series of local committees and through two 'sections', established in Glasgow and Edinburgh. The Glasgow section was responsible for the Outer Isles, Argyll and western Inverness-shire; the Edinburgh section for Skye, the eastern mainland and Orkney and Shetland.

The origins of schemes for directed out-movement of Highland labour lie in a resolution of the Free Church Synod of Argyll in September 1846, although there is evidence from 1836–37 of landlords assisting tenants to emigrate.[42] The Synod argued

> . . . that great benefit would be conferred by a number of steamers being sent round the west coast and islands of Argyleshire [*sic*] to convey the young and able-bodied of the population to the Lowlands, and such parts as have lines of railway in progress of construction, and where demand for labour exists, this being rendered necessary by the poverty of the people.

Initially proposed to the Free Church Destitution Committee, the idea came into operation in the early months of 1847 and was quickly adopted by other bodies. Eventually, the Free Church merged its relief schemes with those of the Central Board, and this programme of organised migration was administered by the Employment Committee of the latter body. This strategy was significant because the level of organisation was good, with the Church approaching railway companies before sending men south, and because support was given to the families until money began to be sent home. It is also true that the schemes for labour movement, and for relief more generally, were planned so as not to interfere with established social relations in the affected districts. The Government view was that schemes for labour mobility 'must be left entirely to the proprietors and the labourers themselves without any interference on the part of the Government'.[43] Direct intervention was considered inappropriate within those doctrines of *laissez-faire* and notions of good management that the Government sought to instil in the Highland peasantry: 'They felt that if any large portion of the subjects of her majesty were to be impressed with a belief that they had a right to rely upon the interposition of the State in order to supply them with food, the strongest motives to foresight, industry, and frugality would be withdrawn, and a principle would be laid down, inconsistent with the well-being of society'.[44] The Free Church Destitution Committee responded to this view on five counts: no one would be moved unless there was a job waiting; families were supported in the absence of male heads of household; local Free Church ministers were to be used to induce men to migrate; the Government was not to be involved unless specifically requested by the Free Church; and, since normally there was virtually no communication in the winter months, the fact of the assisted passage over the winter of 1846–47 was not to be taken as an indication of its continuing thereafter.

By December 1846, the Free Church Destitution Committee had 'made arrangements with some of the Railway Companies for the employment of about 3,000 labourers'.[45] Its concern to recruit them from the west and Argyll was not only a reflection of the geography and extent of destitution. The Committee noted a difference in migration practices between 'western and northern Highlanders'. The latter (meaning those from the north and north-east mainland) were accustomed to 'transmitting to their families and relations a portion of their earnings'. The Committee considered that 'to create similar feelings and habits in the Islanders and western Highlanders, would be the first great step towards their improvement'.[46] Nominal lists of migrants kept by the Central Board provide details of how many people went where: the surviving 'List of Men sent to Railway Contractors' covers the years 1847, 1848 and 1849, and numerous other lists document other male migrants and the movement of females to agricultural work. Even with this information, it is difficult to know total numbers. A total of 1,263 migrants is known to have moved between October 1846 and early 1848, but this was chiefly to railway work, and many others moved outwith this period and to other employment between 1846 and 1854. Figure 3.2 shows the pattern of total known movements between 1846 and 1849. The majority of those for whom we know their native parish came from north-west Skye. There was relatively little out-movement towards west-central Scotland or from the east and north mainland Highlands. Most employment was focused on railway construction in Fife and the eastern central Lowlands, but this pattern of movement varied between years. In 1847, the most severe year of famine, temporary migration was dominated by male migration from Kilmuir in Skye to Dysart in Fife. Movement in 1848 and 1849 was heavy from Skye and tended to go to East Lothian. Most of the 263 known female movers moved from Skye to East Lothian and were directed to 'country service'. Of those migrants for whom the return journey may be traced, it appears the average time spent away was six weeks. This geography of temporary migration is partly explained by the concern of the Free Church Destitution Committee to focus on the islands and western Highlands. Explanation rests chiefly, however, in the role and wishes of landlords and tenants, in the varying success of other relief

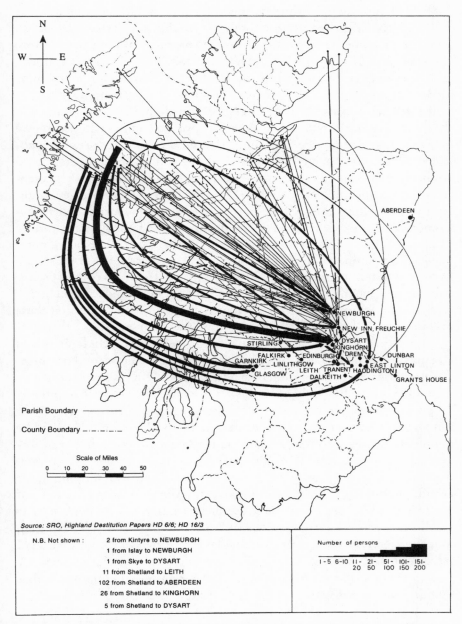

N.B. Not shown :
2 from Kintyre to NEWBURGH
1 from Islay to NEWBURGH
1 from Skye to DYSART
11 from Shetland to LEITH
102 from Shetland to ABERDEEN
26 from Shetland to KINGHORN
5 from Shetland to DYSART

Figure 3.2   *Patterns of known famine relief migration from the north-west Highlands, 1846–1849*

schemes, and, principally, in the relative geography of destitution since most migrants were drawn from predominantly potato-dependent areas in which the crop had almost totally failed for successive seasons. In northern Skye, between 56 and 72 percent of the local populations were receiving parochial relief in the three years from 1847. The great majority of listed heads of household in this area were 'lotters', an increasingly landless class by this period, for whom relief through temporary migration was vital to continued subsistence. But it should also be understood that such migration was, as a customary practice, familiar to them and many others. The famine lent emphasis and direction to already established trends. Even so, it is difficult to know how the famine and its related temporary displacement of people directly influenced the permanent relocation of people, either within the Highlands or in terms of Highland-Lowland migration. Some have argued for a migratory movement from west to east within the Highlands during the famine. But it is now considered that any such movement was neither large-scale nor permanent.[47] The famine did prompt emigration, however, much of it directly from the western Highlands and Islands. Although there is contemporary commentary on increases in the numbers of Highlanders asking for support in Glasgow in 1847, and records of St Columba's Church there in 1850 being 'besieged by people from the Highlands in a state of destitution',[48] it is almost impossible to say that these people or others like them permanently relocated in the cities in consequence of the famine. For those on relief schemes managed through their native parishes, such permanency was impossible. Yet there is evidence of a network of support for poor Highlanders who did arrive in the city and of a broader network of funding support for relief of destitution in the Highlands during the famine. Large donations, managed via the Glasgow and Edinburgh sections, came from individual Highlanders and others at home and abroad. Analysis of subscription lists for 1847–8 reveals many of Edinburgh's Gaelic community to have contributed, as did the Gaelic congregations of Aberdeen and Inverness, Highland regiments, and overseas bodies such as the Boston Scots Charitable Society.[49] In Glasgow, the Rev. Norman MacLeod, *Caraid nan Gael* (The Highlanders' Friend), who, as we shall see, was much involved in the affairs of Glasgow's Gaelic population, considered (in evidence to the 1841 Select Committee on Emigration) that such support was apparent within and beyond the city:

You say there is a great deal of charity remitted by the Highlanders in Glasgow to their friends? – There is.

Is there much charity among the Highlanders in Glasgow towards others who fall into distress? – A great deal.

Charity from individuals or from benevolent societies? – From societies instituted strictly for their relief, such as the Highland Strangers' Friend Society and Celtic Dispensary, &c.

Elsewhere, he commented upon the sense in which such support marked the Highland community:

You think the relief which a Highlander would derive from his countrymen in Glasgow would be greater than that which would be derived by the Irish or the Lowlanders? – Decidedly, I never knew a Highland family in circumstances of great destitution that I did not know where to get some relief; and I would add, with gratitude, I seldom knew the want of a pound for such a purpose.[50]

This is not to claim that relief was not forthcoming for destitute Highlanders from non-Highland migrants or from other bodies altogether. It is to suggest, however, that there was a strong cultural bond between resident urban Highlanders and Gaels and temporarily resident and destitute Highlanders at the time of the famine, and to speculate that such connections influenced the decision to migrate permanently.

STEPPED MIGRATION AND TEMPORARY MIGRATION AS A PROCESS OF CULTURAL CHANGE

If temporary migration and the circulation of labour brought many Highlanders into regular contact with the Lowland economy, charting the actual patterns of movement of such people, as for those who made the move permanently, is not always easy. We should not simply suppose a direct single movement since there is evidence both that temporary migrants circulated within the Highlands before moving south and that, once in the Lowlands, occupational mobility was, for some at least, closely allied to geographical mobility as migrants moved around before returning home. Occasionally, however, we are afforded glimpses of the 'stages' of movement or the stepped migration paths followed by migrants: of one 'Widow MacDonald', for example, born in the Highland Perthshire parish of Kenmore in 1793, who moved residence five times before settling in Perth in 1836.[51] In this context, there is some limited evidence of patterns of what is usually called 'stepped' or 'step-wise' movement underlying temporary and permanent migration and some partial evidence to hint at the circulation of labour as a cultural process. We may speculate, too, that those temporary migrants for whom we can trace a stepped migration path to the cities, especially where the journey took a long time, were undergoing, simultaneously, geographical mobility and processes of social and cultural change.

The concept of stepped or stepwise migration has been the focus of attention since 1885 and Ravenstein's second 'law' of migration that 'migration proceeds step by step'.[52] Using Poor Law evidence, particularly the *General Register of Poor*, one study has shown how material on 'particulars of settlement' for applicants seeking poor relief in Lowland towns can trace intermediate locations, and the duration of stay at them, between the Highlands and arrival in the town. Under the 1845 Poor Law (Scotland) Act, paupers were required on application to indicate those places through which they had earlier travelled and, if relevant, received relief before their application for support. Some individuals demonstrate that sense of mobility as a way of life that others have seen for engineers 'on the tramp' and other occupational groups in nineteenth-century society more generally.[53] Consider Donald Ferguson, for example, an unmarried 49–year-old blacksmith applying for poor relief in Glasgow on 7 March 1867. The parochial clerk recorded how Ferguson '[had] been resident in Renfrew, Port Glasgow, Greenock, Dublin, Birkenhead, Chester, Partick, Govan, High St. Anderston [Glasgow] and various quarters in town and country: Not been above 3 years at one time in any parish in Scotland since he became of age, to work for himself'. It is, of course, one thing to be able to recapture the complexity of such movement and quite another to know just how such movement was, if it was at all, a means of assimilating the migrant into Lowland culture. Of a sample of 334 Highlanders moving to Glasgow between 1852 and 1898 for whom stepped migration can be proven, 50 per cent made the move in two steps (i.e., can be shown to have had only one intermediate location between native parish and enumeration in Glasgow). Many, however, took a series of steps in moving south: 15 per cent took five or more steps. The average time taken to complete the move south was a little over twelve years. Most stepped migration that involved two or more intermediate locations was from a rural parish to a smaller town and then to Glasgow. It is difficult to know the extent to which such migration should be considered a process of acculturation, not least because this is to presuppose the Highland migrant as some sort of cultural archetype, possessing purely 'Highland' qualities until touched by similarly absolute 'Lowland' cultural characteristics. But the findings do highlight the complexity of these patterns of movement underlying the presence of Highland migrant populations in the Lowlands, either as residents or as gangs of harvest labourers.[54] It is also to suggest that such stepped migration, especially where it took a year or more in the case of the temporary mover, served to draw the Highlander into the culture and experience of Scotland more generally and more slowly than is sometimes supposed, just as it probably familiarised others with the sight and presence of migratory Highlanders (see Figure 3.3).

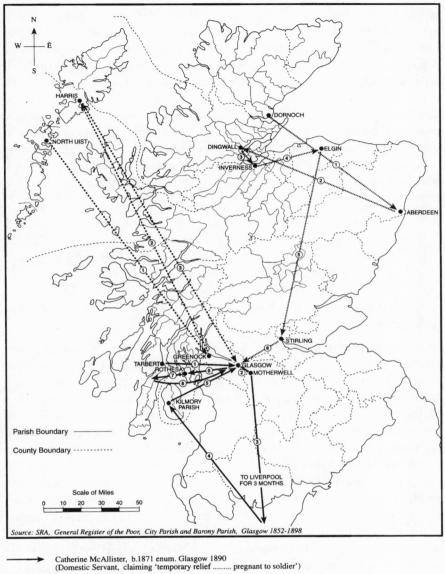

Source: SRA, *General Register of the Poor, City Parish and Barony Parish, Glasgow 1852-1898*

→ Catherine McAllister, b.1871 enum. Glasgow 1890
(Domestic Servant, claiming 'temporary relief .... pregnant to soldier')

•••••••••► Norman Maclean, b.1806 enum. Glasgow 1865, Carpenter

••••••••••► James Leckie, b.1829 enum. Glasgow 1873, Coach wheel maker

Figure 3.3 *Examples of stepped Highland-Lowland migration, c.1806–1890*

There is abundant evidence to point to temporary migration as a means of language change. In Kilmore and Kilbride parish, for example, and in Lochgoilhead and in Kilmorich and in South Knapdale, English was being introduced into still very strongly Gaelic-speaking parishes by returning seasonal migrants in the 1790s: 'The English has of late spread considerably, owing, in a great measure, to young people travelling to the low country, and returning home after they have acquired the language' [of South Knapdale in 1797]. Even on Barra in the Western Isles, we are told that 'by their frequent excursions to Glasgow, the people have introduced a number of English words'. By the mid-nineteenth century, this process of language change through returning temporary migrants was more widespread than earlier. In Gairloch parish in 1836, we are told how:

> Some young men . . . consider they are doing a great service to the Gaelic, by interspersing their conversation with English words, and giving them a Gaelic termination and accent. These corrupters of both languages, with more pride than good taste, now and then, introduce words of bad English or bad Scotch, which they have learned from the Newhaven or Buckie fishermen, whom they meet with on the coast of Caithness during the fishing season. The Gaelic, however, is still spoken in as great a purity by the inhabitants in general, as it was forty years ago.[55]

In Kilfinichen and Kilvickeon, Kilmartin, Portree, and Strath parishes, and in the far north-west parish of Tongue, similar patterns of language change were occurring as a result of seasonal and temporary migration.[56] Quite the reverse happened, of course, in those Lowland parishes periodically filled with Highlanders whose presence, however regular in terms of annual labour demands, either necessitated Gaelic-speaking catechists, or put a strain on available accommodation. In Campbeltown in Kintyre in 1755, the minister noted how difficult it was to give an estimate of his Highland congregation given 'the many strangers coming yearly to this place both to ye land and ye sea services'.[57] There, and more widely, connections between the Highlands and the Lowlands were not founded on permanent departure from the former and residence in the latter but were apparent in the regular circulation of labour between the two regions determined by different demands within their economies.

CONCLUSION

Highland migration to the Lowlands was not, then, only to establish and reinforce a resident migrant population. The temporary and seasonal circulation of Highland labour was commonplace from the end of the seventeenth century, and, in terms of labour for the harvest and other agricultural purposes, did not fully decline until the late 1890s. For women, the demands of the crofting sector in particular and the rhythms of the urban economy in general directed many towards domestic service, to textile production and, in the northern Highlands especially, to fishing on the eastern coasts. For men, construction work, notably on the railways in the 1840s, and seasonal agricultural work, were the main causes of their widespread temporary and seasonal movement from the Highlands in this period. We know that the population of the north and west Highlands in particular was reliant upon the income derived from such temporary movement from at least the early 1700s. Parishes in the south and east Highlands equally welcomed the cash such migration brought, but that region was not so critically dependent, especially from the 1840s, upon the short-term circulation of labour. Such movement was, in general terms, from north and west to south and east, but there are important variations on this general picture. First, temporary migration took place within the Highland region, chiefly from the north-west to the north-east parishes in association with seasonal demands within the fishing industry. Second, temporary and seasonal migration from the south-west and central Highlands was probably chiefly directed to the western central Lowlands. From the 1830s harvest migration by Highland women within this host area was increasingly overshadowed by the presence of Irish-born women. In the arable districts of the north and east Lowlands, however, and excepting areas around Aberdeen and Banff which drew upon local labour, Highland women persisted in that seasonal supply of labour so vital to Scottish agriculture.

These patterns of seasonal and temporary migration were accentuated by those schemes of directed labour mobility associated with the relief of the Highland population at the time of the Highland potato famine. For some then, as for others before and after, the journey south lasted but six weeks and was made only because circumstances in their native parishes demanded they go. For others, like the Waternish crofter who spent half of his life in East Lothian in the twenty years before 1851, short-term migration was a way of life, integral to the maintenance of the crofting system and to certain sectors of the Lowland economy. It is probable that many such temporary migrants moved south in a series of stages, determined by the availability of transport and the presence of fellow-migrants, and it has been shown, too, how temporary migrants could switch jobs and residence in the Lowlands prior to returning home. For some, the short-lived move south was facilitated by the presence of fellow-Highlanders able and willing to help them obtain a job and, if need be, assist with the journey home. The minute books of the Uist and Barra Association for 5 October 1892 make mention, for example, of many

'. . . young women coming from the Highlands to obtain situations [as domestic servants in Glasgow] for the first time' and of how arrangements were made with 'Mr Bell's Registry Sauchiehall St. by which all girls coming for the first time to Glasgow shall have situations obtained for them at the Association's expense'. In 1896, special support was given to '. . . a destitute old man, newly discharged from the Infirmary and a native of South Uist' to assist in his passage home and in order that he might get work in Fort William as a means to do so.[58] The picture is, of course, not so clear for the vast majority of temporary migrants. But this illustration alone highlights the ways in which permanent settlement in the urban Lowlands was underlain and reinforced by the complex circulation of temporary and seasonal migrants.

NOTES

1. A. G. Macpherson, 'Migration fields in a traditional Highland community, 1350–1850', *Journal of Historical Geography*, 10 (1), 1984, pp. 1–14: I. Carter, 'Marriage patterns and social sectors in Scotland before the eighteenth century', *Scottish Studies*, 17 (1) 1973, pp. 51–60.

2. R. A. Gailey, 'Mobility of tenants on a Highland estate in the early nineteenth century', *Scottish Historical Review*, XL, 1961, pp. 136–145; on comparable evidence for parts of Lowland Scotland, see R. A. Houston, '"Frequent flitting": geographical mobility and social structure in mid-nineteenth-century Greenlaw', *Scottish Studies*, 27, 1983, pp. 31–47; *idem*, 'Geographical mobility in Scotland, 1652–1811: the evidence of testimonials', *Journal of Historical Geography*, 11 (4), 1985, pp. 379–394; I. D. Whyte and K. A. Whyte, 'Geographical mobility in a seventeenth-century Scottish rural community', *Local Studies*, 32, 1984, pp. 45–53.

3. I. R. M. Mowat, *Easter Ross 1750–1850* (Edinburgh, 1982); D. Omand (ed.), *The Ross and Cromarty Book* (Golspie, 1984); E. Richards, *The Leviathan of Wealth* (London, 1973); L. Leneman, *Living in Atholl: a social history of the estates 1685–1785* (Edinburgh, 1986).

4. M. Flinn *et al* (eds.) *Scottish Population History* (Cambridge, 1977), pp. 316–348.

5. R. A. Houston and C. W. J. Withers, 'Population mobility in Scotland and Europe, 1600–1900: a comparative perspective', 1990 *Annales de Démographie Historique*, pp. 285–308; J. Lucassen, *Migrant Labour in Europe 1600–1900* (Beckenham, 1987); E. François (ed.), *Immigration et société urbaine en Europe occidentale, XVIe-XXe siècles* (Paris, 1985); C. Tilly, 'Migration in modern European history', in J. Sundin and E. Soderlund (eds.), *Time, Space and Man: essays on macrodemography* (Stockholm, 1979), pp. 175–197; N. P. Canny, *Europeans on the Move* (Oxford, 1994); L. P. Moch *Moving Europeans; migration in Western Europe since 1650*, (Bloomington, Indiana, 1992).

6. Moch, *op.cit.*, p. 6.

7. Lucassen *op.cit.*, pp. 105–115.

8. T. M. Devine, 'Temporary migration and the Scottish Highlands in the nineteenth century', *Economic History Review*, XXXII, 1979, pp. 344–359.

9. OSA, XIII, 1794, p. 224.

10. Census Enumerators' Schedules for Highlands parishes for 1841, 1851, 1861: see T. M. Devine, *The Great Highland Famine* (Edinburgh, 1988), Appendix 8, pp. 317–319.
11. H. Jones, 'Evolution of Scottish migration patterns: a social-relations-of-production approach', *Scottish Geographical Magazine*, 102 (3), 1986, p. 155: on this issue from a methodological point of view, see J. A. Agnew and K. Cox, 'Urban in-migration in historical perspective: an approach to measurement', *Historical Methods*, 12 (4), 1979, pp. 145–155.
12. NLS, MS 33.5.16, f.3.
13. *Chronicle of Perth 1210–1668* (Maitland Club, 1831), p. 24; *Register of the Privy Council of Scotland*, XIII, pp. 807–8; *Extracts from the Royal Burgh of Stirling, 1519–1666* (Scottish Burgh Records Society 1887, 1889), II, pp. 157–8; C. W. J. Withers, *Gaelic in Scotland 1698–1981: the geographical history of a language* (Edinburgh, 1984), pp. 183–4.
14. W. Sime, *History of the Church and Parish of St Cuthberts or West Kirk of Edinburgh* (Edinburgh, 1829), p. 115.
15. W. Howatson, 'The Scottish hairst and seasonal labour 1600–1870', *Scottish Studies*, 26, 1982, pp. 13–36; P. G. Mewett, 'Occupational pluralism in crofting: the influence of non-croft work on the patterns of crofting agriculture in the Isle of Lewis since about 1850', *Scottish Journal of Sociology*, 2 (1), 1977, pp. 31–49.
16. R. J. Adam, *Sutherland Estate Management 1802–1816* (Edinburgh, 1972), II, p. 85.
17. *NSA*, VII, 1842, p. 214; Devine, *Highland Famine, op. cit.*, pp. 147–150.
18. A. R. B. Haldane, *The Drove Roads of Scotland* (Edinburgh, 1952); Howatson, *op. cit.*
19. The historiography of this argument is best outlined in Devine, 'Temporary migration and the Scottish Highlands . . .', *op. cit.*, pp. 347–349.
20. *Ibid.*, p. 349 and see also M. Gray, 'North East Agriculture and the Labour Force, 1790–1875', in A. A. Maclaren (ed.), *Social Class in Scotland: past and present* (Edinburgh, 1976), pp. 86–104; *idem.*, 'Farm workers in North-East Scotland', in T. M. Devine (ed.), *Farm Servants and Labour in Lowland Scotland 1770–1914* (Edinburgh, 1984), pp. 10–28.
21. I. D. Whyte, 'Population mobility in early modern Scotland', in R. A. Houston and I. D. Whyte (eds.), *Scottish Society 1500–1800* (Cambridge, 1989), pp. 37–58; I. D. Whyte and K. A. Whyte, 'The geographical mobility of women in early modern Scotland', in L. Leneman (ed.), *Perspectives in Scottish Social History* (Aberdeen, 1988), pp. 83–104; for a discussion of these trends within Europe, see those works cited in n. 5 above. Comparable material in the British context is reviewed in P. Clark and D. Souden (eds.), *Migration and Society in Early Modern England* (London, 1987), and D. Baines, *Migration in a Mature Economy: emigration and internal migration in England and Wales 1861–1900* (Cambridge, 1985).
22. A. O'Dowd, *Spalpeens and Tatti Hokers: history and folklore of the Irish migratory agricultural worker in Ireland and Britain* (Dublin, 1991) is by far the best detailed survey of this sort of material: no comparable detailed study exists for Scotland, but see I. MacDougall, *Hoggie's Angels: Tattie Howkers Remember* (East Linton, 1995).
23. BPP, *Fourth Report on the Employment of Children, Young Persons and Women in Agriculture*, 1870, XIII, Appendix Part II, pp. 112–116.

24. J. Williams-Davies, '*Merched y Gerddi*: a seasonal migration of female labour from rural Wales', *Folk Life*, 1979, pp. 12–23.
25. T. C. Smout, 'Aspects of sexual behaviour in nineteenth-century Scotland', in MacLaren (ed.), *op. cit.*, pp. 36–54; A Blaikie, *Illegitimacy, Sex and Society: Northeast Scotland, 1750–1900* (Oxford, 1993).
26. C. W. J. Withers, *Gaelic Scotland: the transformation of a culture region* (London, 1988), pp. 190–194.
27. R. D. Lobban, 'The Migration of Highlanders into Lowland Scotland c. 1750–1890, with particular reference to Greenock', (unpublished PhD thesis, University of Edinburgh 1969).
28. *NSA*, 1841, XIX, p. 403.
29. BPP, *Commission of Inquiry into the Condition of Crofters and Cottars in the Highlands and Islands of Scotland*, 1884–1885, XXXII-XXXVI (Napier Commission report), Vol 1, Q 258, p. 17, (Evidence of Neil Macpherson, Braes parish Skye, 8 May 1883).
30. SRO, CH3/983/1. (Minutes and Records of the Free Church of Scotland's Gaelic Home Mission Committee).
31. SRO, AF 67/402, f 7 Report on the Cottar Population of the Lews 1888.
32. BPP, *Royal Commission on Labour: Minutes of Evidence*, Appendix XIXA, p. 61; see also J. H. Treble, 'The seasonal demand for adult labour in Glasgow, 1890–1914', *Social History*, 3 (1), 1978, pp. 43–60.
33. Devine, *Highland Famine*, op. cit., pp. 160–161.
34. *The Stirling Observer*, 30 September 1847, p. 6.
35. BPP, *Report to the Board of Supervision by Sir John McNeill GCB on the Western Highlands and Islands*, 1851, XXVI, p. xii.
36. The best discussion by far is Devine, *Highland Famine*.
37. BPP, *First Report from the Select Committee on Emigration, Scotland, together with the Minutes of Evidence and Appendix*, 1841, VI, p. 4.
38. Devine, 'Temporary migration and the Scottish Highlands', *op. cit.*, p. 356.
39. SRO, Highland Destitution Papers, (hereafter HD), 7/8 f. 29; SRO, GD 46/13199 ff. 1, 3, 7–8; GD 46/13/213; GD 46/13/215 Parts (1)-(6).
40. Devine, *Highland Famine*, op. cit., p. 157.
41. SRO, HD 7/28, 6 October 1846.
42. C. W. J. Withers, 'Destitution and migration: labour mobility and relief from famine in Highland Scotland 1836–1850', *Journal of Historical Geography* 14 (2), 1988, pp. 128–150.
43. BPP, *Relief of the Distress in Scotland: correspondence, from July 1846 to February 1847, relating to the measures adopted for the relief of the distress in Scotland*, 1847, LIII, p. 24 (Resolution of the Free Church of Argyle (sic), 2–3 September 1846).
44. NLS, MS 1054, f. 197v. Letter on distress in Highlands 1837.
45. BPP, *Relief of the Distress in Scotland*, op. cit., p. 212 (Lord Advocate to Sir George Grey, 10 December 1846).
46. *Ibid.*, p. 222 (Lord Advocate to Charles Trevelyan, 20 December 1846).
47. Devine, *Highland Famine*, op. cit., p. 195.
48. *The Witness*, 21 December 1850; Devine, *ibid.*, p. 196.
49. SRO, HD 16/123 (List of Districts under the charge of the Glasgow Section of the Highland Relief Board for 1848); HD 16/70 (Subscriptions for relief of Highland Destitution, 1847–1848), Sections 1–13.

50. BPP, *First Report from the Select Committee on Emigration*, 1841, VI, pp. 119–120.
51. C. W. J. Withers, *Highland Communities in Dundee and Perth 1787–1891* (Dundee, 1986), pp. 35–38.
52. D. B. Grigg, 'E. G. Ravenstein and the "laws of migration"', *Journal of Historical Geography* 3, 1977, pp. 41–54.
53. D. Friedlander and R. J. Roshier, 'A study of internal migration in England and Wales (Part I)', *Population Studies*, 19, 1965, pp. 259–279, (Part II); *ibid*, 1966, pp. 45–59; S. Nicholas and P. R. Shergold, 'Internal migration in England, 1818–1839', *Journal of Historical Geography*, 13, 1987, pp. 155–168; Baines, *op. cit.*, H. Southall, 'The tramping artisan revisits: labour mobility and economic distress in early Victorian England: *Economic History Review*, 44, 1991, pp. 247–269.
54. C. W. J. Withers and A. J. Watson, 'Stepwise migration and Highland migration to Glasgow, 1852–1898', *Journal of Historical Geography*, 17, 1991, pp. 35–55; issues to do with the process of acculturation during migration are also addressed in E. R. Brennan, 'Secular changes in migration between birth and marriage', *Journal of Biosocial Science*, 15, 1983, pp. 391–406.
55. NSA, 1836, XIV, pp. 95–96.
56. NSA, 1842, XVII, p. 307; 1844, XVII, p. 562; 1841, CXIV, p. 226; 1840, XIV, p. 308.
57. SRO, GD 95.11.5.16.8 (1), 21 November 1755.
58. Uist and Barra Association, Minutes 1 May 1890 – April 1896 (5 October 1892; 26 October 1896). I am very grateful to the Secretary of the Association, Mrs McCoard, for granting me access to the Association's Minute Books and other records.

CHAPTER 4

The Geography of Permanent Highland-Lowland Migration, c.1750–1891

Permanent rural-urban migration was a major element of demographic change throughout Europe from the later eighteenth century.[1] For Britain, although much is known about early modern rural-urban migration from sources such as apprenticeship registers,[2] no systematic source is available to document internal migration at parish level until the 1851 Census. From this date, it is possible to document at decennial intervals the lifetime migration of urban migrants, recognising, however, that recorded differences between parishes of birth and enumeration may obscure stepped or seasonal movement (see above, pages 61–80). Other difficulties include knowing age at arrival and, thus, the length of residence of urban migrants. Notwithstanding these problems, the Census provides an invaluable source for considering the geography of population displacement in Britain from the mid-nineteenth century.[3]

This chapter examines the patterns of permanent migration of all Highland-born persons resident in Glasgow, Edinburgh, Leith, Greenock, Paisley, Aberdeen, Dundee, Perth, and Stirling. Particular attention is paid to the 1851 Census and, for several towns or individual parishes, to the 1891 Census. Other sources are used to supplement this material. Much evidence is presented as maps in order to summarise and to illustrate, on a parish-by-parish basis, the geography of Highland-Lowland permanent urban migration from 1851 to 1891. From this, conclusions and explanations are advanced about the geography, the nature and the cause of permanent population movement from the Highlands to the urban Lowlands.

EVIDENCE FOR PERMANENT MIGRATION BEFORE 1851

It is difficult to know patterns of Highland-Lowland population movement before 1851. There is evidence that urban Scotland had permanently-resident Highlanders from the end of the eighteenth century, even from the early 1700s. But few sources if any allow us to know their places of origin. The movement of apprentices and domestic servants to Inver-

84

ness, Edinburgh and Aberdeen in the eighteenth century suggests, for the few Highlanders involved, that the two towns drew upon Highland parishes nearest each town.[4] Highland surnames have been used to infer resident Highlanders in Greenock from the later seventeenth century and, to judge from later evidence, most of that town's early Highland population came from contiguous parishes in Argyll with Highlanders coming from farther afield only later in the nineteenth century.[5] Highland surnames appear in trades directories and other name-based sources from the later 1700s for several Lowland towns, but surname use is problematic: some Highlanders changed their name when moving south; and surnames alone cannot distinguish between Highlanders recently arrived and those of second- or third-generation Highland descent.[6] There are no biographies for urban Highlanders in the eighteenth and nineteenth centuries like that for '*Murchadh Ruadh*' ['Murdo of the Red Hair'], the Assynt-born Highland policeman who joined the Lanarkshire police in 1928, aged 20, and who became that county's Chief Constable in 1967.[7] Some institutional records, notably for Gaelic chapels in the Lowlands, allow an estimate of numbers of resident urban Highlanders before 1851 although they are virtually silent on the parishes of origin of such Highland populations. There were about 500 Highlanders in Edinburgh in 1707 when the Rev. Neil MacVicar was translated to the city's West Kirk from Fort William.[8] In 1717, we are told only of 'considerable numbers of persons having the Irish language residing in the City of Glasgow and the town of Grinok'.[9] More reliable figures are available for the later 1700s. Edinburgh's Gaelic chapel opened in 1769 with seating for 800 persons, and was twice enlarged, in 1776 and 1790, to accommodate 1,100 and 1,800 persons. There were about 800 Gaelic speakers resident in Aberdeen and its immediate neighbourhood in 1788. In Glasgow, sittings in the Ingram Street Gaelic chapel were 1,090 in 1820, with Duke Street having 1,300 and the Gorbals Gaelic Chapel a further 1,050 sittings.[10] Such statistics should be interpreted with care. For one thing, the congregations of Gaelic chapels never filled all seats available. The sums involved in paying seat rents excluded the less well-off: what one commentator noting this circumstance of Dundee's Highland congregation in the 1850s called 'those falling off . . . from poverty and neglect'.[11] For another, these institutional records give little indication of the origins of the congregations, although attempts were made in this direction. In the mid-1830s, the Rev. Dr. Norman Macleod of St. Columba's in Glasgow undertook to prepare a 'Gaelic Census' in order better to inform the work of Church Commissioners then examining ecclesiastical provision in the city. In evidence to the Poor Law Inquiry in 1843, Macleod noted:

I ought to have mentioned that when the Church Commissioners were here a few years ago, I considered it proper to prepare myself for the examination by ascertaining the actual condition of the Highlanders in Glasgow; and I employed ten individuals to visit every house in the city and suburbs. We took down the names of every individual we could find who was born in the Highlands. The statement occupies two large folio books like atlasses [*sic*], and shows that there were 23,000 native Highlanders whose names were arranged in columns. Then there was the number of families, the churches they attended, their condition in life, and the state of each family. We found 11,000 of the lowest class of Highlanders who were not looked after by any minister appointed for that purpose. Such was the state of the Highland population in Glasgow at that time, and it is much the same now.[12]

Surviving records that allow for assessment of migration before 1851 provide only patchy evidence. The 1821 Census for Paisley lists the county birthplace of the town's inhabitants. Returns for the Highland counties suggest perhaps 7 per cent of the town were Highland-born, the majority from Argyllshire.[13] Some hospital admissions' rolls for Glasgow show the same predominance with a declining proportion of patients from the more distant Argyll parishes and Inverness-shire. Of the 215 persons admitted in 1842 by the Glasgow Celtic Infirmary, 129 were from Argyll, 27 from Inverness-shire, 4 from Ross and 1 each from Perthshire and Sutherland. A further 53 persons were born in the Lowlands 'but of Highland Parentage'.[14] Membership records of the Glasgow Highland Society, begun in 1727, show, for members outwith Glasgow in the period 1727–1800, a pronounced concentration in Argyllshire and west Highland towns: Fort William, Inveraray, Oban, Stornoway. But this is more an indication of Glasgow's commercial sphere of influence and of the residence of Highland-born mercantile classes than it is a reliable guide to birthplace and migration.[15]

For the period before 1851, it is probable, from what Lobban has documented of Greenock and from other limited evidence, that the towns of west-central Scotland drew the majority of their Highland-born from mainland Argyll and the nearer insular parishes, from southern Inverness-shire and, for a few, from more distant small towns like Stornoway. It is probable, too, that Highlanders in urban east Scotland came from central Highland parishes and the eastern seaboard of Ross and Cromarty and Sutherland rather than from Argyll. But what we know of the geography of Highland-Lowland migration before 1851 is in some measure based on inference backwards from what is known in detail of 1851 and later.

HIGHLAND-LOWLAND MIGRATION IN 1851

Assessment of the county of origin of the Highland-born population in each of the principal towns of Scotland in 1851 reveals marked differences in size of resident Highland migrant populations and in geography of origin (Table 4.1). Glasgow had the largest Highland migrant population and like Greenock and Paisley drew most of its migrants from Argyll. In contrast, Edinburgh's Highland population came almost equally from Inverness-shire and Ross and Cromarty. The same is true of the small Highland population in Leith. Dundee, and more markedly Perth, took the great proportion of their migrant Highlanders from Highland Perthshire. Stirling, centrally positioned between larger urban centres to west and east, drew upon a more diverse hinterland for its small Highland population in 1851: some from Argyll and from Inverness-shire, most from Highland Perthshire. Highland migrants in Aberdeen, the eastern- and northern-most Lowland town, came in almost equal measure from Inverness-shire and Ross and Cromarty, although as for Edinburgh and in contrast to the west-central towns a relatively high proportion were natives of Sutherland.

This evidence is suggestive of pronounced though not exclusive geographical differences in source area for Scotland's urban migrant Highlanders in the mid-nineteenth century. But there are several reasons why we should treat this evidence with caution. Firstly, we must not isolate Highland-Lowland migration from the bigger picture of inter-county migration in 1851. Highland-Lowland permanent urban migration, in terms of the main trends of Scottish population movement in the nineteenth century, was overshadowed by migration into the towns from the rural Lowlands and Borders.[16] Secondly, Highland-born migrants were less numerous than the Irish, especially in Glasgow and Dundee.[17] Thirdly, the Census documents the *place* of birth for enumerated Highland-born populations, but not the *date* at which they left the Highlands: we are thus given a static 'moment' of a longer-running dynamic process. For, say, that 85–year-old Uist-born woman recorded as an unemployed seamstress in Dundee's Nethergate in 1851, and more generally for the older Highlanders in all towns, the statistics in Table 4.1 mask the fact that migration recorded in 1851 may have occurred before then, for some possibly in the later eighteenth century, and possibly involved other locations on the way. Lastly, evidence at this scale obscures significant parish-based variation within the Highlands in the geography of migration. In order both to illustrate this and to allow comparison with the 1891 census and other evidence, movement to the west-central towns and to the eastern Lowland towns is examined separately.

Table 4.1

BIRTHPLACE OF THE HIGHLAND-BORN POPULATION IN THE PRINCIPAL TOWNS OF SCOTLAND, 1851*

Highland County	Aberdeen	Dundee	Edinburgh	Lowland Towns[+]			Paisley	Perth	Stirling
				Glasgow	Greenock	Leith			
Argyll	2.3	6.7	15.59	70.69	78.67	21.14	80.0	2.3	26.0
Bute	0.2	0.6	1.10	6.58	9.30	3.17	3.8	0.7	1.9
Inverness	34.7	27.2	26.60	13.64	9.18	26.84	11.8	12.3	19.5
Ross and Cromarty	40.4	15.8	25.10	4.46	2.09	23.25	1.8	3.1	7.9
Sutherland	15.8	4.8	9.18	2.58	0.23	9.53	0.4	1.6	5.6
Highland Caithness	4.3	1.4	4.79	0.23	0.07	6.76	0.3	–	–
Highland Moray	1.5	0.1	0.28	0.08	–	0.21	–	0.3	–
Highland Perth	0.6	43.0	17.20	1.68	0.44	8.68	–	79.6	39.0
Highland Nairn	0.2	0.4	0.16	0.06	0.02	0.42	1.0	0.1	–
TOTAL NO. OF HIGHLAND-BORN	1,762	809	4,303	14,959	4,243	473	1,584	1,200	215
HIGHLAND POP. AS % TOTAL URBAN POP.	2.44	1.02	2.68	4.54	11.33		3.30	5.03	1.67

* From *Census of Scotland* Enumerators' Books 1851

+ All of the Lowland towns here indicated are based on the Parliamentary Burghs

The geography of Highland migration to urban west Scotland:
Glasgow, Greenock, Paisley

Figures 4.1 and 4.2 reveal a more complicated geography of permanent population movement from the Highlands into Glasgow by 1851 than is evident from county-based data. For the Highlands as a whole (Figure 4.1), the leading parish of supply was Inverness, with smaller flows of people from, for example, Kiltearn, Tain, Stornoway, Kilmallie, and Weem parishes. The eastern parishes of Ross and Cromarty and Inverness-shire, together with east Sutherland, supplied only small numbers. Apparently few people can be shown by individual parish to have come from Skye and the Outer Isles. This is unlikely actually to have been the case, given the numbers from Skye (229 persons), from Inverness-shire (384), from Lewis and from Ross whose parish of birth is not given in the enumerators' returns and who are, therefore, not shown in Figure 4.1.

Several features are noteworthy in this detailed geography. Firstly, Campbeltown on the Kintyre peninsula supplied nearly one in ten of Glasgow's Highlanders by 1891 (1,471 persons in a total population of 14,959 Highland-born). The great proportion of the population of this parish was located within the town: numbers in the landward districts were always low. What this suggests, for this particular migration flow anyway, is that Glasgow drew its Highland population rather more from smaller Highland towns than it did from the widespread but less heavily populated rural parishes. Secondly, and in substantiation of this claim, several other Highland parishes with small towns were important sources of supply: Rothesay on Bute, Inveraray, Kilmore and Kilbride (with Oban), and Kilmichael Glassary parish (including Lochgilphead). This picture is complicated by the large numbers for whom parish of birth was not enumerated. Many of those moving to Glasgow from Kilninian and Kilmore parish in Mull, for example, moved from Tobermory, and most migrants from Islay for whom we know parish of birth came from Kilarow and Kilmeny parish. It is impossible, however, to know the parish of birth of the other 476 Mull-born and 728 Islay-born persons in Glasgow in 1851 and to know if they were drawn particularly from any one parish or group of parishes. Thirdly, the smaller and more distant island parishes within the inner Hebrides – Tiree and Coll, for example – were the source of few migrants. It is also the case that there was variation within Glasgow's parishes in terms of the source areas for Highlanders (Table 4.2). The proportion of Argyll-born Highlanders in Shettleston and Maryhill, for example, was higher than for the city as a whole and much greater than for, say, St John's parish where, in contrast, relatively large numbers of the Highland-born were from Bute, chiefly from Rothesay. Almost all those Argyll-born Shettleston Highlanders for

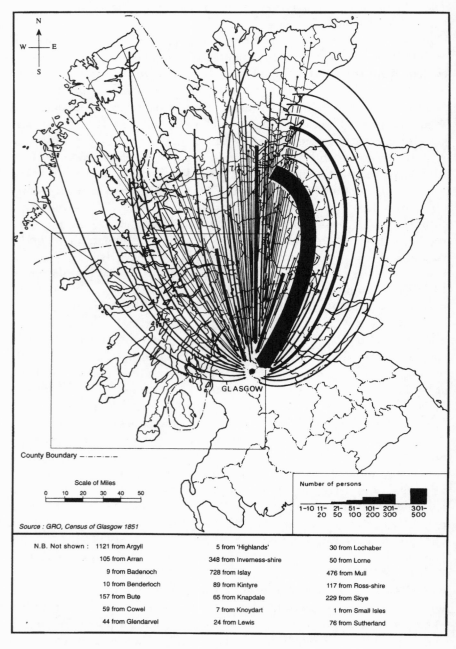

Figure 4.1 *Highland migration to Glasgow, 1851*

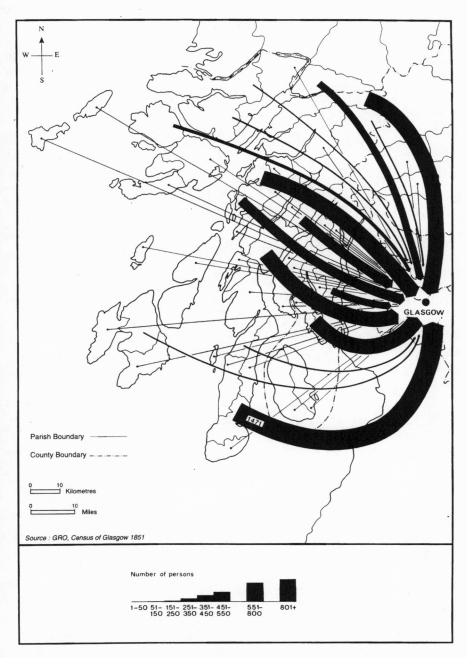

Figure 4.2 *Highland migration from Argyll to Glasgow, 1851*

Table 4.2

BIRTHPLACE OF THE HIGHLAND-BORN POPULATION OF GLASGOW, BY PARISH, 1851*

Number of Highlanders born in indicated county, as a percentage of total Highland-born population, by parish

Highland County	Glasgow parishes[+]															City of Glasgow
	(a)	(b)	(c)	(d)	(e)	(f)	(g)	(h)	(i)	(j)	(k)	(l)	(m)	(n)	(o)	
Argyll	66.42	72.97	61.68	66.37	70.17	62.82	66.29	63.67	76.20	68.05	73.43	68.31	81.76	86.85	73.44	70.69
Bute	7.13	6.25	8.74	5.69	4.39	5.82	3.48	11.43	5.17	4.47	6.16	7.34	0.55	1.15	7.82	6.58
Inverness	14.80	13.64	16.19	14.76	15.85	20.39	18.61	15.33	11.72	15.38	12.66	15.18	14.94	5.14	10.87	13.64
Ross and Cromarty	5.16	3.69	6.86	5.50	3.46	5.01	4.65	4.70	3.79	5.75	3.96	4.93	1.10	4.00	4.45	4.46
Sutherland	3.37	1.61	2.80	3.73	3.46	3.76	3.87	4.05	1.75	3.51	1.98	3.04	0.55	1.71	2.14	2.58
Highland Caithness	0.39	–	–	0.17	–	–	–	–	–	0.31	0.35	0.24	–	–	0.16	0.23
Highland Moray	0.04	–	0.31	0.50	0.33	–	–	–	–	0.62	0.08	–	–	–	–	0.08
Highland Perth	2.65	1.84	3.42	3.28	1.25	2.09	3.10	1.12	1.37	1.91	1.38	0.96	1.10	1.15	1.12	1.68
Highland Nairn	0.04	–	–	–	1.09	0.11	–	–	–	–	–	–	–	–	–	0.06

[+] Key to Glasgow parishes: (a) West or St. George (b) St. Enoch (c) Southwest, St. Mary or Tron (d) Northwest or St. David's (e) East, Outer High or St. Paul's (f) North, Inner High or St. Mungo (g) South, Blackfriars or College (h) St. John (i) Middle or St. Andrew's (j) St. James (k) Barony (l) Calton (m) Maryhill (n) Shettleston (o) Gorbals (such as lies within the City or Glasgow)

* From *Census of Scotland* Enumerator's Book 1851.

whom we know parish of birth came from Campbeltown. Argyll-born Highlanders in St John's parish came in almost equal proportion from Kilmore and Kilbride, Campbeltown, and Dunoon and Kilmun. We should be cautious in reading too much into this geographical variation in receiving parishes, not least because persons may have arrived and lived elsewhere before being enumerated in the 1851 Census. It is possible to hint, nevertheless, that, in addition to the points made above, Highland migration to Glasgow was, knowingly, from and to particular parishes. We may even speculate that migrants followed an established 'migration itinerary' determined either by personal knowledge of circuits of temporary labour mobility or by following other locals or fellow parishioners, with whom connections were maintained, into particular parts of the city. Evidence given by the Rev. Dr. Norman Macleod to the Poor Law Commissioners on the occupational support given by Glasgow-resident Highlanders lends this view credence:

> I think the Highlanders find it more easy to get respectable employment than the Irish; the Highlanders have many friends in Glasgow to whom they apply. They come with letters of recommendation to countrymen and clansmen who are in comfortable circumstances; we are very clannish; and those who come from one Island do it for the men from that Island who have to get employment – the Macdonalds for the Macdonalds and the Macleods for the Macleods and so on, so that they find very little difficulty in getting work.[18]

What the Uist and Barra Association was doing in Glasgow in the 1890s in respect of temporary migration (see above page 80), migrant institutions like the Glasgow Argyllshire Society, the Glasgow Northern Highland Benevolent Society (begun in 1836), and bodies like the Glasgow Skye Association (1865), the Glasgow Sutherland Association (1857), and *An Comunn Ileach*, the Glasgow Islay Association (1862), did for Highlanders from those parts seeking permanent residence.

Few of Greenock's Highlanders resident in 1851 came from the north and west mainland, although there were relatively significant numbers born in the Skye parishes of Portree and Sleat. Inverness parish was an important source. The eastern districts of Ross and Cromarty, Inverness-shire and Highland Perthshire were the source of few migrants (Figure 4.3). Greenock's Highland migration field by 1851 was overwhelmingly from Argyll (Figure 4.4). Campbeltown, Rothesay, and Kilmichael Glassary parishes all provided large numbers. Yet, and mindful of the fact that the parish of birth is not known for some, there are some important elements to note of Highland migration from Argyll to Greenock by 1851. Proportionately, many fewer Highlanders were from the north-west

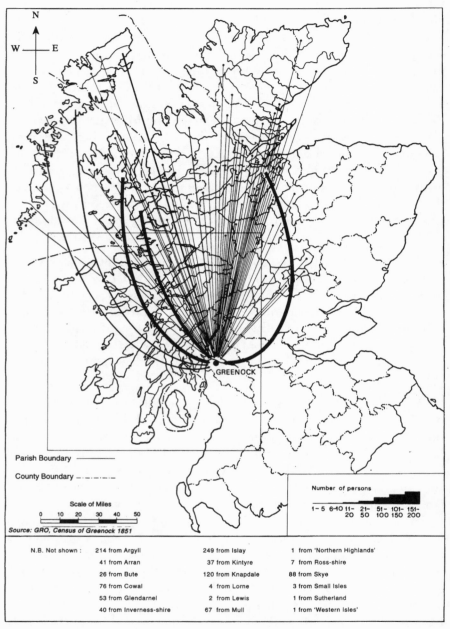

Figure 4.3 *Highland migration to Greenock, 1851*

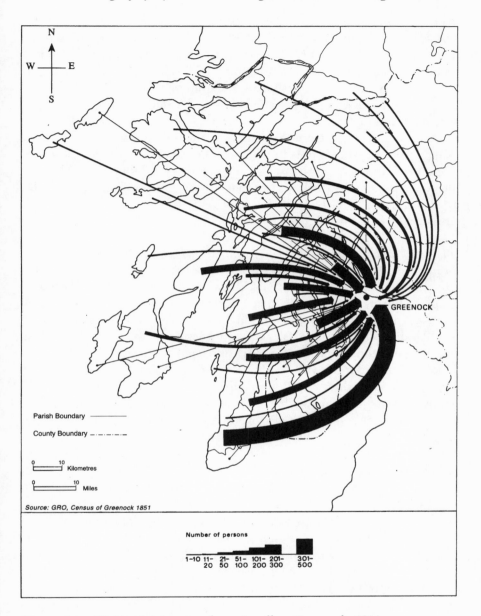

Figure 4.4 *Highland migration from Argyll to Greenock, 1851*

Argyll mainland than from the south. Most Kintyre peninsula parishes outside Campbeltown were important source parishes. Jura, insignificant for Glasgow, was the source of large numbers of Greenock's Highlanders. Further north, however, Kilmore and Kilbride and Kilbrandon and Kilchattan parishes were for Greenock unimportant.

Longer-distance Highland migration to Paisley in 1851 was, as for Glasgow and Greenock, from the eastern seaboard and from Inverness with little movement from the north-west mainland and islands (Figure 4.5). Within Argyll, Campbeltown and Kilmichael Glassary parishes were important, and, in contrast to Greenock, Paisley drew more evenly from the northern mainland parishes of that county. Out-movement from Islay to Paisley, particularly from Kilarow and Kilmeny parish, is notable amongst individual 'lines' of migration.

The geography of Highland migration to urban east Scotland:
Edinburgh, Leith, Perth, Dundee, Aberdeen, Stirling
Highland migration into the Scottish capital by 1851 was evenly drawn from the northern mainland, especially from the eastern seaboard. Few of Edinburgh's Highland population in 1851 came from the far north-west mainland, from the Outer Isles or from the islands of Mull, Tiree, Coll and Islay. Within Argyll, important source parishes were Campbeltown, Kilmore and Kilbride with smaller flows from Kilmichael Glassary and Inveraray and Rothesay on Bute (Figure 4.6). Within this general picture, several eastern parishes within Ross and Cromarty and Inverness-shire were important sources, as also were the Highland Perthshire parishes (Figure 4.7). Notable in this respect is movement from the small Highland towns of Dingwall and Cromarty, the evenly-balanced, low-level out-movement from the eastern parishes of Inverness-shire and the handfuls of migrants drawn more or less equally from north-west Highland Perthshire. Standing out as a major supply parish is Inverness. There is no significant variation within this picture for Highland migration into Leith in 1851, then a separate burgh from Edinburgh, excepting that the high proportion moving from Highland Caithness (Table 4.1) was almost entirely migration from the parish of Latheron (22 of 29 Highland Caithness-born persons in Leith in 1851) (Figure 4.8). Migration to Leith from Inverness, Dingwall, Cromarty, Campbeltown, Oban (in Kilmore and Kilbride parish) and Rothesay mirrors Highland migration to Edinburgh. There was considerable within-city residential variation in terms of county of origin of Edinburgh's Highland population in 1851 (Table 4.3; *cf.* Table 4.4 for Glasgow). St. Mary's parish, for example, had nearly seven times as many Argyll-born Highlanders as Old Greyfriars parish which, together with Tolbooth parish, had high

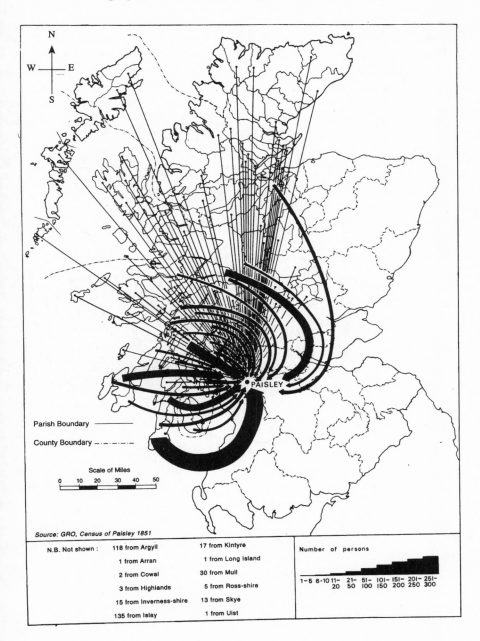

Figure 4.5 *Highland migration to Paisley, 1851*

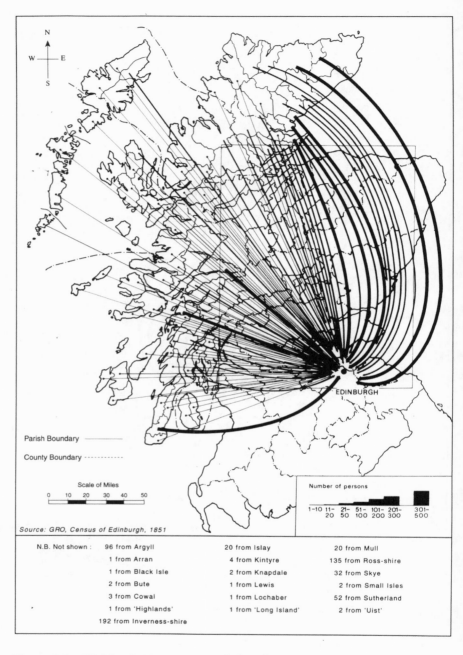

Figure 4.6 *Highland migration to Edinburgh, 1851*

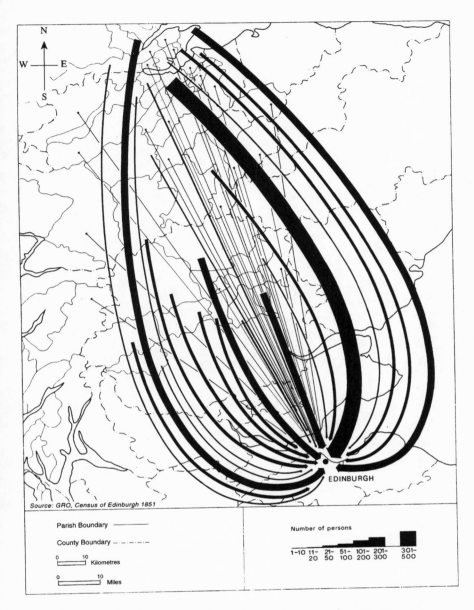

Source: GRO, Census of Edinburgh 1851

Parish Boundary ——————

County Boundary —·—··—·—

Number of persons

1–10 11– 21– 51– 101– 201– 301–
      20   50   100 200 300 500

Figure 4.7   *Highland migration from the north-east central Highlands to Edinburgh, 1851*

Table 4.3

BIRTHPLACE OF THE HIGHLAND–BORN POPULATION OF EDINBURGH, BY PARISH, 1851*

Number of Highlanders born in indicated county, as a percentage of total Highland-born population, by parish

Highland County	(a)	(b)	(c)	(d)	(e)	(f)	(g)	(h)	(i)	(j)	(k)	(l)	(m)	(n)	(o)	(p)	(q)	(r)	City of Glasgow
Argyll	11.74	3.09	11.65	3.72	9.80	15.78	3.92	6.79	15.65	5.40	18.30	14.82	20.99	16.24	8.75	10.31	18.76	20.25	15.59
Bute	–	–	–	–	1.96	–	–	0.97	1.79	–	0.79	1.19	1.77	1.38	–	0.93	1.40	1.28	1.10
Inverness	27.86	19.58	27.18	55.55	33.33	35.08	36.27	24.27	23.47	28.12	28.97	22.09	22.77	24.53	33.75	36.25	24.36	27.84	26.60
Ross and Cromarty	24.59	28.86	27.18	11.11	13.72	28.07	21.90	38.83	20.86	23.43	19.62	24.12	23.48	17.59	30.00	29.06	26.77	26.58	25.1
Sutherland	6.55	17.55	13.59	12.96	17.64	10.52	7.64	18.47	20.86	11.80	5.03	6.97	6.97	5.09	2.50	11.25	8.40	7.59	9.18
Highland Caithness	1.67	12.37	1.96	5.55	7.84	1.78	9.80	3.88	6.95	20.31	2.96	4.65	3.55	2.77	5.00	4.37	3.97	6.34	4.79
Highland Moray	–	–	–	–	–	–	1.07	–	0.88	–	0.26	–	0.76	–	–	–	0.35	–	0.28
Highland Perth	27.86	18.55	18.44	11.11	11.76	8.77	9.80	6.79	9.56	10.93	24.13	25.87	19.92	32.40	20.00	7.83	15.74	10.12	17.20
Highland Nairn	–	–	–	–	3.95	–	–	–	–	–	–	0.29	–	–	–	–	0.25	–	0.16

(Columns (a)–(r) are the Glasgow parishes+)

+ Key to Edinburgh parishes: (a) Lady Yesters (b) Old Greyfriars (c) New Greyfriars (d) St John (e) New North Church (f) Tron Church (g) Old Church (h) Trinity College Church (i) High Church or St Giles (j) Tolbooth Church (k) St George (l) St Stephen (m) St Mary (n) St Andrew (o) Greenside (p) Canongate (q) St Cuthbert (such as lies within the Parliamentary Burgh of Edinburgh) (r) South Leith (such as lies within the Parliamentary Burgh of Edinburgh)

* From *Census of Scotland* Enumerators' Books 1851

concentrations of the city's Caithness Highlanders. Over half of the Highlanders in St. John's parish were, by contrast, natives of Highland Perthshire. In part, these patterns may be explained in the same way as for Glasgow and the urban west. In part, too, particular patterns of movement are discernible in relation to occupation: that from Latheron to North Leith and Newhaven was of sailors, fish curers, and others connected with maritime employment; the high concentration of men from Sutherland and Highland Caithness in St. Giles parish in 1851 was because they were soldiers in Edinburgh Castle.

Highland migration to Perth in 1851 was overwhelmingly from Highland Perthshire with few persons moving from longer distance, except from Inverness (Figure 4.9). Movement from the north-west mainland parishes was minimal, non-existent from some insular parishes. In contrast, Dundee's Highland population in 1851, chiefly from Highland Perthshire parishes, drew reasonably large numbers from Argyll (within which county Kilmore and Kilbride and Campbeltown parishes were important), and from eastern parishes in Inverness-shire and Ross and Cromarty, as also from the north Skye parish of Kilmuir (Figure 4.10). Dingwall, Cromarty, and Tain parishes were individually important source parishes within the eastern districts. The picture given for migration to Dundee in the Census of 1851 is reinforced by what we know of the place of birth of Highlanders buried within St. Peter's churchyard in Dundee from 1837 to 1854, and the 881 Highland-born persons buried in the city's Howff Churchyard between 20 February 1821 and 22 December 1854 (Figure 4.11). More clearly than the Census, this evidence documents movement over a period, and, since the Howff burial register for Highland-born includes men of 96 as well as infants of six months, provides for a few individuals anyway a surrogate record of lifetime migration into the city from the 1740s, if not earlier.[19] For some Highlanders in Perth or Dundee, as noted of the stepped migration of some Highlanders in Glasgow's City and Barony parishes from 1852–1898, their appearance in the town masked a series of moves prior to urban residence. One 'Widow MacDonald', a Highland-born woman in Perth, was questioned by members of the parochial board there on 1 November 1843 on matters concerning poor relief payments. She revealed she was born in Kenmore parish in Highland Perthshire in 1793 and married in Crieff in 1823. Sometime between 1823 and 1824, she moved with her husband to Edinburgh where they remained for ten years before moving to Denny in Stirlingshire for a further two years. From Denny, they moved to Cardross, and, following the death of her husband there, she moved to Perth in the summer of 1836. Consider, too, Mary McDougall, born in Fortingall in 1753 and a servant in the parish of Little Dunkeld for

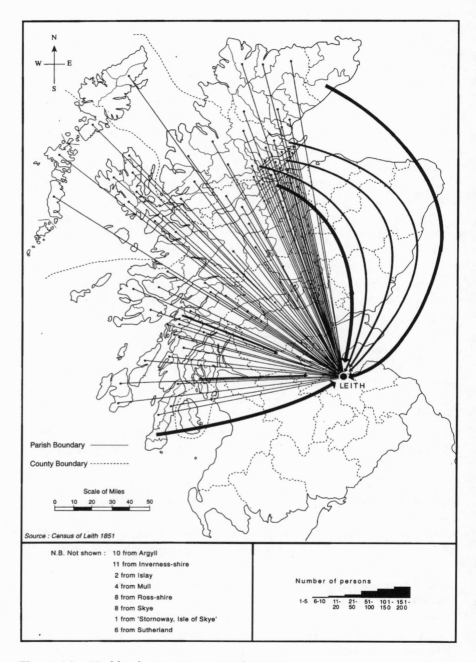

Figure 4.8 *Highland migration to Leith, 1851*

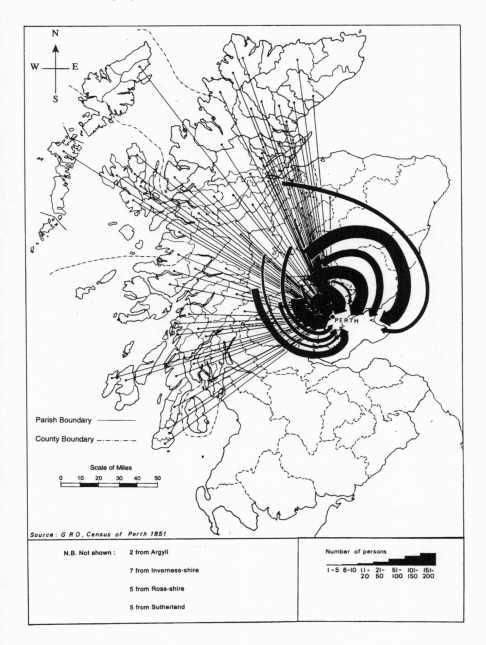

Figure 4.9 *Highland migration to Perth, 1851*

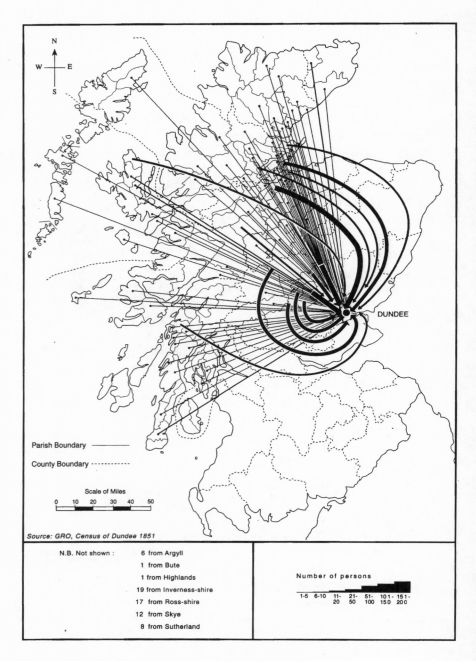

Figure 4.10 *Highland migration to Dundee, 1851*

40 years. She left both parish and job when over 60 years old and moved to Auchtergaven where she worked for eight years before making the move to Perth in 1841. For Donald McDonald, a 62–year-old in 1843, the move for himself and his family from Fortingall was more simply motivated and direct: he was 'put out of his farm where he lived all his life, for being unable to pay the rent, 7 years ago', and moved, with his wife and six children, directly to Perth.[20] Thus, when William Arnot of Perth noted in testimony to the 1843 Poor Law Commissioners that 'This city has, for a great many years back, been completely inundated from the surrounding rural, especially Highland parishes',[21] he was referring in simple terms to patterns of migration we can with reasonable certainty say were complex in motivation and in their geography and apparent rom at least the late eighteenth century.

Aberdeen's Highland migration field in 1851 was predominantly from the eastern parishes of Ross and Cromarty and Inverness-shire. Inverness parish was an important source (Figure 4.12). Highland parishes along the eastern Grampians were common source parishes for Aberdeen, as also were parishes in east Sutherland and in Highland Caithness: areas unimportant for Perth and for Dundee. The parishes of the west Highlands and Islands were insignificant source areas although small numbers did move from Campbeltown, Oban in north Argyll, and from Lochbroom, Lochcarron and Stornoway in the west. Set between the north-east source areas for Aberdeen, and, to some degree, Perth and Dundee and the south-western Highlands source areas for urban west-central Scotland, is evidence for the few Highland-born in Stirling (Figure 4.13). Most of Stirling's Highlanders came from Highland Perthshire, notably from Killin and Balquhidder. The Argyll-born within the town were taken from across that county. The north and west Highlands were unimportant as a source region, with the exception of small numbers from Kilmuir in Skye.

HIGHLAND-LOWLAND MIGRATION IN 1891

Highland migration to the urban Lowlands by 1891 shared, at county level (Table 4.4), the same broad geographies of source area as for 1851. Table 4.4 is not directly comparable with the evidence of 1851 (Table 4.1), since for some towns it lists figures for the 'traditional' Highland counties only and not the detailed enumeration of the Highlands as here understood. Yet it is clear that by the end of the century, Glasgow, Greenock, and Paisley still drew substantially upon Argyll for their Highland migrants, but that an increased proportion of the Highland population in these towns was from Ross and Cromarty and Inverness-shire.

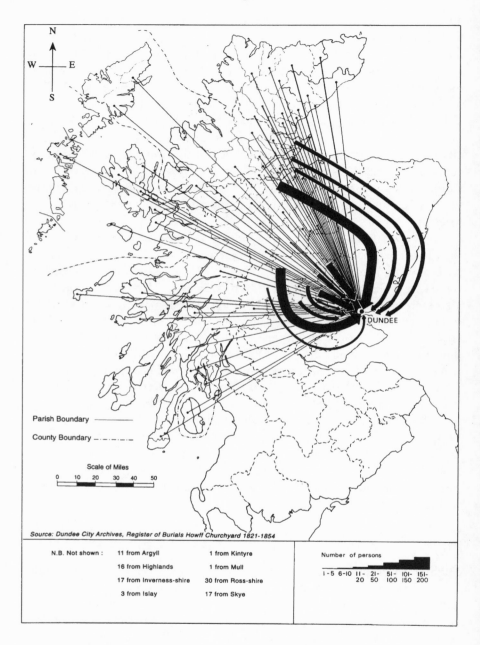

Parish Boundary ——————

County Boundary –·–·–·–·–

Scale of Miles

0 10 20 30 40 50

Source: Dundee City Archives, Register of Burials Howff Churchyard 1821-1854

N.B. Not shown :

11 from Argyll

16 from Highlands

17 from Inverness-shire

3 from Islay

1 from Kintyre

1 from Mull

30 from Ross-shire

17 from Skye

Number of persons

1 -5 6-10 11 - 21- 51- 101- 151-
              20   50 100 150 200

Figure 4.11 *Highland migration to Dundee, 1821–1854*

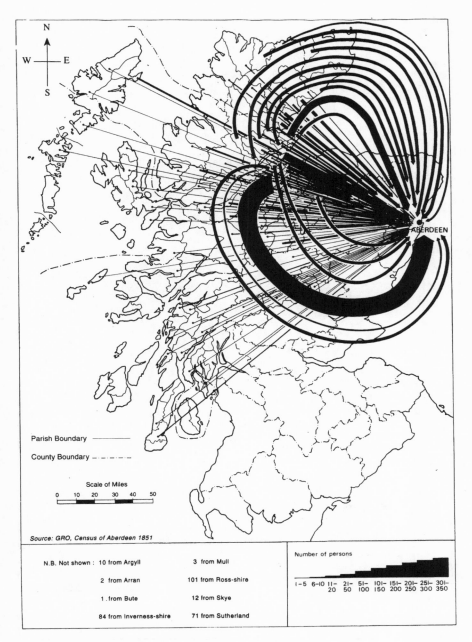

N

W——E

S

Parish Boundary ——————

County Boundary —·—·—·—·—

Scale of Miles

0   10   20   30   40   50

Source: GRO, Census of Aberdeen 1851

ABERDEEN

N.B. Not shown : 10 from Argyll   3 from Mull

2 from Arran   101 from Ross-shire

1 . from Bute   12 from Skye

84 from Inverness-shire   71 from Sutherland

Number of persons

1–5 6–10 11– 21– 51– 101– 151– 201– 251– 301–
            20   50   100 150 200 250 300 350

Figure 4.12   *Highland migration to Aberdeen, 1851*

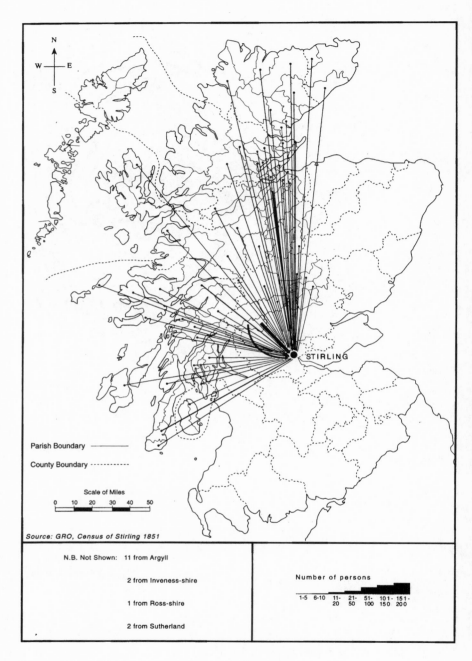

Figure 4.13 *Highland migration to Stirling, 1851*

Table 4.4

BIRTHPLACE, BY HIGHLAND COUNTY, OF THE HIGHLAND-BORN POPULATION IN THE
PRINCIPAL TOWNS OF SCOTLAND, 1891*

Highland County	Aberdeen	Dundee	Lowland Towns +						
			Edinburgh	Glasgow	Greenock	Leith	Paisley	Perth	Stirling
Argyll	7.0	16.25	17.16	55.51	68.95	17.58	68.18	11.59	36.9
Inverness	46.38	50.31	33.94	26.16	22.41	31.98	19.84	56.77	35.71
Ross and Cromarty	36.85	31.08	36.85	14.27	7.55	33.23	8.56	22.78	23.51
Sutherland	9.77	2.36	12.05	4.06	1.09	17.20	3.41	8.86	3.87
TOTAL NO. OF HIGHLAND-COUNTY BORN	1,468	1,126	6,576	18,536	3,601	1,035	1,144	509	336
TOTAL NO OF HIGHLAND-BORN+ +		1,277	–	–	–	–	–	1,117	336
HIGHLAND POP. AS % OF TOTAL URBAN POP.	1.20	0.81	2.51	3.27	5.67	1.50	1.72	3.73	2.24

* From *Census of Scotland* (1892), *BPP.*, Vol. XCIV, Table XIV
+ All of the Lowland towns here indicated are based on the Parliamentary Burghs
+ + Highland – born as here defined (see page 00).

Edinburgh and Leith, as in 1851, drew equally from these two northern counties but in increased proportion from earlier in the century. Both places, notably Leith, had a larger proportion of Highland population from Sutherland by 1891. Stirling's Highland source area continued to be relatively evenly spread across the Highlands by 1891. The migration fields for Perth, Dundee, and Aberdeen were predominantly from Inverness and Ross and Cromarty. Within this general picture, the study of individual parishes and certain towns allows greater precision in understanding of the geography of Highland migration by 1891.

The geography of Highland migration to Partick parish, Glasgow

In 1891, Partick, then recognised as a 'Highland' part of Glasgow, had a Highland-born population of 3,456 persons (using the detailed definition of Highland-born), about 6.85 per cent of the total parish. The great majority were from Argyll, and, recognising large numbers to be not locatable by parish of birth, important source parishes were Tobermory on Mull, Kilmore and Kilbride and other northern mainland parishes such as Kilbrandon and Kilchattan, Ardnamurchan, and Lismore and Appin (Figure 4.14). Campbeltown was not important and southern Argyll was less important than the northern mainland and island parishes of that county. From further afield, Partick's Highlanders came from eastern Ross and Cromarty and Inverness-shire, and in large numbers within that area from Inverness, Cromarty, Tain, and Dingwall. Also notable is movement from the north and west mainland and island parishes, with migrant streams from Lochbroom (41 persons), eastern Skye, and Stornoway parish (98 persons). The numbers involved are small (although Partick's Highland population was then about the same size as Greenock's), and we should not readily suppose this parish to be typical of Glasgow as a whole. But this evidence does illustrate in more detail what is hinted at in comparison between Tables 4.1 and 4.4: that, by the later nineteenth century, larger numbers of urban Highlanders had come from further afield in the Highlands. Argyll was the principal source county for Glasgow and for Partick, but within that county, northern rather than southern parishes were more important than previously. Parishes within the north-east farming Highlands with a town or village continued to be individually important. This evidence also suggests that the north and west was, with the exception of Sutherland, more important as a region of supply to urban west Scotland by 1891 than in 1851. Sutherland Highlanders, to judge from Table 4.4 and, for an earlier period, from Figures 4.6 and 4.8, were drawn more towards the east Lowlands than to the west. Figure 4.14 also suggests how the regional emphasis of more migrants from the north and west Highlands later in

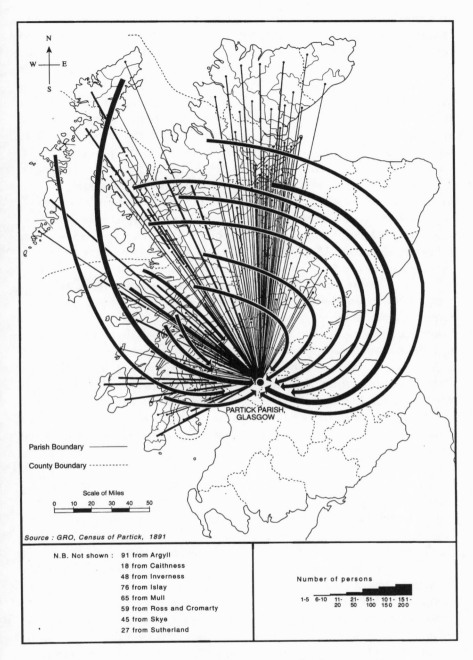

Parish Boundary ————

County Boundary -------------

Scale of Miles
0 10 20 30 40 50

Source : GRO, Census of Partick, 1891

PARTICK PARISH,
GLASGOW

N.B. Not shown : 91 from Argyll
18 from Caithness
48 from Inverness
76 from Islay
65 from Mull
59 from Ross and Cromarty
45 from Skye
27 from Sutherland

Number of persons

1-5 6-10 11- 21- 51- 101- 151-
20 50 100 150 200

Figure 4.14   *Highland migration to Partick parish Glasgow, 1891*

the nineteenth century itself had local internal variation. Using the 1891 Census to substantiate and elucidate that local variation for Highland migration to the whole of Glasgow, Greenock and Paisley and for the constituent parishes within each town must be the subject of further research. Yet from what is known of Highland migration to the urban west from other sources it is likely that this south-north regional variation by the second half of the nineteenth century did obtain more widely, and that what we have seen of movement to Partick from parishes in Skye, Wester Ross, the Outer Isles and from other Highland parishes with a town or village was more widely apparent. Lobban's work on Greenock shows that an increasing proportion of the town's Highland population came from the northern Highlands by the later nineteenth century.[22] Place-of-birth statistics within the registers of Glasgow's police between 1826 and 1891 show an increased proportion from farther afield later in the period (Figure 4.15). Even if evaluated on a year-by-year basis, the picture of greater movement from further away does not alter.[23] Similarly, the lifetime migration of Highlanders receiving poor relief in Glasgow's City and Barony parishes between 1852 and 1898 shows large numbers from northern Argyll (as well as from Campbeltown), from Tobermory and Kilmore and Kilbride in particular, as well as out-movement from Inverness and from Stornoway (Figure 4.16). As a picture of *direct* movement, this is misleading since many Highlanders within this sample moved within Scotland between quitting the Highlands and registering for poor relief in Glasgow (see above page 76 and Figure 3.3). But as an indication of native parish, it substantiates other evidence on the nature of migration to the urban west in the second half of the nineteenth century.[24]

The geography of Highland migration to urban east Scotland: Perth, Dundee, Aberdeen, Stirling

Perth's Highland-born population in 1891 of 1,117 persons represented 3.73 per cent of the town's population. (In 1851, the town's 1,200 Highlanders constituted a little over 5 per cent of the total). As in 1851, Perth's Highland migration in 1891 was predominantly from Highland Perthshire (Figure 4.17). Longer-distance movement was largely from eastern Ross and Cromarty with Inverness and Dingwall important parishes. Argyll was the source of few Perth Highlanders, but Campbeltown was important within movement from that county. Migration to Dundee in 1891 was largely from Highland Perthshire, from eastern Ross and Cromarty and Inverness-shire, but, in contrast to Perth then and to Dundee in mid-century (Figures 4.10 and 4.11), was also from the north and west mainland and Outer Isles and in greater numbers from Highland

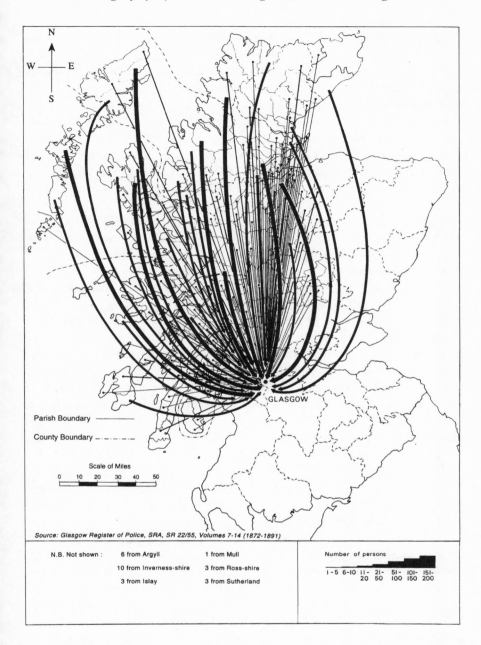

Figure 4.15   *The migration of Highland-born Glasgow policemen, 1872–1891*

Caithness and from Campbeltown in the south (Figure 4.18). Kilmuir parish in north Skye was an important source area for Dundee's migrants in 1851 and 1891. The evidence of the 160 Highland-born paupers registered in Dundee's East Poorhouse between 1856 and 1878 illustrates something of Highland migration to Dundee for the inter-censal period and highlights individual parishes such as Inverness and Cromarty within the north-eastern coastal Highlands (Figure 4.19).

The evidence for Dundee as a whole between 1821 and 1891 shows, in the second half of the century, an increase in migration from Ross and Cromarty, a small increase from Argyllshire, and a more marked decrease in movement from the parishes in Highland Perthshire (Table 4.5). Although this broadly supports the distance-decay relationship evident in Highland migration to urban west Scotland in the same period, the rise in numbers of Argyll-born within Dundee and the constantly low proportion of Highland migrants from Sutherland and Highland Caithness should be noted. What is clear about the evidence for Dundee is the variation *within* the counties of Ross and Cromarty and Inverness between 1851 and 1891.

Aberdeen's Highland migration field in 1891 was overwhelmingly from Inverness-shire, particularly from Inverness, and from the eastern portions of the northern mainland in general (Figure 4.20). Argyll was unimportant though most parishes were the source of a few migrants. From the north-west Highlands, Stornoway on Lewis and Portree on Skye were important source parishes together with Lochbroom and Gairloch on the mainland. The east-west distinction within Sutherland in terms of parishes of supply is more marked for 1891 than for 1851 (Figure 4.12), excepting the farthest north-west mainland parishes of Durness, Eddrachillis and Assynt. The evidence of birthplace of Highland-born students matriculated in the University of Aberdeen between 1860 and 1890 (Figure 4.21) and for earlier periods supports the Census-based evidence of Aberdeen's largely north-east Highlands migration field.[25]

Stirling in 1891, in contrast, took its Highland population of 376 persons almost equally from Argyll (98 persons, 26 per cent of the total), Inverness-shire (94 persons, 25 per cent), and Highland Perthshire (90 persons, 24 per cent). Important individual source parishes were Inverness, Ardersier, and Dingwall from the north-east coastal districts, and Kilmore and Kilbride and Campbeltown from Argyll. The north-west was unimportant as a source region (Figure 4.22). This geography of migration holds also for the few Highland-born paupers in the town between 1845 and 1891.[26]

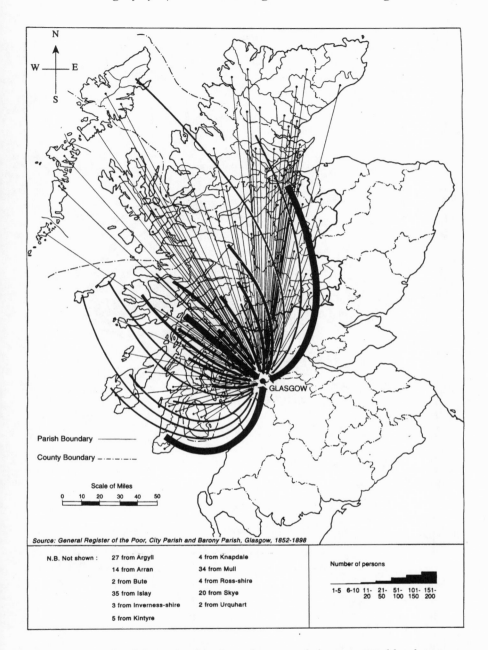

Figure 4.16 *The 'lifetime' migration of poor and destitute Highlanders in City and Barony parishes Glasgow, 1852–1898*

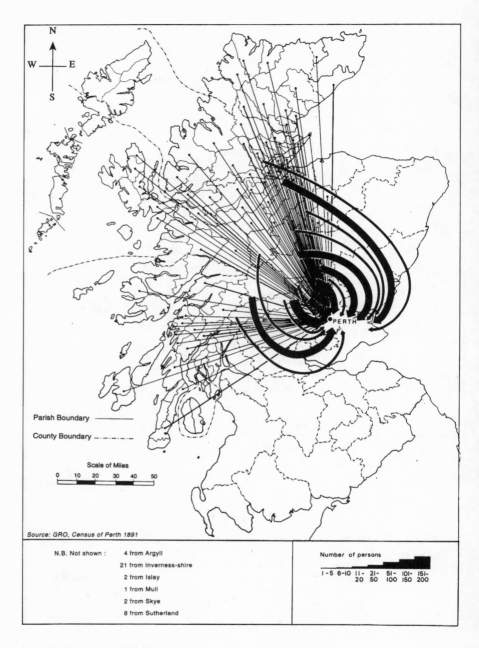

Figure 4.17 *Highland migration to Perth, 1891*

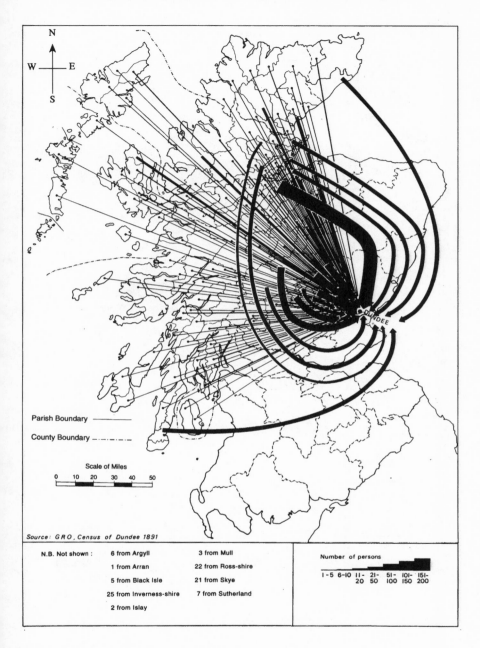

Figure 4.18 *Highland migration to Dundee, 1891*

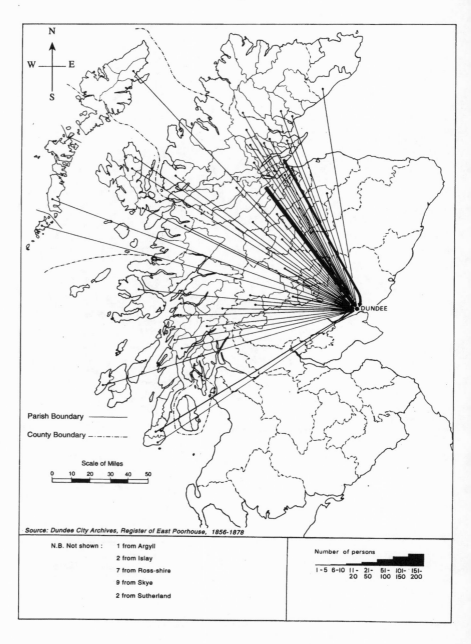

Figure 4.19 *Highland migration to Dundee's East Poorhouse, 1856–1878*

Table 4.5

BIRTHPLACE OF THE HIGHLAND-BORN POPULATION OF DUNDEE, 1821–1891

Numbers of Highlanders born in indicated county and as a percentage of Highland-born population, by source

Highland County	1821–54[1]		1837–54[2]		1851[3]		1856–78[4]		1891[5]	
	No	%	No	%	No	%	No	%	No	%
Argyll	37	(4.2)	1	(5.0)	54	(6.7)	18	(11.3)	92	(7.2)
Bute	2	(0.2)	–	–	5	(0.6)	–	–	11	(0.9)
Inverness	250	(28.4)	2	(10.0)	220	(27.2)	71	(44.4)	364	(28.5)
Ross and Cromarty	105	(11.9)	2	(10.0)	128	(15.8)	32	(20.0)	263	(20.6)
Sutherland	76	(8.6)			39	(4.8)	7	(4.4)	44	(3.4)
Highland Caithness	11	(1.2)			11	(1.4)	3	(1.9)	27	(2.1)
Highand Moray	5	(0.6)	1	(5.0)	1	(0.1)	1	(0.6)	7	(0.5)
Highland Perth	391	(44.4)	14	(70.0)	348	(43.0)	28	(17.5)	466	(36.5)
Highland Nairn	4	(0.5)			3	(0.4)	–	–	3	(0.2)
	881	(100.0)	20	(100.0)	809	(100.0)	160	(100.0)	1,277	(100.0)

1. Register of Burials, Howff Churchyard 1821–1854
2. Register of Burials, St Peter's Churchyard, Feb 1837 – Dec. 1854
3. Census Enumerators' Books, 1851
4. Register of Inmates, Dundee East Poorhouse, 1856–1878
5. Census Enumerators' Books, 1891

119

CONCLUSION

Three main points may be made of the geography of permanent Highland-Lowland migration. Firstly, each Lowland town drew largely but not exclusively upon particular parts of the Highlands. The south-west and north-east geography of supplying districts, first clearly identifiable for 1851, was probably extant from the 1750s. Glasgow, Greenock and Paisley took the majority of their Highland-born from Argyll, mainland and insular, and, to a lesser extent, from eastern Ross and Cromarty and Inverness-shire. Stirling's Highland migration field was equally from Argyll, Highland Perthshire, and Inverness-shire. Highland migration to Perth and Dundee was principally from Highland Perthshire and the eastern central and coastal Highlands. Argyll, the Hebrides and the north-west mainland were not important source areas. Aberdeen drew heavily upon eastern north Scotland, to a lesser degree upon Highland Perthshire, and hardly at all upon Argyll. Highland migration to Edinburgh and Leith was from the north-east Highlands with higher proportions than elsewhere from Sutherland and Highland Caithness. Secondly, by the later nineteenth century, more Highlanders were coming from distant Highland parishes. This has been noted of Greenock: 'The pull of Greenock on the Highlands reached out in a wave-like motion, affecting first districts close at hand, and later the more distant places within an ever-widening radius in successive periods through the eighteenth and nineteenth centuries'.[27] This distance-decay relationship over time did not conflict with the geographical variation in migration fields within the Highlands. But it is not a wholly applicable generalisation. It holds less well for certain towns than others: Highland movement from Argyll to Dundee increased in the later 1800s, for example, and declined from Sutherland in the same period. Thirdly, various individual Highland parishes were important sources for Highland migration, particularly parishes with a small town or village. This movement is applicable for Highland migration to all Lowland towns. From the north-east, Inverness and, to a lesser extent, Dingwall, Cromarty, and Tain were important in this respect. Inverness was an important source parish for all the study towns. Within the south and south-west Highlands, Campbeltown was the most important.

Highland-Lowland migration should not, then, be seen as an unstructured outpouring characterising all parts of the Highlands equally. It had a fairly precise geography, partly captured here, involved some districts and particular parishes more than others, and was, in general, more common from the south-west, central and north-east Highlands than from the north and west until later in the nineteenth century. It is less easy

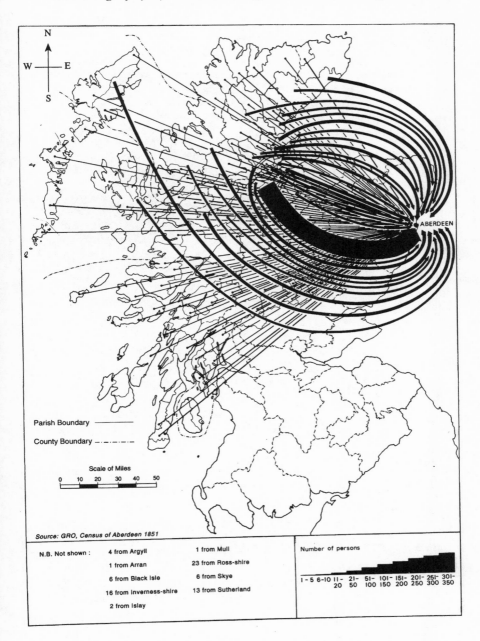

Figure 4.20 *Highland migration to Aberdeen, 1891*

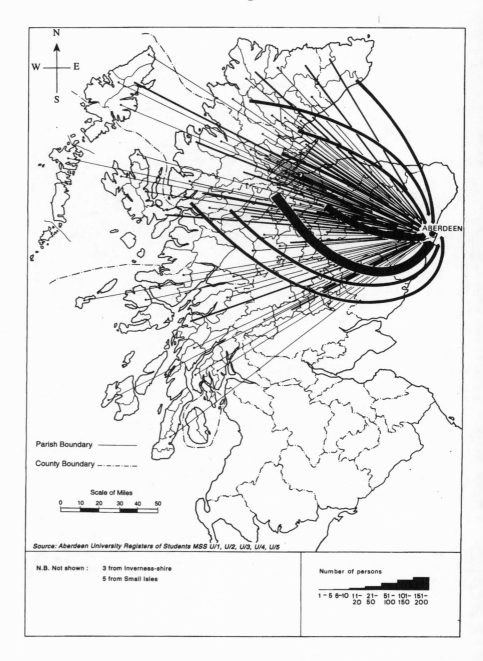

Figure 4.21   *The migration of Highland-born students to the University of Aberdeen, 1860–1891*

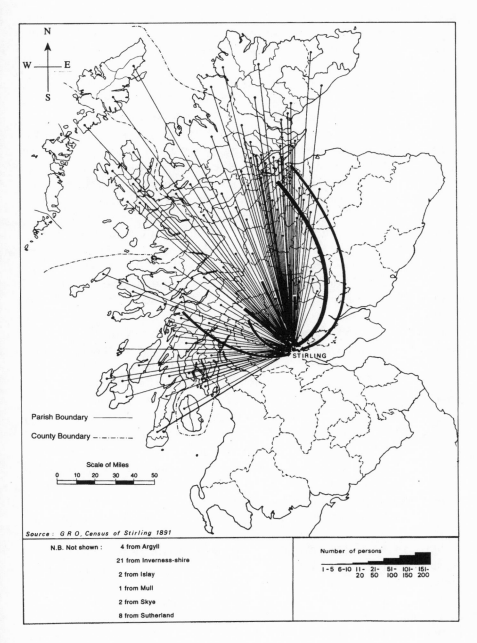

N
W — E
S

Parish Boundary ————
County Boundary —·—·—·—

Scale of Miles
0   10   20   30   40   50

STIRLING

Source: G R O, Census of Stirling 1891

N.B. Not shown :   4 from Argyll
                     21 from Inverness-shire
                     2 from Islay
                     1 from Mull
                     2 from Skye
                     8 from Sutherland

Number of persons
1 - 5 6-10 11- 21- 51- 101- 151-
            20   50 100   150   200

Figure 4.22   Highland migration to Stirling, 1891

to know in detail, however, who was moving and quite why. Known age-at-arrival statistics for a handful of Dundee's Highlanders show only great variation in the ages at which people may be presumed first resident.[28] Being told only that a great many Highlanders who came to Glasgow by the later 1830s did so between the ages of 16 and 22 is little use as a basis for generalisation.[29] Given the evidence for stepped movement, we should not simply suppose known age at arrival to be indicative of age at departure from the Highlands. For Dundee, as for other towns, permanent Highland migration was underlain by circuits of temporary labour mobility. Even where the recorded birthplace of children in the enumerators' volumes allows identification of intervening places and, thus, of familial mobility prior to enumeration in the Lowlands, it is not easy to generalise from the wealth of individual experience. Overall, migration in the first half of the nineteenth century and earlier involved the younger age ranges with older persons participating more commonly from the later 1800s.[30] It is possible to distinguish between 'wholly-Highland families' where both parents and all recorded children are Highland-born, and 'part-Highland families' where both parents were Highland-born but none of the children were Highland-born or where one parent and the eldest child were Highland-born. In addition, we should note the presence of the Highland-born man or woman married to a non-Highland partner with no Highland-born children recorded, and the unmarried Highland-born individual. In Dundee in 1891, only a little over 6 per cent of the town's Highland population are represented in the enumerators' books as a wholly Highland family.[31] If we may use such limited evidence more generally, we might hypothesise that most migrants, certainly in the later eighteenth and early nineteenth centuries, moved as young, predominantly single people. Highland families moved more commonly as a unit only later when, as for the McDonald family in Fortingall in 1836, changes in local circumstance demanded wholesale departure rather than the temporary absence of the head of household or of the younger members in domestic service and harvest work.

This geography is principally migration from the farming Highlands. As several commentators noted from the later eighteenth century, agrarian change in the south and west Highlands – notably commercial sheep farming, engrossment of holdings and the gradual removal of runrig and other customary practices (see above, pages 33–40) – was a major cause behind people leaving the land. Evidence of 1792 for Ardchattan and Muckairn in northern Argyll is indicative:

> Several families have removed to the Low country, where the wages are high. The principal cause of the decrease of population is the engrossing

and uniting several farms, and turning them into sheepwalks. Farms that formerly occupied 8 or 9 families are now occupied by only 2 or 3, and, in some places, solely by one shepherd.[32]

As was noted of Glenorchy and Inishail in Argyll fifty years later, options other than 'removing to some of the manufacturing towns of the south' were available: emigration, or staying put in some new 'assigned locality' (see above page 40). Migration to the towns was the choice of many from the farming Highlands because the region had close connections with the Lowlands and was better able to shed labour. In the crofting districts, the customary practices of temporary migration delayed permanent departure and emigration, rather than Lowland migration, was more common when social and agrarian change forced people from the land. Since such change came later to the north-west mainland and to the Hebrides than to the southern and north-east coastal Highlands, it is possible to see the numbers moving from these more distant parishes later in the century as one result of the later transformation of rural society in the northern Highlands. The greater severity of the potato famine from 1846 in the north and west Highlands and Islands should also be recognised. On Skye, destitution was most severe in the northern parishes. We may speculate that the temporary directed labour mobility from Kilmuir in particular from 1846–1849, of females to domestic service and of males to railway construction in East Lothian and Fife, was a prompt to many to leave the island altogether by 1851.[33] Since one of the relief schemes was stocking knitting and other textile work, it is not unreasonable to suggest that the Highland women moving in the migration stream from Kilmuir to Dundee by 1851 did so both because they had prior knowledge of the area and relevant skills to bring.

Knowing exactly how the decision to move permanently was influenced by familiarity with the Lowlands through trade or temporary mobility is likewise difficult. But it is clear that migration was, for many Highlanders, not a response to change but a normal part of daily life, especially in the farming Highlands. The picture we get from Fortingall in Highland Perthshire for 1790–1 hints at a complexity of movement typical of many places then:

> It is almost incredible to tell, what swarms leave the country every year, and go to the south for service. Almost all the boys, from 10 to 15, go to tend sheep or cattle, and learn a little English. – Many of them afterwards go into service, or to handicraft employments and never return. Besides these, crofters, cottagers, and day-labourers, who can earn no bread at home, set out for the great towns to get employment.[34]

Not all moved directly to the towns. Out-movement from individual parishes in the Highlands with a town or village – Inverness, Campbeltown, Oban, Dingwall, Cromarty, and, later in the nineteenth century, Stornoway – is partly to be explained by the population levels there: migration was greater because there was the demographic potential. What is also clear is that these towns and villages were drawing in the local Highland populations before chanelling them south. In Perthshire and in parts of Easter Ross, planned villages took many cleared from the land.[35] In Kilcalmonell and Kilberry in mid-Kintyre, 19 per cent of the parish population in 1792 was born outwith the parish.[36] In Campbeltown at the same time, incoming Highlanders were adding to the town's poor roll:

> This uncommon proportion [a high number of paupers] is partly owing to the number of poor families who come here from other parts of the Highlands, in hopes of getting some employment and bread, many of whom are soon a burden on the community. The prospect of pursuing the trade of begging to greater advantage, in a place more populous than the neighbourhood, probably induces others to take huts here; from which they are not hindered, if they pay, or promise, a few shillings of rent.[37]

There is no single trend for Highland towns as a whole: Inverness, Campbeltown and Stornoway steadily increased in population as parliamentary burghs from 1801; Cromarty declined each decade from 1841; and Dingwall declined in population as a parliamentary burgh from 1871. But assessment of the 1851 enumerators' returns for Campbeltown, Inverness and Oban shows the same story: growth by in-migration, principally from nearby Highland parishes and from more or less discrete migration fields, just as Lowland towns did on larger scales across the Highlands. What little we are told in 1844 for several Highlanders listed among those 'Poor Persons who have come from country parishes into the town of Inverness, in the hope of bettering their condition' adds an individual humanity to this picture: of William Callum, his wife and six children from nearby Kirkhill, for example, 'Came into Inverness about four years since, disabled from palsy; turned out of croft, and cow sold to pay rent; is with family in a destitute state'.[38] For some persons, then, if not perhaps for this family, permanent migration to the Lowlands was preceded by moves from the croft and clachan to and through the small Highland towns. For others, the move south was more direct and its motivation clearer. Many left Barra for Glasgow in the 1780s, invited south by the industrialist David Dale to work in his mills. Illness, and trade slumps, meant that some returned home.[39] For some Mull Highlanders, intended permanent migration was not realised: 'Most of the families that went to the Low country in 1792, returned back in 1793, for the same reason they left the country, want of employment'.[40]

126

For tens of thousands of others, however, migration to the urban Lowlands was permanent and with a particular geography. Regional distinctiveness in source area has been identified. Yet it is unlikely, given the generally common features of cottar and crofter life throughout the Highlands, that this distinctiveness meant that Glasgow's Highlanders were in any particular sense different from, say, Edinburgh's simply by virtue of different origin. Nor is there any reason to suppose that the presence of more Argyll-born in one Glasgow or Edinburgh parish than another was alone the basis of differences in Highland urban culture. Most migrants, together with the cause and the exact route of their movement, will always remain unknown. A few, like William Callum moving into Inverness in 1839, have lives revealed only in the stark tones of official enumeration: 'Betty Muir, aged sixty. Born in Ross-shire. Has been in Aberdeen since she was eighteen years old. She has 3s a month. Her rent is 1s 4d. per month. Very infirm. Small house, but kept decent. Has a poor bed a very little furniture. Used to get something by going out, but she cannot get out now'.[41] For many, life for the urban Gael meant occupational change and, perhaps, attendance at a Gaelic chapel or membership of a Highland society in the south as well as geographical mobility.

NOTES

1. R. A. Houston and C. W. J. Withers, 'Population mobility in Scotland and Europe, 1600–1900: a comparative perspective', *Annales de Démographie Historique*, 1990, pp. 285–308; J. Lucassen, *Migrant Labour in Europe 1600–1900* (Beckenham, 1987); N. P. Canny, *Europeans on the Move* (Oxford, 1994); L. P. Moch, *Moving Europeans: Migration in Western Europe since 1650* (Bloomington, Indiana, 1992).
2. A comprehensive review of migration in the early modern period is provided by P. Clark and D. Souden (eds.), *Migration and Society in Early Modern England* (London, 1987).
3. D. Mills and C. Pearce, *People and Places in the Victorian Census: a review and bibliography of publications based substantially on the manuscript Census Enumerators' Books, 1841–1911* (Cheltenham, 1989) provides a full review of scholarly work on the Census and documents the difficulties encountered in using it as a source for migration. 'Lifetime migration' is understood as the move between given parish of birth and parish of enumeration on the relevant Census night.
4. A. A. Lovett, I. D. Whyte and K. A. Whyte, 'Poisson repression analysis and migration fields: the example of the apprenticeship records of Edinburgh in the seventeenth and eighteenth centuries', *Transactions, Institute of British Geographers* 10(3), 1985, pp. 317–332; I. D. Whyte and K. A. Whyte, 'Patterns of migration of apprentices into Aberdeen and Inverness during the eighteenth and early nineteenth centuries', *Scottish Geographical Magazine* 102, 1986,

pp. 81–91; I. D. Whyte and K. A Whyte, 'The geographical mobility of women in early modern Scotland', in L. Leneman (ed.), *Perspectives in Scottish Social History: essays in honour of Rosalind Mitchison* (Aberdeen, 1988), pp. 83–106.

5. R. D. Lobban, 'The migration of Highlanders into Lowland Scotland, c.1750–1890, with particular reference to Greenock', (unpublished Ph.D., University of Edinburgh, 1969), pp. 25–29.

6. G. F. Black, *Surnames of Scotland* (Edinburgh, 1926), p. 553.

7. T. Macdhomhnaill, *Murchadh Ruadh Poileasman Gàidhealach air Ghalldachd* (Motherwell, 1983).

8. I. Macdonald, 'The beginning of Gaelic preaching in Scotland's cities', *Northern Scotland* 9, 1989, pp. 45–52.

9. S.R.O., CH2/557/5, f.171.

10. S.R.O., CH2/766/1, f.40; CH2/766/3, ff. 56–59; *Aberdeen Journal* 12 June 1788; A. Gammie, *The Churches of Aberdeen* (Aberdeen, 1909), p. 187; J. Cleland, *Enumeration of the Inhabitants of Glasgow* (Glasgow, 1820), p. 33.

11. S.R.O., CH3/322/2 f.50.

12. BPP, *Second Report of the Commissioners of Religious Instruction, Scotland*, 1837–8, XXXII, Appendix II, p. 32.

13. T. M. Devine, 'Highland migration to lowland Scotland, 1760–1860', *Scottish Historical Review* LXII, 1983, p. 138.

14. BPP, *Poor Law Inquiry Commission for Scotland*, 1844, XX, p. 643, 5 May 1843.

15. C. W. J. Withers, 'Highland Clubs and Gaelic Chapels: Glasgow's Gaelic Community in the eighteenth century', *Scottish Geographical Magazine*, 101 (1), 1985, pp. 16–27.

16. R. H. Osborne, 'The movements of people in Scotland, 1851–1951', *Scottish Studies* 2, 1958, pp. 1–46; H. Jones, 'Population patterns and processes from c. 1600', in G. Whittington and I. D. Whyte (eds.), *An Historical Geography of Scotland* (London and New York, 1983), pp. 93–118.

17. J. A. Jackson, *The Irish in Britain* (London, 1963); T. M. Devine (ed.), *Irish Immigrants and Scottish Society in the Nineteenth and Twentieth Centuries*, (Edinburgh, 1991).

18. BPP, *First Report from the Select Committee on Emigration, Scotland, together with the Minutes of Evidence and Appendix*, 1841, VI, p. 118 [Q. 1250].

19. C. W. J. Withers, *Highland Communities in Dundee and Perth, 1787–1891* (Dundee, 1986), pp. 20–21.

20. BPP, *Poor Law Inquiry*, 1844, XXII, pp. 175, 259–260.

21. *Ibid.*, p. 241 [Q. 479].

22. Lobban, *op cit.*, Table 8, p. 461.

23. C. W. J. Withers, ' "The long arm of the law": migration of Highland-born policemen to Glasgow 1826–1891' *Local Historian* 18, 1988, pp. 127–135.

24. C. W. J. Withers and A. Watson, 'Stepwise migration and Highland migration to Glasgow, 1852–1898', *Journal of Historical Geography* 17, 1991, pp. 35–55.

25. C. W. J. Withers, 'Highland migration to Aberdeen, c. 1649–1891', *Northern Scotland* 9, 1989, pp. 21–44.

26. Central Region Archives, *General Register of Poor for Stirling*, SB 11/1/1–11, 1845–1891.

27. M. Flinn *et al.*, *Scottish Population History* (Cambridge, 1977), p. 459.

28. Withers, *Highland Communities in Dundee and Perth*, pp. 36–37.

29. BPP, *First Report from the Select Committee on Emigration*, 1841, VI, p. 119 Q. 1260.

30. Devine, 'Highland migration to lowland Scotland', pp. 140–141; *idem*, 'Temporary migration and the Scottish Highlands in the nineteenth century', *Economic History Review* XXXII, 1979, pp. 344–359.
31. Withers, *Highland Communities in Dundee and Perth*, p. 35.
32. OSA, VI, 1792, p. 177.
33. C. W. J. Withers, 'Destitution and migration: labour mobility and relief from famine in Highland Scotland, 1836–1850', *Journal of Historical Geography*, 14, 1988, pp. 128–150.
34. OSA, II, 1790–1, p. 454.
35. This point is made of the rural Lowlands by M. Gray, 'Scottish emigration: the social impact of agrarian change in the rural Lowlands, 1775–1875', *Perspectives in American History* 7, 1973, pp. 95–174; on movement to planned villages, see D. G. Lockhart, 'Patterns of migration and movement of labour to the planned villages of north-east Scotland', *Scottish Geographical Magazine* 98, 1982, pp. 35–49; *idem*, 'Migration to planned villages in Scotland between 1725 and 1850', *Scottish Geographical Magazine* 102, 1986, pp. 165–180; for Easter Ross, see I. R. M. Mowat, *Easter Ross 1750–1850* (Edinburgh, 1982); on Perthshire, see L. Leneman, *Living in Atholl: a social history of the estates, 1685–1785* (Edinburgh, 1986); on connections between such short-distance movement to towns and villages on the Highland margins and protoindustrialisation, see I. D. Whyte, 'Protoindustrialization in Scotland', in P. Hudson (ed.), *Regions and Industries* (Cambridge, 1989), pp. 228–251.
36. OSA, X, 1792, p. 59.
37. OSA, X, 1791–2, pp. 546.
38. BPP, *Poor Law Inquiry Commission for Scotland*, Part II 1844, XXI, p. 506.
39. OSA, XIII, 1793, p. 338.
40. OSA, XIV, 1792, p. 196 (for the parish of Kilfinichen and Kilviceon).
41. BPP, *Poor Law Inquiry*, Part II, 1844, XXI, p. 664.

PART THREE

The Making of Urban Gaelic Culture

CHAPTER 5

Patterns of Work and Residence

If the rhythms of seasonal and temporary labour mobility familiarised some Highlanders with the nature of urban society, permanent residence in the urban Lowlands was a different experience altogether. As circumstances changed in their native parishes and as people increasingly took up permanent residence, Highland migrants were forced to compete in urban society for employment and housing. For some contemporary commentators, the Highlander was ill-suited to urban life by reason of language and what was perceived as an almost innate moral and physical incapacity. The Commissioners of Inquiry into the Poor Law in 1844 considered that the cause of what they took to be an almost endemic poverty in the Highlands was '. . . the imperfectly formed habits of the Highland labourer, in respect of provident and persevering industry. Under the stimulus of immediate reward, he is capable of making very great exertions, but the task accomplished, and the price paid, he relapses into his wonted lethargy'. Further:

> The truth is, – and intelligent Highlanders themselves will be the first to acknowledge, that it may be stated in explanation of the fact now mentioned, without any invidious reflection, or view of disparaging the many excellent qualities of their countrymen, – that the labouring population in the Highlands, regarded as a whole, are behind their neighbours in other parts of the country in the march of civilization. They are deficient in the knowledge of letters, they are still more deficient in that practical education of civilized life, which results from the mutual attrition and jostling of parties endeavouring to outstrip each other in the acquisitions of industry; and hence their habits, instead of being fully formed to patient application, still partake, to a large extent, of the character impressed upon them by the institutions of a state of society which now no longer exists. Were we required to point out the cause, which has had the principal effect in retarding in the case of the labouring classes in the Highlands, the progress of improvement, we should, without hesitation, assign as that cause, their ignorance of the common language of the United Kingdom. By this ignorance they are prevented from bringing their labour to the general market, and cut off from innumerable advantages of an almost equally important character which they might otherwise enjoy.[1]

Despite, like the Irish, being thus ethnologically characterised as 'lazy' Celts in opposition to industrious Saxon 'natives',[2] there is no certain evidence to suggest that the Highlander was greatly hindered by having Gaelic. For some, of course, lack of familiarity with the customary practices of urban labour markets and with particular technical skills did debar them from employment. Sir Walter Scott considered that the wrench Highlanders felt in leaving home to take up jobs in Glasgow's manufactories was 'like tearing a pine from its rock'.[3] The facts of permanent migration and urban employment perhaps were the cause of psychological trauma: this has been hypothesised for Highland emigrants.[4] But, in truth, the feelings of being uprooted by social change and by the move to new city environments were shared by many in urban Scotland, not just Highland migrants.

This chapter examines the jobs undertaken by urban Highlanders from the late eighteenth century, notes the social and cultural support systems that operated within Highland populations when migrants were ill or out of work, and discusses migrant residential patterns. No systematic source is available to determine either occupation or residence in relation to migrant status until the 1851 Census, but by piecing together evidence from various sources, it is possible to know something of the Highlanders' place in the labour market in late eighteenth- and early nineteenth-century urban Scotland. Urban life and work in this period defies easy generalisation. From the second quarter of the 1800s, Scotland's cities changed greatly as a new technology of gaslight, trams and, latterly, sanitary and housing reform and piped water brought changes to the environment, and, in time, improvement in living conditions and control over infectious diseases. The urban economy, for the working classes at least, was characterised by changes in the division of labour, by the displacement of one industry by another and by the substitution of handicraft skills by waged labour and industrialised machinofacture.[5] Migrant Highlanders moved to cities undergoing dynamic change and they actively participated in that change.

PATTERNS OF OCCUPATION

Several commentators, in the past and more recently, have claimed that Highland migrants came from and fitted into the lower orders of society.[6] Some evidence supports this view. Robert Heron commented in 1797 upon Highlanders moving south to work at the harvest, as chairmen, porters and in manufacture, and Thomas Newte, in 1791, certainly considered Edinburgh's Highlanders to be part of the unskilled underclass: 'As the offices of drudgery, and of labour, that require not any skill, are generally performed in London by Irishmen, and Welsh people of both sexes, so all such inferior departments are filled in Edinburgh by the

Highlanders'. In the capital, 'as well as into other cities of note in Scotland', there was a constant influx [of Highlanders] 'to supply the places of porters, barrowmen, chairmen and such like'.[7] Edinburgh's City Guard was almost entirely Highland in the second half of the eighteenth century.[8] Census evidence certainly shows Highlanders in semi- and unskilled occupational categories (see below). But it also records some in skilled and managerial positions. Indeed, there is abundant evidence to show Highlanders in all sorts of jobs within urban society and, thus, to allow correction of the above views.

The records of the Glasgow Highland Society, established in 1727, show many Highlanders with employment in managerial/ professional jobs, and in a range of skilled and semi-skilled manual tasks such as printing, coopering, inn-keeping, and in textiles and in occupations connected with maritime commerce (Table 5.1). This evidence must

Table 5.1
OCCUPATION OF MEMBERS OF GLASGOW
HIGHLAND SOCIETY, 1787–1861*

	Year		
Occupational Group†	1787	1831	1861
Managerial/Professional	22.1	30.1	23.3
Intermediate non-manual	30.8	34.4	25.8
Skilled manual	15.2	9.4	6.6
Semi-skilled manual	7.2	2.2	1.5
Unskilled manual	2.6	1.2	0.1
Textile workers	5.7	4.0	5.1
Mine workers	–	–	–
Agricultural workers	0.1	0.1	–
Scholars/students	0.1	–	–
Not given	16.2	18.6	37.6
[Total number of members]	1,066	1,607	735

* From *Glasgow Highland Society List of Regulations thereto and List of Members* (Glasgow, 1861). Figures expressed as a percentage of the total number of listed GHS members.
† From the 1951 *Census*; List of Occupations and Industries

be treated with caution. Firstly, some members were resident in Highland towns like Stornoway (some lived as far afield as Guiana and the Caribbean). Secondly, because cost of entry precluded those reliant upon wage labour, it is not necessarily fully representative of Glasgow's Highland population. Even so, there is no doubt that many Highlanders were established in the middle ranks of urban society. Of 1,066 listed members between 1727 and 1787, for example, nearly 300 are recorded as 'merchants': a further 463 merchants are given for the period 1787 to 1831, mostly in Glasgow, Port Glasgow, and Greenock. We know that several Highlanders became prominent local industrialists: Robert Macfie in Greenock's sugar refinery, for example, and Archibald Campbell in the glassworks there in 1793.[9] Probably the most notable was George Macintosh, born in 1739 at Newmore in Rosskeen parish, Ross and Cromarty, who, by 1777, had established the Dunchatten 'cudbear' dye works at Dennistoun, then on the north-east outskirts of Glasgow. All the employees were Highlanders and a role call was taken in Gaelic every morning. His son, Charles, continued to support Highland labour: in giving evidence to the Select Committee on the State of the Irish Poor in 1838, he was the only Glasgow employer to indicate a preference for Highland labour. George Macintosh raised 700 men – the Glasgow Highland Volunteers – from amongst his workforce in 1803. He was first president of the Gaelic Club of Gentlemen in Glasgow, and a good friend to other prominent Highlanders in the city and of the ministers of the Gaelic chapels.[10] Macintosh was a close friend to David Dale, who, as shown (page 126), specifically advertised for Highland labour for his New Lanark factories.[11] Both men were involved in the establishment in 1791 of the cotton mill and weaving factory at Spinningdale on the Dornoch Firth in Sutherland, a capital venture which failed by 1804, despite the fact that, in 1803, it had employed 80–100 weavers. One of the reasons why returns were so poor was because, for the mill-owners anyway, '. . . the habits of the highlanders were found very ill-suited for such occupation'.[12]

Strang in 1856 considered that the presence of higher-status Highlanders in Glasgow as merchants and manufacturers dated from the second half of the eighteenth century: '. . . it was not till some years after the last Rebellion in favour of the Stuarts, [1745–46], that the scions of the Gael were found seated in the high places of Glasgow society'. He, too, hinted at Highlanders' supposed innate aversion to the demands of urban-industrial labour:

> To confine a Highland gentleman, a couple of centuries ago, to the drudgery of a shop or a countinghouse, or, what was worse, to that of a workshop or a manufactory, would have been felt a degradation and a punishment never to be submitted to. The chivalrous spirit of the child of "the mountain and the flood," eschewed disdainfully at that period the profitable employment of the shuttle, and everything akin to weaverism and chapmanship.[13]

The presence of men like George Macintosh might prove Strang right in terms of timing. The fact that so many members of the Glasgow Highland Society resident in the urban Lowlands were established as merchants or as manufacturers by the later eighteenth or early nineteenth century would suggest that the facts of economic necessity generally prevailed over any self-image as either a 'chivalrous spirit' or as a people innately incapable of industry.

What is difficult to know for the occupations of urban Highlanders is quite how the discernible facts of geographical mobility were linked with occupation. One study has suggested that many Highlanders who migrated from the small towns and villages of north and west Argyll in the later nineteenth century took up the same trade they had left behind.[14] Certainly, it is reasonable to suggest that for the migration we have seen from Inverness, Campbeltown, Oban, Fort William, Dingwall, Inveraray and other Highland villages, a proportion of those moving retained the same occupation. For them, as for some step-wise movers to Glasgow in the later nineteenth century, Highland-Lowland migration was an urban-urban movement with no associated occupational mobility. And even for some from predominantly rural parishes, like the fishermen moving from Latheron to North Leith between c.1790 and 1851 (see above, page 96), the fact of migration did not mean a change of job. Lobban has shown that the relatively large numbers of Highland-born persons in Greenock in the later eighteenth century and early 1800s connected with the customs services and with coastal commerce likewise indicated a change of residence but not one of occupation.[15] For a select group like the Gaelic-speaking ministers transferred to Lowland charges from Highland parishes, their move was only geographical. Only occasionally are we afforded a glimpse of the detailed occupational circumstances motivating moves to the urban Lowlands: in a letter of 5 January 1773 to his kinsman James Grant, for example, Dr Gregory Grant, younger son of Grant of Burnside in Strathspey, appealed for his support in obtaining the vacant post of physician at the Infirmary in Edinburgh with reference to his own ability in Gaelic: 'His Grace of Argyle, I doubt not, has that feelling [*sic*] attachment to the poor of his people, which makes a great man appear good, so that as many come to this Hospital from his Grace's country & yours, who can not speak English, and that no other Physician here can speak their language, might not my knowledge of it, be some additional advantage to the poor & the hospital?'[16] Such evidence should not be presumed typical. More commonplace as a general experience, both of the patterns of mobility and in terms of occupation, were the circumstances of men like Robert McDougal and his wife, Ann Stewart, admitted into Aberdeen's Poor House in July 1841. McDougal, aged

51, was Glasgow-born, but his 53–year-old wife was from Skye. He had been a weaver in Paisley for 23 years and she had also been employed in textiles: 'but, in consequence of the present scarcity of work, had been obliged to come north seeking employment. Have three of a family in Paisley, all out of work'.[17] The difficulty of knowing the extent to which the social transition of migration was also an occupational one has been identified in other migrant groups, in Britain and in an international context. One study of Welsh emigrants to the eastern United States, for example, has shown, from the evidence of migrants' obituaries, that for those moving overseas from the iron-working districts of south Wales, there was a clear rural-to-urban transition as rural migrants, after first moving to the industrial towns, undertook new jobs before, both because of declining wages in Wales and the new opportunities afforded in Pennsylvania, they moved to better jobs overseas.[18]

For one group of urban Highlanders, it is possible to know something of their experiences before arrival, and, thus, to understand better the relationships between occupational transition and migration. Sloan's study of Highland-born recruits within Glasgow's Registers of Constabulary for 1856 and 1857 shows that most were young single men, that about half of the Highland recruits were from Argyll with relatively large numbers coming from the north and north-west Highlands, and shows, for one contemporary commentator at least, that these recruits had no prior experience of policing: 'Young men from the country districts and the Highlands of Scotland, who have never been in a large City before, ignorant of the localities in Glasgow, and without knowledge of the duties of a constable, or the manner in which these duties should be performed . . . are the principal sources from which the force is recruited'.[19] Assessment of the previous employments recorded for the 114 Highland-born recruits to the Glasgow constabulary in these two years shows that, in fact, 13 of them had formerly been policemen. Seventy-two had been 'labourers' with a further 10 in agricultural occupations and six formerly in the army. Also clear is the high rate of turnover amongst Highland recruits: a little over one-third of Highland recruits left the force within six months, 'dissatisfied with the delay and ordeal through which they have to pass, and the meagre remuneration given to them, before they can possibly better their position on the force'.[20] This evidence can be substantiated by what is known of the previous occupations of those Highland migrants who joined Glasgow's police force between 1826 and 1891. We have already seen increasingly large numbers to have come from the northern Highlands by the third quarter of the nineteenth century (see Figure 4.15). Assessment of the previous occupations held by Glasgow's Highland-born policemen from 1826 shows an increasing number with prior experience of police work, some of whom were joining Glasgow's police force a second time, and some of whom had been employed as policemen in Edinburgh, Haddington, Inverness or in other towns. It also reveals several from the skilled manual occupations as well as a predominance from the categories 'unskilled manual' and 'agricultural worker' (Table 5.2). Mean age at arrival was 24 years.

Table 5.2
PREVIOUS LISTED OCCUPATION OF GLASGOW'S HIGHLAND-BORN
POLICEMEN, 1826–1891*

Occupational Group	1826–185		1852–1871		1872–1891	
	No	% of total	No	% of total	No	% of total
Managerial/Professional	–	–	8	0.88	21	1.85
Intermediate non-manual	6	3.28	22	2.44	41	3.64
Skilled manual	7	3.74	61	6.78	61	5.38
Semi-skilled manual(†)	24	13.33	152	16.89	288	25.44
Unskilled manual	52	28.57	575	63.89	627	55.41
Textile workers	6	3.28	9	1.0	–	–
Mine workers	–	–	3	0.35	1	0.08
Agricultural workers	87	47.80	70	7.77	91	8.03
Scholars/students	–	–	–	–	2	0.17
Not given	–	–	–	–	–	–
[Totals]	182		900		1132	

* Mitchell Library, SR 22/55, Vols 1–14.
(†) Of which category, there were, in each of the three periods respectively, 0, 61 and 95 persons listing their prior occupation as 'policeman'.

Accounts given of some Highland-born policemen confirm the view of one commentator that these were 'raw, ill-instructed and uncultured lads'.[21] Donald McDonald, a Skyeman who joined the police on June 10 1850 aged 21, had a long, if chequered, career. Found on more than one occasion in a public house whilst on duty, he was several times admonished, disciplined and reduced in rank before good work secured promotion through the ranks of constable to sergeant. But found 'much the worse of liquor' on 15 September 1871, he was dismissed the force in October 1871. Others made the police their career: Alexander Bethune, for example, from Snizort, who joined on 5 June 1878 aged 18 as a probationary constable, was an Inspector (2nd Class) by 1891. He resigned in 1923 with an annual salary of £430 *per annum*.[22] There is some correlation between place of birth, migration and previous occupation: all those listed between 1826 and 1851 as coming from the slate-working parish of Kilbrandon and Kilchattan in Argyll, for example, had prior employment as quarrymen. But for the great majority, with listed rural occupations such as farm servant or shepherd, and even for those with prior urban-industrial experiences as boilermaker or iron moulder, becoming a policeman in nineteenth-century Glasgow was a wholly novel experience.

Such evidence serves as an important qualification in respect of Census material which, from 1851, allows more complete understanding of occupations pursued by urban Highlanders (Table 5.3). Large numbers of Highlanders in Dundee and Paisley and in Aberdeen in 1851 were employed in textiles. The relatively high proportions of scholars listed in Aberdeen reflect the presence of Highland students at the University (see Figure 4.21). More generally, this evidence points to the range of occupations engaged in by urban Highlanders. Between about one-quarter and one-third of all Highlanders in the sample towns here had employment in skilled manual categories. With the exception of Paisley, one in every ten employed Highlanders had a job in the managerial/ professional occupations. In Paisley, there was a more clearly-split occupational division amongst the Highland-born between the skilled manual trades, and employment in textiles. Census evidence is only a surrogate measure of occupation in other periods, however, and, for the reasons given above, it should not be taken as indicative of the occupational background of Highlanders prior to urban residence. It is quite possible, of course, given the rurally-based nature of much textile manufacture in Highland Perthshire – the source area for much of the Highland population in Dundee throughout the nineteenth century (see Figures 4.10, 4.11, 4.18, 4.19) – that many of those urban Highlanders employed in textiles in that town in 1851 and 1891 (about one in four persons within the economically-active population) had prior experience of spinning, weaving, and other aspects of the textile trades. But such skills would not necessarily have prepared those Highlanders or others either for mill work or for the shift from coarse linen working to jute production in the later 1850s and 1860s.[23] The same issues hold true for the large numbers of Highlanders employed in textiles in Paisley in 1851. In the Paisley area in 1816, about 600 Highlanders were employed as farm servants and labourers, with a further 800 engaged in the printfields and in the bleachfields. By the early 1840s, the occupation of bleachfield worker in the area was almost entirely dominated by Highland women, whose menfolk worked elsewhere, in the mills and in various trades.[24] Some textile mills and factories in the area, from at least 1836, employed Gaelic-speaking foremen to instruct Highlanders in

Table 5.3

OCCUPATION OF THE HIGHLAND POPULATION IN SELECTED LOWLAND TOWNS IN THE NINETEENTH CENTURY AS A PERCENTAGE OF THE TOTAL EMPLOYED HIGHLAND-BORN POPULATION

Occupational Group	Dundee 1851	Dundee 1891	Perth 1851	Perth 1891	Stirling 1851	Stirling 1891	Aberdeen 1851	Aberdeen 1891	Paisley 1851	Glasgow 1852–1898 (males only)
Managerial/Professional	10.27	7.47	7.55	9.09	22.36	17.05	6.85	14.14	2.38	2.4
Intermediate non-manual	7.87	10.41	10.58	13.96	6.83	14.24	10.63	11.22	5.04	1.5
Skilled manual	23.45	25.59	28.96	31.35	31.05	23.21	26.23	27.22	31.08	24.8
Semi-skilled manual	14.72	7.70	14.88	15.67	11.80	19.39	11.52	12.04	8.98	17.8
Unskilled manual	16.09	16.87	22.09	11.98	18.02	5.18	17.22	15.18	9.34	25.9
Textile workers	24.14	26.16	4.76	6.71	3.73	4.18	15.78	4.55	33.92	4.4
Mine workers	–	–	–	–	1.25	0.32	–	–	–	0.2
Agricultural workers	0.51	–	1.62	1.84	4.96	6.43	2.00	0.70	6.41	0.5
Scholars/students	4.62	5.77	9.53	9.35	–	–	9.77	14.95	2.85	–
Not given	–	–	–	–	–	–	–	–	–	22.5

* Census Enumerators' Books 1851 and 1891; Mitchell Library, D/HEW 10/1/3–10/6/41; D/HEW 14/11–14/35.

the nature of textile work.[25] In these two towns at least, then, the picture we are afforded from the Census in 1851 probably is indicative of the occupations followed by Highlanders there in earlier periods.

In Dundee, the occupational records, where given, of the Highland-born individuals entered in the Howff Burial Register between 1821 and 1854, and of the Highlanders receiving relief through the town's East Poorhouse between 1856 and 1878 show large numbers engaged in textile manufacture (Table 5.4). Such statistics disguise the nature of the work in

Table 5.4

PLACE OF BIRTH AND NUMBERS OF HIGHLAND–BORN INDIVIDUALS
RECEIVING POOR RELIEF IN EDINBURGH, 1844*

| Highland County | (a) Temporary Outdoor | | Indoor Relief | | | (b) |
	Aid	Pensioners	Males	Females	Total	
Argyll	–	16	1	1	2	6
Caithness	1	28	1	12	13	5
Inverness	0	30	3	7	10	7
Ross and Cromarty	3	31	2	4	6	8
Sutherland	1	23	6	5	11	6

* *Poor Law Inquiry Commission*, 1844, PP., Vol. XX, pp. 148–149.
(a) Numbers of paupers receiving relief in the Edinburgh Charity Workhouse; (b) Birthplace of unemployed operatives or labourers aided by the Edinburgh Local Committee

certain sectors within that industry. We can only speculate, for example, about the work routines and cause of death of men like James Mackay, an Inverness-born weaver, who died on 27 May 1830 of 'asthma', aged 37, or of Angus McPherson from Skye, a workman at Claverhouse Bleachfield who died of the imprecise but all-too-common 'mill fever', aged 23, on 5 May 1836.[26] We can more clearly see how particular occupational branches suffered a reduction in wages or, in the case of flax hecklers and the handloom sector, virtual disappearance with the advent of technical change: there were 11 handloom weavers amongst the Highland population in 1851, but none by 1891. One such, 70–year-old James Campbell from Glenelg, spent his last years in and out of Dundee's East Poorhouse as trade cycles, wage slumps and structural under-employ-ment gave way between 1864 and 1876 to dismissal and death.[27]

In general terms, Dundee's textile economy shifted from the hand manufacture of linen products in 1851 to the machinofacture of jute fabrics by the later 1800s. The relative numbers of Highlanders employed in the working of flax and linen in 1851 and in the jute industry in 1891 (figures obscured in the overall Census returns: Table 5.3) would suggest that they held a more prominent position in the latter trade than in the former and that there was a gender division of Highland labour, with women predominating over men in several of the stages of jute manufacture. The main processes of production – preparing, reeling, weaving and finishing – had different rates of wages, and within each process wages differed between men and women and between the distinct occupations involved in each stage such as 'softeners', 'batchers', and 'rovers' in preparing, 'twisters' and 'shifters' in spinning, 'tenters' and 'weavers' in weaving, and 'lappers' and 'lumpers' in finishing. Each stage had overseers, always men, who were paid the highest wages of all. Of the 221 individuals listed in the Dundee enumerators' books in 1851 and 1891 as being directly connected with jute, 18 were overseers (we are not told of which stage), 22 were spinners, 36 weavers, and 13 preparers, with small numbers engaged as lappers, warpers, winders, reelers and a further 106 described only as 'millworker'. Highland children, some but by no means all of whom also attended school, were employed at piecework rates in several menial tasks. John McEwen, a Perth mill-owner, in evidence to the Select Committee on Hand-Loom Weavers' Petitions in 1834, considered that 'the mills are occupied mostly by the children which come from the Highlands', and noted also that Highland children, in being prepared to accept lower wages, kept out the local-born children.[28]

In 1841, one commentator observed:

> There are very few works in Glasgow in which Highlanders are not found: the classes who have received the benefit of education are employed in warehouses; they are employed as clerks, and so on: the other classes, the uneducated, are employed at various public works.[29]

Studies of the occupational patterns of Glasgow's Highland-born between 1851 and 1891 reveal a greater diversity in employment than this claim would suggest. Mackenzie's examination of Highlanders in the Broomielaw, Kingston, and Plantation areas of the city shows, for the first-named district for 1851 and 1891, a few male Highlanders in the managerial/professional group as employees, greater numbers employed in skilled trades, and handfuls in most other occupations, notably in sea- and harbour-related occupations such as portering. Highland women in that district, if listed as employed at all, were commonly domestic servants or lodging-house keepers. In Kingston, by contrast, with a smaller Highland population, a relatively large number of male Highlanders over the same period were employed as policemen. Servants, washerwomen, and lodging-house keepers were the dominant categories for employed Highland women. In the Plantation district, numbers of Highland men found employment in shop work and as clerks: a large proportion of the employed Highland women were domestic servants. In general, Highlanders in these areas were not commonly employed in industrial manufacture.[30] This may well have been, as Mackenzie notes, because some larger industrial employers had a notable prejudice against Highland labour: 'A great majority of the West Highland hands are quite useless; they are deficient in the aptitude to learn, and they do not work so heartily; in general, they are a lazy, idle set; we decidedly prefer the Irish to these Highlanders'.[31] Certainly, her study identifies a preference for employment in the service sector with Highlanders being much more commonly employed in domestic service, in seafaring and in harbour-based occupations such as carters, porters and dock labourers.

In Anderston in 1851, in contrast, male Highlanders were chiefly employed in metal-working, and in the machine- and ship-building industries, with other high proportions in transport and in the construction industry. In contrast to the experience of the Irish and of the total employed male population, and in marked distinction to the Highland-born in either Paisley or Dundee, only a little over 3 per cent were engaged in textile manufacture. It is possible that this occupational pattern would not have held there before about 1831 since the first three decades were marked by a pronounced decline in handloom weaving and a growth in engineering, metal working and ship-building. Most jobs in the new urban industries in Anderston were for skilled men or their apprentices and the development of associated new technologies, especially in ship-building, also prompted new opportunities for established trades such as wright, joiner, and painter. Spinning was a common source of employment for women, followed by domestic service.[32] The evidence that 22 per cent of Highland-born males in Anderston in 1851 were employed as transport workers supports Mackenzie's data for the nearby Broomielaw district. As Sloan notes, 'The ability of the menfolk among the Highlanders in Anderston and the Broomielaw area to find employment as sailors, firemen and stewards in the river, coastal and ocean-going vessels plying their trade to and from Glasgow harbour largely accounts for the unusually high proportion of Highlanders who were transport workers'.[33] Evidence from Glasgow's City Porter Register from March 1834 onwards shows that Highlanders took about one-third of the 282 licences granted to porters in that year, took a declining proportion between 1840 and 1853 and about one-quarter of the 146 badges given as formal entitlement of position to harbour porters from 1834 to 1868.[34] In parts of central Glasgow, by contrast, the employed male Highland population was more evenly spread across the construction industries, metal and machinery, food and clothing manufacture, and, for one in every ten, the police. For employed Highland women in Anderston in 1851, the dominant occupation by far was service (75 per cent of all employed Highland women there), especially for the younger age cohorts. Only 9.1 per cent of the employed Highland-born females worked in the local printworks or as steam-loom weavers: these were jobs dominated by Irish women.[35]

The picture of general occupational specialisation within the Highland-born male population in relation to the industrial characteristics of different towns or parishes – textiles in Paisley, coarse linen and jute in Dundee, the transport trades in the Broomielaw and in Anderston in metal working and engineering – is repeated in Greenock between 1776 and 1891 where large numbers of Highlanders were employed as porters, dock labourers, coopers, in the customs and excise service, and in other ways connected with the sea as well as in textiles. This pattern persisted throughout this period. Highland women there worked in the bleach-fields or as domestic servants.[36] But in Greenock, as elsewhere in the urban Lowlands, not all Highland migrants found employment, and, even when they did, the vagaries of the economy meant many faced periods without work.

UNEMPLOYMENT, HEALTH AND HIGHLAND SOCIAL WELFARE

Evidence to the 1844 Poor Law Commissioners shows the urban authorities coping with an influx of destitute Highlanders in consequence of potato famine and the effects of longer-run agricultural change (see above, pages 70–75). It also records the experiences of already resident urban Highlanders for whom resort to the poor relief system was an unwelcome but vital necessity. In-migrants had to be resident for three years in urban parishes to claim parochial relief. For this reason, knowing that in Edinburgh in 1844, for example, there were about 200 Highland-born persons receiving various forms of poor relief (Table 5.4) is to know nothing of other Highlanders there not formally qualified for support. And even for this total and for similar cases in other towns, it is difficult to know if such people were relatively recent rural arrivals seeking support because they had not yet entered the job market, or longer-term resident migrants seeking temporary relief following unemployment occasioned by an industrial downturn. Of the seven Dundee Highlanders paid poor relief in the presence of the Commissioners on 7 October 1843, for example, all had been resident for longer than ten years, with the longest there, one Alexander Forbes from Inverness, resident in Dundee since 1792. Others were more recently arrived, their life's circumstances reduced to a single paragraph:

Margaret McLean, a single woman, aged twenty-six. Born at Lairg, Sutherlandshire. Came to Dundee with her mother in June 1839, to live with her sister, a labourer's wife. She received relief from Dundee after she had been in it 3 years and 3 months. The cause of her receiving relief was, that she became palsied on one side. She was quite well when she came first to Dundee. Allowance 1s 6d per week.[37]

Where longer-run poor law records survive – for Barony in Glasgow 1852–1868, for Stirling 1868–1891, for some parishes of Perth between 1855 and 1890, and for Dundee's East Poorhouse between 1856 and 1878[38] – it is possible to document the circumstances over time of some pauperised Highland families, and, for others, to chart their appearance in and out of the poorhouse. Alpin McGrigor, for example, a 32–year-old unemployed labourer from Killin, living in Spittal Street in Stirling in May 1868, had nothing but parochial relief to keep himself, his wife and their five children. To judge from his declaration of their circumstances and from the birthplace of the children, the McGrigor family had been destitute in Glasgow in 1860, briefly employed in Thornhill between 1860 and 1863, and employed for only a short while after arrival in Stirling in 1863.[39] Some, like Annie McRae, a 48–year-old knitter from Inverness living in Cowan Street in Stirling in 1891, had been a pauper chargeable to her native parish in 1886. At her death in March 1915, she had been dependent upon parochial relief for 33 of her 72 years.[40]

It was precisely such circumstances that prompted the foundation of institutions of social welfare for urban Highlanders. In testifying to the Select Committee on Emigration in 1841, the Rev. Norman Macleod, commenting on the then 'great distress among the low Highland population in Glasgow', noted how:

> Distress comes upon families sometimes suddenly by accident, by disease, by death before they have acquired a domicile in Glasgow. To meet such cases we have established a Highland Stranger's Friend Society; and I think within the last three years we have distributed from 800l. to 1,000l. for the relief of Highland strangers in Glasgow, by strangers meaning those who have not acquired a domicile[41] [three years' industrious residence].

This body had been founded in 1814 in association with the Duke Street Gaelic Chapel, its object being 'the temporary relief and transmission of poor Highlanders to their respective parishes [i.e., back to the Highlands] before they obtain a legal residence'.[42] Macleod was also much involved with the establishment in 1837 of the Celtic Dispensary in Glasgow, begun 'with the object of providing medical advice and medicine, and in urgent cases medical attendance in their own houses, for poor strangers coming from the Highlands in quest of employment but who have not yet acquired a settlement in Glasgow, and who therefore had no legal claim on the various charitable institutions in the city'.[43] The Highland Society of Glasgow also mobilised support amongst the better-off Highlanders in the city and amongst landlords in the Highlands, and several more locally-based institutions such as the Glasgow Argyllshire Society, begun in 1851, raised funds 'which shall be applied in affording pecuniary relief in such a way as may be considered proper to deserving persons connected with the county by birth, parentage, marriage or residence'.[44] Gaelic chapels were central to the network of Highland charitable institutions (see below, pages 170–171). Macleod comments on how the Highland Stranger's Friend Society got and used its money:

> We make occasional collections through the year, but we have many wealthy Highland merchants in Glasgow, most benevolent persons. There are some who sit in my own church in the afternoon, and who, though they don't understand Gaelic, attend the church where their fathers worshipped in their own language. They very often give me sums for the Gaelic population. I have many who don't wait to be asked, and they put 5l. into my hand at a time. I have only to apply to some of them in cases of exigency. I keep a sort of open account with some individuals, and there are several persons who receive from the fund thus realized; but I confine that to individuals connected with my own church.[45]

For many commentators, being a pauper in the Highlands at least had the advantage of 'free [clean] air and fresh water'. Access to both was not common in the cities. In Glasgow, as elsewhere, poverty and disease were closely associated:

> The Highlanders who come here, and their families, are poor people, or the children of poor people ejected from crofts. They come from a place where they have been paying 10l. or 12l., till they come down to wretched villages; then they are rouped out, and, leaving their native place, are at length landed at the Broomielaw, where they are left without labour and work. The next time we hear of them is, that they are in the infirmary for some infectious complaints; and they are sometimes here for a year or two in the lowest state of misery.[46]

It is not always possible to know in detail exactly what diseases urban Highlanders had, or to know their causes. Even where that can be known, there is, in the absence of detailed comparative data for the rest of the population, no direct way in which to assess the medical history of migrant populations. Macleod certainly considered that 'the proportion of Highlanders who have especially suffered from small-pox and measles is much greater that that of any others of the population in Glasgow'.[47] The evidence to support this view is contradictory. In one sample of 95 smallpox victims in 1843, for example, 70 had come from the Highlands. Lobban's assessment of the 1855 Registers of Death for Glasgow and for Greenock shows a relatively high mortality amongst Glasgow's Highlanders as a result of smallpox with relatively low mortality from consumption and typhus, but typhus to have been the predominant cause of death amongst Greenock's Highland population, with smallpox no higher for Highlanders than it was for Lowlanders.[48] Of the 215 Highland persons admitted to the Celtic Infirmary in 1842, only eight persons were registered as having smallpox, a smaller number than the 12 fever cases, the 12 bronchitis cases and the 22 reported with 'Indigestion'.[49] Diseases in nineteenth-century cities anyway tended to have age-specific characteristics: smallpox and measles, for example, along with scarlet fever, cholera and other zymotic diseases were more common as causes of infant and juvenile mortality than they were amongst older age cohorts where respiratory diseases were more prevalent. The typhus outbreak in Glasgow in 1846–47 was known as 'famine fever' because it was seen to heighten in the city with the arrival of the Irish and Highland poor fleeing the potato famine. But whatever connections there were in the minds of some between migrancy and medical condition were more imagined than real.[50] Where it is possible to know cause of death by age amongst urban Highland populations, as for Dundee between 1821 and 1854 (Table 5.5), the picture we are afforded is, in detail, of smallpox and measles being killers of the young and of lung-related diseases like consumption [tuberculosis] more common amongst working adults and the elderly, and, in general, of great complexity as to cause of death.

Migrant Highlanders suffered what diseases they did, then, because of their working and living conditions, not because they were more prone than others to particular diseases. To some contemporary physicians, the deterioration in health amongst Highland girls was directly attributable to working in the bleachfields and in the textile mills.[51] Many branches of the textile industry in which Highlanders worked involved long hours of outdoor or piece work or periods spent standing soaked by wet cloth. Poor wages meant a restricted diet and, in turn, lowered resistance to illness. Of the 110 Dundee Highlanders who intimated illness or disability as the reason for their application for poor relief through the town's East Poorhouse between 1865 and 1878, for example, 32 noted lung-related diseases, by far the most common justification. One such was Catherine McNaughton, a 66–year-old from Blair Atholl employed as a waste

Table 5.5

PRINCIPAL SPECIFIC CAUSES OF DEATH IN THE HIGHLAND-BORN POPULATION IN DUNDEE, 1821–1854

Principal Specific Cause of Death	Age Cohorts and Numbers of Deaths in Each Cohort																					Total Deaths by Cause
	0–4	5–9	10–14	15–19	20–24	25–29	30–34	35–39	40–44	45–49	50–54	55–59	60–64	65–69	70–74	75–79	80–84	85–89	90–94	95–99	100–	
Accidental[1]	–	–	–	1	2	2	3	3	1	4	–	2	–	–	5	–	–	–	–	1	–	24
Asthma	–	–	–	–	–	1	1	2	1	7	7	10	15	25	5	4	1	–	–	1	–	80
Bowel diseases[2]	1	–	2	1	–	7	2	2	3	2	3	2	4	3	6	4	1	–	–	–	1	44
Cancer	–	1	1	–	–	–	–	–	1	1	3	2	2	2	–	–	–	–	–	–	–	12
Cholera[3]	–	–	1	–	2	2	3	5	5	3	9	7	9	4	4	2	1	1	–	–	–	58
Consumption[4]	1	1	1	4	11	13	12	13	18	13	14	9	14	2	1	1	–	–	–	–	–	128
Dropsy	–	–	1	1	1	–	–	1	1	5	4	4	6	1	1	4	1	1	–	–	–	32
Heart attack	–	–	–	1	–	–	2	2	2	5	2	2	8	6	2	3	–	–	–	–	–	35
Influenza	1	–	–	1	–	–	–	–	2	–	–	2	5	4	1	–	2	–	–	–	–	18
Measles	3	2	1	–	–	–	–	–	–	–	–	–	–	–	–	–	–	–	–	–	–	6
Scarlet fever	2	1	1	1	–	1	–	1	–	–	–	–	–	–	–	–	–	–	–	–	–	7
Smallpox	6	2	2	–	4	1	–	1	–	–	–	–	–	–	–	–	–	–	–	–	–	16
Typhus	–	–	1	2	6	2	5	4	11	3	4	5	3	2	–	2	–	–	–	–	–	40
Venereal disease	–	–	–	–	1	–	1	–	1	–	–	–	–	–	–	–	–	–	–	–	–	3
Whooping cough	4	–	–	–	–	–	–	–	–	–	–	–	–	–	–	–	–	–	–	–	–	4
Total Deaths by Cohort	18	7	10	12	27	29	29	34	46	43	46	45	66	49	25	20	6	2	–	2	1	547

From Dundee City Archives, Register of Burials Howff Churchyard 1821–1854

[1] Including one murder and three suicides

[2] Including 'flux'; dysentery; 'Illiac passion' (inflammation of the ilium); diarrhoea

[3] The first recorded case among the Highland-born population was that of Jean McIntosh from Kirkmichael parish Perthshire, who died aged 78 on 10 September, 1826

[4] This does not include deaths attributable to 'inflammation of lungs'

picker in a jute mill, who first entered the poorhouse on 19 July 1861, only to be dismissed on August 16. Almost a decade later, she was re-admitted and, on February 14 1871, her death due to 'chronic bronchitis and debility' was entered in the Poorhouse Register.[52] For her, as for others, one's experience of urban life, and the causes of one's death there, depended greatly upon where in the city one lived.

QUESTIONS OF RESIDENCE

When J. P. Kay wrote in 1836 of Manchester's 'Little Ireland' and of the 'Irish town' there, he was drawing attention to a phenomenon common-place in many British cities in the nineteenth century. For Kay, some contemporaries and for a number of recent scholars, the facts of ethnic residential differentiation in cities were important not just as a major element of Irish or other migrant distinctiveness, but as part of the making of the modern city itself.[53] Questions such as 'Where did urban Highlanders live in the cities of Lowland Scotland ?' and 'How did the facts of residence contribute to any sense of migrant identity ?' are, however, easier to pose than answer.

There was a Gaelic Lane (in Aberdeen) and a Highland Close (in Greenock), but there does not seem to have been any marked resi-dential segregation and certainly not any identifiable Highland 'ghet-to'. In Dundee, in 1851 and in 1891, many Highlanders employed in the textile industries lived in the Hawkhill and Scouringburn parts of the city. But this pattern was probably more a reflection of their place in the working populations and of their capacity to afford access only to certain sectors of the housing market than it was of a desire to maintain a Highland identity through residential proximity. For some, the job determined residence as for the seven Highland-born servants in the Queen's Hotel on Dundee's Perth Road in 1891. On a smaller scale, the pattern of live-in Highland domestic servant is repeated in many of the larger houses and private residences of the middle and upper-middle classes in Dundee and in Perth as it is in the other Lowland towns. Elsewhere in Dundee, many of those Highlanders employed in shore-portering lived close to their work, and many unmarried women employed in the jute mills were housed in pur-pose-built accommodation near to the bleachfields and mills.[54] Where it is possible to confirm the identification of individual Highlanders across different sources, we can see, for some, a clear separation between residence, workplace and place of meeting with other High-landers. The records of Meadowside Gaelic Church in Dundee and of St Stephen's Gaelic Chapel in Perth, for example, show a number of

Highland-born to have had shops or workshops in the centre of the town and homes in the less central streets. Peter McIntyre, for example, is recorded in the communion roll for 3 April 1850 of the Gaelic Church in Meadowside in Dundee as resident at Perth Road. Cross-reference with the 1850 *Dundee Directory* and with the 1851 Census shows his home address as 17 Thomson Street, Perth Road, and his business as a wine merchant and grocer to have been conducted at 95 Nethergate in the town centre.[55]

Smith has argued of late nineteenth- and early twentieth-century Glasgow that it was 'not a city of ethnic neighbourhoods, either of the Irish or the Highlanders'.[56] Using the distribution of Gaelic speakers rather than place-of-birth statistics as an indication of the Highland-born, Mackenzie has suggested that Glasgow's Gaelic-speaking population in Glasgow in each of the census years of 1881, 1891 and 1901 was not evenly spread but rather concentrated in certain areas. Broadly, the east end of Glasgow was less Gaelic-speaking by the later nineteenth century than the western districts of the city: 'the areas which contained the highest percentage and numbers of Gaelic speakers were those to the west of the city centre: on the north bank of the Clyde from Broomielaw to Partick and on the south bank from Kingston to Govan'.[57] Commentators like the Rev. Norman Macleod certainly thought of the Broomielaw district as one of 'Highland' settlement, but, as Mackenzie notes, numbers of Highland women were scattered throughout the city given their place as domestic servants. The concentration in areas like the Broomielaw owed much to the occupations available there and to the movement into the area of Gaelic chapels from the east of the city (see below). But even within the less Highland east end and central parts of Glasgow, there is some evidence of Highland residential concentration. Many of Glasgow's Highland-born policemen and their families lived in and around George Street in 1851, for example, and in generally better-quality housing stock with less overcrowding within individual tenements than the Glasgow Irish.[58] For some individuals, we can know something not only of the geographical separation between home and workplace, but of their residential mobility within the city. Alexander McLachlan, an agricultural worker from Ardnamurchan, for example, joined Glasgow's police force as a 20–year-old on 3 September 1866. His first lodgings were at 29 Brown Street, but during the course of the next five years before leaving the force in December 1871, he moved six times within the city (Figure 5.1). From poor law returns we can identify in detail the residential mobility of others within Lowland cities: Christine Johnston, for example, a 50–year-old domestic servant born in Inverness who made 16 moves, mainly within central Glasgow, between arriving as a young

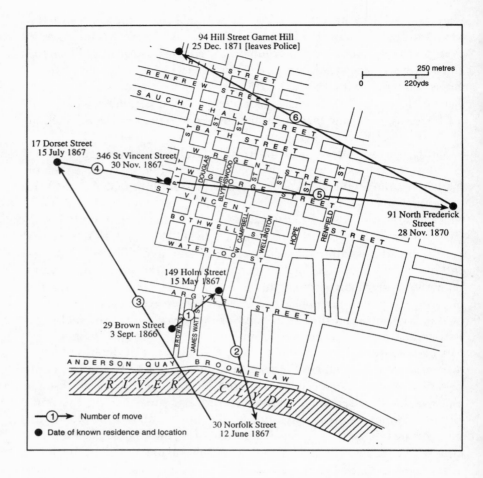

Figure 5.1 *The residential mobility in central Glasgow of Alexander MᶜLachlan, Highland-born policeman, 3 September 1866–25 December 1871*

woman of 17 in 1819 and registering for poor relief in August 1852 (Figure 5.2). A larger sample of 157 Highland paupers in Glasgow's City parish between 1857 and 1897 suggests no simple relationship between length of residence in Glasgow and frequency of residential change for the Highland poor. Very few of the more recently-arrived migrants had moved more than twice. In contrast, nearly half of those Highland migrants who had been resident longer than ten years had moved six or more times, many of the moves being literally 'across the stair' within the same tenement (Table 5.6).

Table 5.6

RESIDENTIAL MOBILITY AND LENGTH OF RESIDENCE IN GLASGOW
OF A SAMPLE OF 157 HIGHLAND-BORN RESIDENTS IN CITY PARISH,
GLASGOW, 1851–1897*

Length of residence in Glasgow	Number of listed residences in Glasgow since arrival					
	1	2	3	4	5	6
Less than 1 year	9	1	1	–	–	1
1–2 years	–	4	–	–	–	–
2–5 years	1	2	9	2	7	7
5–10 years	4	7	6	12	5	16
10 years +	8	9	8	9	6	23
Totals	22	23	24	23	18	47

* Mitchell Library, Glasgow City Parish, General Registers of Poor and Applications for Relief, DHEW (1851–1855) (1855–1862) (1864–1871) (1874–1883) (1884–1889) (1894–1897)

Sub-letting and sharing was a common residential experience in the nineteenth century amongst those for whom rent was the greatest single drain on the wage, and the shortage of appropriate affordable housing aggravated the problem. Many Highlanders lived as lodgers, often with relatives, and, in addition to Highland institutions like the Uist and Barra Association finding accommodation for Highland girls from those parishes who had come to Glasgow to get work as domestic servants, there is evidence in all the towns studied of young men and women, boarders and lodgers, coming from the same parish as the head of household. We should not automatically presume a shared sentiment or Highland identity merely by virtue of this widespread occurrence, even when, as we have seen, there is contemporary testimony pointing to support for Highlanders from one island or parish from fellows already resident (see above, page 80). But it is reasonable to suggest that familial and local links influenced where one lived in the city and with whom, as they also did the decision to migrate at all. Lodging with relatives or fellow parishioners was probably more important upon first arrival, with later contact being maintained through familial visits, the workplace and shared membership of chapels and Highland associations rather than through shared residence. For most Highland-born, the decision on where to live was much more a matter of constraint – the location of the job, the fact that wage levels demanded a walk to work, their place in the wider urban economy – than it was a deliberate and consciously-maintained choice to promote, through residential patterns, a communal sense of Highland identity.

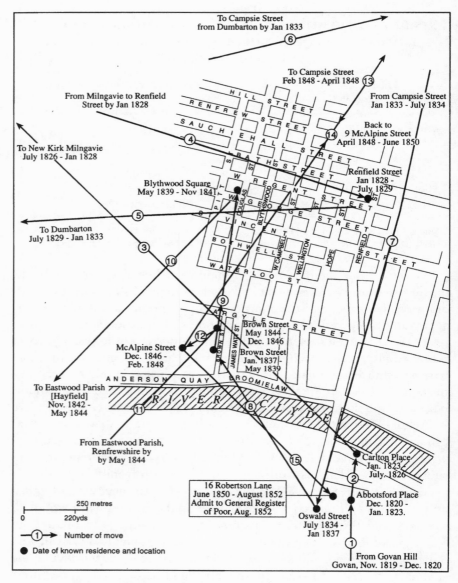

Figure 5.2   *The residential mobility in Glasgow and west Scotland of Christine Johnston, Inverness-born domestic servant, November 1819–August 1852*

CONCLUSION

This chapter has sketched the outlines of Highlanders' occupational and residential place in urban society and illuminated our general understanding with reference to the experiences of a few individuals. Some issues have not been considered. Questions about generational changes in occupational patterns – did the Lowland-born sons and daughters of migrant Highlanders remain within the same occupational ranges as their parents? – have not been addressed. Nor has it been possible to document for all the intricacies of the relationships between migration, employment, occupational mobility and home life in the cities. But it is possible to advance some general claims.

Urban Highlanders did not come from, and fit only into, the lower working classes in Scotland. From the early eighteenth century, Highland-born merchants were established in Lowland towns, especially where maritime commercial links with the Highlands were important. By the later eighteenth and early nineteenth centuries, merchants and Highland-born manufacturers like George and Charles Macintosh were using their success to provide employment for other, less well-off, Highlanders. As the permanently-resident Highland population grew, so Highlanders found employment across the range of urban occupations. Where certain towns or districts within them had particular industries, the Highland migrant population tended to concentrate in certain occupational groupings: cotton textiles in Paisley, coarse linen and jute in Dundee, the customs service in Greenock, and, in Glasgow, in the service and transport sectors in and around the Broomielaw and, in central districts, in the police force. There is no doubt that some local factory owners did have an aversion to Highland labour. But we would be quite wrong to suppose, as some did in 1844, either that Highlanders were innately incapable of industrial labour or, in being capable of it, that they filled only certain sectors as part of an ethnic division of labour.

For some, urban life was a change of residence but not of job. For the majority, the facts of mobility were occupational as well as geographical. As for most people, the nature of employment governed access to the necessaries of life, including the nature and location of one's home. Residential location certainly influenced one's life chances. For one commentator on the health of Glasgow in 1840, no city was worse 'as regards the points of cleanliness and health'. The city exhibited 'a rate of mortality inferring an intensity of misery and suffering unequalled in Britain'. There were, he noted, about 30,000 people making up 'the dense and motley community who inhabit the low districts of Glasgow . . . they consist in a great portion of the Irish and of Highlanders'.[59] For some

Highland paupers on the margins of society, living in a back close off the Broomielaw and receiving only limited charitable help, Symons' view on the moral condition of the poor is exactly right. It was for just such people that Highland charitable and medical institutions were established and that migrant associations had poor funds. Such people lived as they did, and caught the diseases they did, however, because they were amongst the throngs of nineteenth-century urban poor, not because they were Highland-born. Of the Highland population as a whole, then, Symons is quite wrong. Many Highlanders lived as domestic servants, held full-time employment in industry or in commerce, and, if circumstances did turn against them, could turn to kin to help get by. Gaelic chapels in these towns also served to provide relief and as one means by which the different groups within the Highland populations could come together.

NOTES

1. BPP, *Poor Law Inquiry Commission for Scotland*, 1844, XX, p. xlix.
2. On this moral and racial positioning of peoples, the Irish including the Celts in nineteenth-century society, see G. Stocking, *Bones, Bodies, Behaviour: essays on biological anthropology* (Madison, Wis, 1988) and *idem, Victorian Anthropology* (New York and London, 1987) and more generally P. Jackson and J Penrose (eds.), *Constructions of Race, Place and Nation* (London, 1993).
3. Sir Walter Scott, *Rob Roy* (Edinburgh, 1890 edition), p.228.
4. This point has been argued by Eric Richards, for example, of nineteenth-century Highland emigration: E. Richards, 'Varieties of Scottish emigration in the nineteenth century', *Historical Studies* 21, 1985, pp. 470–487.
5. R. J. Morris, 'Urbanisation and Scotland', in W. Hamish Fraser and R. J. Morris (eds.), *People and Society in Scotland Volume II, 1830–1914* (Edinburgh, 1990), pp. 73–102.
6. J. MacInnes, *The Evangelical Movement in the Highlands of Scotland* (Aberdeen 1951), p. 133; D. E. MacDonald, *Scotland's Shifting Population, 1770–1850* (Glasgow, 1937), pp. 73–74; W. Sime, *History of the Church and Parish of St. Cuthbert or West Kirk of Edinburgh* (Edinburgh, 1829), p. 115; G. Eyre-Todd, *History of Glasgow* (Glasgow, 1934), I, p. 316.
7. R. Heron, *Scotland Delineated* (Edinburgh, 1797), pp. 230–231; T. Newte, *Prospects and Observations on a Tour in England and Scotland* (London, 1791), p. 362.
8. *Ibid.*, Newte (1791), p. 362 and *Scots Magazine* (1766), XXVIII, p. 341.
9. R. D. Lobban, 'The migration of Highlanders into Lowland Scotland, c.1750–1890, with particular reference to Greenock' (unpublished Ph.D., University of Edinburgh, 1969), p. 113.
10. J. Strang, *Glasgow and its Clubs* (London, 1856), p. 126; G. Macintosh, *Biographical Memoir of the late Charles Macintosh, F.R.S.* (Glasgow, 1847), Appendix I, pp. 115–155; R. Bain, 'A Highland Industrial Pioneer: George Macintosh', in *The Active Gael (Transactions of the Gaelic Society of Glasgow)*, 1939, pp. 179–190.

11. *Aberdeen Journal*, June 1810; see also page 126 above for Dale's influence upon Highland migration.
12. Macintosh, *Biographical Memoir*, p. 122.
13. Strang, *Glasgow and its Clubs*, pp. 128–129.
14. I. M. L. Robertson, 'Changing form and function of settlement in South-west Argyll, 1841–1961', *Scottish Geographical Magazine* 83 (1971), pp. 29–45.
15. Lobban, 'The migration of Highlanders', p. 117.
16. S.R.O., GD 248/201/2 (5 January 1773).
17. BPP, *Poor Law Inquiry Commission for Scotland*, 1844, XXI, p. 670 9 July 1841.
18. A. K. Knowles, 'Immigrant trajectories through the Rural-Urban Transition in Wales and the United States, 1795–1850', *Annals, Association of American Geographers*, 85(2), 1995, pp.246–266.
19. Glasgow City Council Archives [formerly Strathclyde Regional Archives], D-TC 14/12/1, Report of the Committee on Watching and Lighting as to Police matters, 10 February 1871; [quoted in W. Sloan, 'Aspects of the Assimilation of Highland and Irish Migrants in Glasgow, 1830–1870', (unpublished M.Phil. thesis, University of Strathclyde, 1987), p. 85.
20. Ibid.
21. Sloan, 'Aspects of the Assimilation of Highland and Irish Migrants in Glasgow, 1830–1870', ibid., p. 98
22. Mitchell Library, MSS 22/55, Volume 1, f.14; Volume 10, f.36.
23. Morris, 'Urbanisation in Scotland', p.80.
24. *Address from the Presbytery of Paisley, to friends interested in the Moral and Spiritual Welfare of the Highlanders, residing out of Paisley, and within the bounds of the Presbytery* (Paisley, 1816), pp. 2–3; BPP, *Children's Employment Commission*, 1843, XV, p. 125.
25. *The Imperial Gazetteer of Scotland* (1861); E. Gauldie, 'Scottish Bleachfields, 1718–1862' (unpublished B. Phil. thesis, University of Dundee, 1967), pp. 459–460.
26. Dundee City Archives, *Howff Burial Ground Burial Register Volume 3 1829–1835; Volume 4 1835–1843*.
27. Charles W. J. Withers, *Highland Communities in Dundee and Perth 1787–1891* (Dundee, 1986), p. 46.
28. BPP, *Report from Select Committee on Hand-loom Weavers Petitions*, 1834, X, p.231.
29. BPP, *First Report from the Select Committee on Emigration, Scotland together with the Minutes of Evidence and Appendix*, 1841, VI, pp.119–120.
30. J. Mackenzie, 'The Highland Community in Glasgow in the Nineteenth Century' (unpublished Ph.D. thesis, University of Stirling, 1987), Tables 4.3, 4.7, 4.12.
31. BPP, *Report on the State of the Irish Poor in Great Britain*, 1836, XXIV, p.114.
32. R. J. Morris, 'Urbanization in Scotland', *passim*.
33. Sloan, 'Aspects of the Assimilation of Highland and Irish migrants in Glasgow, 1830–1870', p. 46.
34. Sloan, ibid., pp.48–51.
35. W. Sloan, 'Employment opportunities and migrant group assimilation: the Highlanders and Irish in Glasgow, 1840–1860', in A. G. Cummings and T. M. Devine (eds.), *Industry, Business and Society in Scotland since 1700* (Edinburgh, 1993), pp. 197–217.

36. R. D. Lobban, 'The Migration of Highlanders into Lowland Scotland', Chapter 5 and pp. 479–480.
37. BPP, *Poor Law Inquiry Commission for Scotland*, 1844, xx, Volume III, Appendix, p. 174.
38. Mitchell Library, D/HEW 10/1/3 – 10/6/41; D/HEW 14/1 – 14/35 [Barony parish 1852–1868]; Stirling Burgh Archives, SB 11/1/7 – 10; Sandeman Library, Perth: Tibbermore Parochial Board Register of Poor 1855–1890 and General Registers of Poor for Kinnoull Parish 1845–1890; Dundee City Archives, Register of Inmates of Dundee East Poorhouse, 1856–1878.
39. Stirling Burgh Archives, SB 11/1/7, p. 221 6 May 1868.
40. Stirling Burgh Archives, SB 11/1/7, p. 382.
41. BPP, *First Report from the Select Committee on Emigration*, 1841, VI, p. 117 Q1242.
42. J. Cleland, *Rise and Progress of the City of Glasgow* (Glasgow, 1832), p. 217.
43. *Memorial from the Celtic Dispensary to the Board of Supervision* (Glasgow, 1846).
44. 'The Directory of Highland and Celtic Societies', *The Celtic Magazine* 4 (1879), pp. 35–38.
45. BPP, *Poor Law Inquiry Commission for Scotland* 1844, VI, p.642 Q 11.
46. Ibid.
47. BPP, *First Report from the Select Committee on Emigration*, 1841, VI, p. 118 Q1245.
48. I. Levitt and T. C. Smout, *The State of the Scottish Working-Class in 1843* (Edinburgh, 1979), p. 220; Lobban, 'The Migration of Highlanders into Lowland Scotland', Tables 49 and 50.
49. BPP, *Poor Law Inquiry Commission for Scotland* 1844, VI, p. 642.
50. The literature on urban mortality, age-specific mortality, and public health in the nineteenth century is a large one: see, in general, M. C. Nelson and J. Rogers (eds.), *Urbanisation and the Epidemiologic Transition* (Uppsala, 1989); G. Kearns, 'Zivilis or Hygaeia: urban public health and the epidemiologic transition', in R. Lawton (ed.), *The Rise and Fall of Great Cities* (London, 1989); R. Woods and J. Woodward (eds.), *Urban Disease and Mortality in Nineteenth-Century England* (London, 1984); R. Schofield, D. Reher, and A. Bideau (eds.), *The Decline of Mortality in Europe* (London, 1991): for a summary of the demographic history of nineteenth-century Glasgow, see Charles W. J. Withers, 'The demographic history of the city, 1831–1911', in W. Hamish Fraser and I. Maver (eds.), *Glasgow Volume II: 1830–1912* (Manchester, 1996), pp. 141–162.
51. Gauldie, 'Scottish Bleachfields', p. 504.
52. Dundee City Archives, Register of Inmates of Dundee East Poorhouse 1856–1878, February 14, 1871.
53. BPP, *Report on the State of the Irish Poor* 1836, XXIV, pp.436–468; for an indication of work on residential segregation of the Irish and the extent to which such segregration is bound up with ethnic differentiation in the nineteenth-century city, see, for example, T. Dillon, 'The Irish in Leeds, 1851–1861', *Thoresby Society Miscellany* 16 (1974), pp. 1–28; L. H. Lees, *Exiles of Erin: Irish Migrants in Victorian London* (Manchester, 1979); R. Swift and S. Gilley, *The Irish in the Victorian City* (London, 1985); J. M. Werly, 'The Irish in Manchester, 1832–1849', *Irish Historical Studies* 18 (1973), pp. 345–358.
54. E. Gauldie, *The Dundee Textile Industry 1790–1885* (Edinburgh, 1969), p.449.

55. SRO, CH3/697/9–15; Census Enumerators' Books 1851, *Dundee Directory*, 1850.

56. J. Smith, 'Class, skill and sectarianism in Glasgow and Liverpool, 1880–1914', in R. J. Morris (ed.), *Class, Power and Social Structure in Nineteenth-Century British Cities* (Leicester, 1991), p. 211.

57. Mackenzie, 'The Highland Community in Glasgow in the Nineteenth Century', p. 87.

58. Sloan, 'Aspects of the Assimiliation of Highland and Irish Migrants in Glasgow, 1830–1870', pp. 174, 180–187, 191–196.

59. J. C. Symons in BPP, *Report of the Select Committee on the Health of Towns* 1840, XI, pp. 362–365.

CHAPTER 6

Gaelic Chapels and Highland Societies: Institutions of Migrant Culture?

From the late seventeenth century, the presence of permanently resident Highlanders in the urban Lowlands was reflected in debates over their spiritual supervision in Gaelic and by the foundation of specifically Highland institutions. We have already seen something, for example, of the ways in which migrant institutions of social welfare such as, in Glasgow, the Highland Strangers' Friendly Society and the Celtic Dispensary, acted to support and care for Highland migrants in that city (see above page 146). Such bodies were not the only sort of Highland migrant institutions. This chapter outlines the range and nature of such Highland bodies, considers what might be understood as their 'core' purpose and examines what these institutions, the Gaelic churches especially, reveal about the social relationships *within* the urban Highland populations.

GAELIC CHAPELS AND URBAN HIGHLAND CULTURE

By the end of the eighteenth century, there were 11 Gaelic chapels in Lowland Scottish cities, the first having been erected in Edinburgh in 1769 (Figure 6.1). Occasional Gaelic preaching for the benefit of migrant Highlanders had been a feature, however, albeit an irregular one, in Edinburgh and Glasgow for nearly a century before the formal establishment of Gaelic chapels. In Glasgow, the Rev. Neil Gillies, a Gaelic preacher noted for his 'ministerial skill in that language', was inducted to the Tron Kirk in 1690 and did much to afford spiritual support to Highlanders in Glasgow until his death in 1701.[1] Not until 1717 was any further concerted effort made to provide for the religious needs of Glasgow's Gaelic Highlanders, and the problem was only effectively solved from 1723 with the appointment of the Rev. John MacLaurin, a Gaelic-speaking minister from Luss in Dunbartonshire, to the Ramshorn Kirk in the city's North West parish. From then until his death in 1754, MacLaurin preached monthly in Gaelic and offered limited charitable support to Glasgow's Highlanders.[2] In Edinburgh, Gaelic language preaching was available from 1701 in the city's West Kirk following

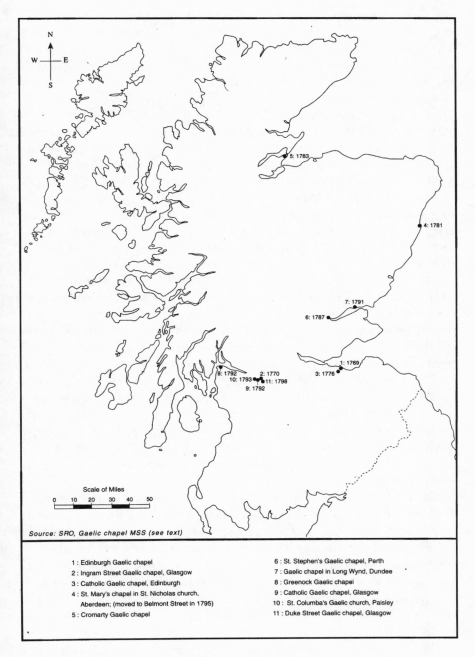

1 : Edinburgh Gaelic chapel
2 : Ingram Street Gaelic chapel, Glasgow
3 : Catholic Gaelic chapel, Edinburgh
4 : St. Mary's chapel in St. Nicholas church,
    Aberdeen; (moved to Belmont Street in 1795)
5 : Cromarty Gaelic chapel

6 : St. Stephen's Gaelic chapel, Perth
7 : Gaelic chapel in Long Wynd, Dundee
8 : Greenock Gaelic chapel
9 : Catholic Gaelic chapel, Glasgow
10 : St. Columba's Gaelic church, Paisley
11 : Duke Street Gaelic chapel, Glasgow

Figure 6.1   *Gaelic chapels in the Lowlands in the late eighteenth century*

the re-location there of the Rev. Neil McVicar from Fort William. The suggestion has been made that McVicar was chosen for his ministerial and not his linguistic abilities, with Gaelic only a factor in his appointment.[3] This is possible, but unlikely given the contemporary concern of the General Assembly of the Church of Scotland and its constituent synods and presbyteries with the religious and civil condition of the Highlands. In 'Overtures for Planting the Highlands' of 1698 and in the 1699 Act anent Planting of the Highlands, the Church had sought to place Gaelic ministers where they were needed most – in Highland parishes – arguing 'that none of them [be] settled in the Low-Country, till the Highland places be first provided'.[4] Later Acts of 1700 and 1701 sought the same end, and, in 1708, the General Assembly forbade all presbyteries to settle 'any minister or probationer having Irish [Gaelic] in any congregation in the Lowlands, unless such persons have been for a year at least in the Highlands supplying vacancies, and no call offered to them'. Even then, such persons were to be translated to the Highland parishes 'as soon as a call comes from any Highland parish needing one having the Irish language'.[5] When the question of McVicar's translation came before the Synod of Argyll, one reason advanced for allowing his departure was the presence of three or four hundred monolingual Gaelic speakers in Edinburgh's West Kirk with no minister to provide for their needs.[6] Given this, and the wider religious context, McVicar's translation probably hinged upon his having Gaelic and the fact that, as a Gaelic speaker, he could 'take inspection of such persons' and of those 'lately come out of the Highlands who do not understand our language' as the presbytery of Edinburgh noted.[7] Other sources speak of McVicar being so anxious to disseminate divine knowledge in the capital 'that every harvest he gathered together the Highland shearers in bands . . . and preached to them in Gaelic'.[8]

The facts of the McVicar case and that of John MacLaurin's move in 1722 from Luss to Glasgow, which, it was noted at the time, ran counter to the 1708 Act,[9] have a broader significance in several respects. The foundation of Gaelic chapels in the Lowlands should not be divorced from matters of wider context, particularly in relation to the Church of Scotland's long-run concern to use religious worship in Gaelic as a means to 'civilise' the Highlands through extending the secular use of English.[10] As was noted in the *Scots Magazine* in 1766:

The design of introducing the English language into the Highlands and Islands of Scotland, hath been long prosecuted by the annual Committees for managing His Majesty's royal bounty, and by the society for propagating Christian Knowledge. This hath been considered as one of the best

means of civilizing these countries, and of promoting in them the knowledge of true religion . . . At the same time they have ordered the masters of
their schools, in all places where Erse only is spoken, to teach their scholars
to read both Erse and English; by which means it is expected, that their
religious instruction, and their knowledge of the English tongue, will be at
once promoted.[11]

For the resident Highlander populations of Edinburgh and Glasgow in
about 1700, having Gaelic preaching may well have been a means to
identify themselves as distinct, a feeling perhaps heightened from the later
eighteenth century by the foundation of specifically Gaelic chapels of
worship. Religious worship in Gaelic was widely welcomed throughout
the Highlands, though not always frequently received, given the shortage
of trained clergy and the scattered population within large parishes,[12] and
it is understandable that migrant Highlanders should be as keen to receive
the word of God in their native language. But secular and Church
authorities saw the matter as one more of spiritual superintendence
for a section of their respective local urban populations otherwise without religious provision than as a matter of maintaining migrant identity
through Gaelic language services: such services were, simply, a means to a
different end however much they were welcomed by urban Highlanders.
And as what follows suggests, English services were introduced into these
Gaelic chapels, in some at a very early stage. Further, the McVicar case
illustrates the more general problem that it is often easier to know about
the ministers and even chart the institutional and denominational history
of the various Gaelic chapels or churches than it is to know who made up
their congregations, where they lived or came from, or how exactly Gaelic
or English was used in church worship.[13] Nevertheless, and from a
varying range of source material, it is possible to consider the origin
and role of Gaelic chapels including the varying use of Gaelic and English
in their services, to reveal something of the social characteristics of their
constituent congregations and to know that they did not serve all urban
Highlanders equally.

The foundation and cultural role of Gaelic chapels
The foundation of Gaelic chapels in the urban Lowlands followed a
general pattern: a group of better-off Highland-born persons in the city,
often with connections to Highland migrant societies and with positions
of influence in Lowland society, sought to promote the interests of their
less influential and more strongly Gaelic-speaking counterparts by establishment of a church in which to receive the word of God in the language
they preferred. Commonly, local persons of influence – merchants,

burgesses – were also involved as initial petitioners. Control of the property and of chapel administration, including an influential say in the appointment of the minister, remained in the hands of this elite group made up of leading members of the urban Highland population and leading locals. There is one exception to this general model: the case of Cromarty in the Black Isle (see Figure 6.1) where the erection of the Gaelic chapel in 1783 was funded by George Ross on behalf of the Highland labourers in his hemp factory there.[14]

In Edinburgh, there is no record of any Gaelic ministry in the twenty years after McVicar's death in 1747. Between about 1765 and his death in 1768, the Gaelic poet Dugald Buchanan had preached to Highlanders in the city and a proposal had even been made to ordain him as minister of a Gaelic congregation in the city.[15] Certainly, an appeal for funds for the support of a Gaelic preacher was circulating during Buchanan's residence in the city and Gaelic services were being held in the College Street Relief Church for the many in the city who had little knowledge of English: '. . . even after residing amongst us for a couple of years, their knowledge of our language, generally speaking, is very imperfect, and they rest satisfied, with so much of it as is necessary to their daily business'.[16] By May 1767, sufficient funds were obtained for building to commence and the Edinburgh Gaelic chapel, in the Castle Wynd, was opened two years later. From the outset, it is clear that Edinburgh's Gaelic chapel was seen by the officers of the Society in Scotland for Propagating Christian Knowledge as a 'charity of the highest importance' in anglicising and civilising, through Gaelic, the Highland population. The *Address to the Public anent Proposals for establishing an Erse Church in Edinburgh*, which had been circulating in the city from July 1766, sought a 'competent fund for providing them in a house for public worship' and it is clear from this *Address* that the question of spiritual supervision rather than maintenance of a Highland community through the use of Gaelic was uppermost in the minds of those proposing the foundation. Subscriptions for the chapel came from two sources: Edinburgh's Highland population as a whole, and prominent individuals within the town, many of whom were of Highland background. For the first group, relatively poor and largely unable to understand English, it is possible to suggest that Gaelic services did provide a bond for them as a group: of the second, it is likely such persons saw in the chapel a means to assist yet anglicise the Highland population and to affirm positions of importance within local society. The largest donation, of £100, came from the Writers to the Signet in Edinburgh, some of whom like Hector MacLean of Torloisk and William Morrison were Highland-born Edinburgh residents: both were also members of the Glasgow Highland Society.[17] Money also came from well-to-do Highlanders further afield: merchants in London and in the West Indies and ship masters in Bristol and in Liverpool.[18] Similar circumstances were apparent elsewhere.

In Aberdeen, large numbers of Highland labourers had been drawn to the city from 1758 when a Mr Adams, a London entrepreneur, had engaged them to work in his granite quarries, and by the last years of the eighteenth century many hundreds of Highlanders lived in or around Aberdeen, together with several dozen Highland-born students in King's and Marischal Colleges. The majority of the labouring Highlanders was described as being 'extremely ignorant of the principles of the Christian religion, and neither understood English nor could express themselves intelligibly in that language'.[19] Gaelic services were held in Aberdeen's East Church from 1785, and by 1790 Aberdeen's Highlanders 'were permitted, by the magistrates, to fit up St Mary's chapel, under the East Church, as a place of public worship, for their accommodation'. Services continued there until 1795, 'when by the assistance of voluntary contributions from benevolent individuals, with collections amongst themselves, they were enabled to build a very neat chapel in Belmont Street, where the ordinances of religion have, ever since, been dispensed to them by their own minister'. The register of subscriptions to the building fund of £850 includes the names of some of Aberdeen's most important citizens, while the largest individual subscription came from a Highland regiment, the Breadalbane Fencibles, then quartered in the town.[20]

In Glasgow, discussions with a view to purchase ground next to Back Cow Lane near Queen Street for a 'Hielan Kirk' began in 1767 through the Gaelic Chapel Society, an off shoot of the Glasgow Highland Society, working in conjunction with the Society in Scotland for Propagating Christian Knowledge.[21] The fifteen Gaelic speakers who headed the petition for Ingram Street Gaelic chapel in Glasgow, opened in February 1770, were all Highlanders with an established position in local society: merchants, manufacturers, bakers, tailors and wrights.[22] Malcolm McGilvra, for example, a prominent woollen and linen merchant in the town, was a chapel manager in 1772, and by 1797 was President of the Managers and a leading figure in the Glasgow Highland Society. George Macintosh, the Ross-shire-born Glasgow manufacturer (see above, page 136), was also involved in the chapel's foundation. Neither was involved, however, in 1797 and 1798 during the petition for a second Church of Scotland Gaelic chapel in Glasgow, in Duke Street, petitioners then claiming to be speaking 'in the name of a numerous body of inhabitants in Glasgow and its suburbs, not near one half of whom can be accommodated in the present Gaelic Chapel'. Duke Street Gaelic Chapel was considered absolutely necessary given what was considered the recent in-movement of large numbers of Highlanders, many prompted by the industrialist David Dale (see above, page 126):

> Every Member of this Reverend Presbytery must be satisfied in their own minds that the Erection of an additional Chapel is absolutely necessary for the accommodation of the very great influx of Highlanders into the City and Suburbs for years past from the encouragement generously given to them by a number of patriotic Gentlemen in this City to prevent their emigration to America, and the Petitioners are happy to say that many of these Gentlemen have very liberally come forward and subscribed towards the intended building for the accommodation of their Servants and numerous families, who have no opportunity at present of hearing the Gospel preached on account of their ignorance of the English language.[23]

Duke Street Gaelic Chapel was to be 'built by the voluntary subscriptions of such persons as wish well to the Undertaking as well as those who wish to be accommodated with seats in it'. The seats were intended only for 'those who speak Gaelic only or chiefly', and it was such people who raised the great part of the £1400 needed to build the chapel. But even with this second chapel in Glasgow, and with the opening of a Gaelic Catholic Chapel in the city in 1792 following the residence in the city of Catholic Highlanders from Inverness-shire who had earlier thought to emigrate under the leadership of Father Alexander MacDonell,[24] not everyone of Highland background in the city could attend Gaelic services. 'Several hundred Highland persons in this City and Suburbs' applied for seats in Duke Street in March 1798. The managers record also the receipt of 'Certificates under the hands of above two hundred highland people, heads of families and others' who had 'applied for accommodation in the Chapel and could not procure seats'.[25] A later entry in the Chapel records suggests the actual numbers without seats may only have been about 170: Ingram Street had room for 1,090 persons and Duke Street for 1,300.[26] But the fact of not all Highlanders being able to get a seat is important for what it suggests about the relative size of the Highland population in Glasgow by about 1800, because it indicates Gaelic services were crucial to the Highlanders' sense of identity and that many could afford to pay for access to such services, and, finally, because it parallels detailed evidence for the middle years of the nineteenth century, considered below, which shows that large numbers of Highlanders, in Glasgow and in other Lowland towns, went without religious supervision altogether, either because they could not or would not pay, from indifference, or from distance from the chapel.

In all the chapels, the original petitioners became the first managers, acting on behalf of the local Highlanders who had subscribed to the building fund and for whose benefit the chapel had been built. The respective committees of management also controlled the property, fixed the level of the seat rents, decided upon the appointment of the minister, the deacon and elders, and, through such men, dictated whether Gaelic only or Gaelic and English were to be used in the services. In the *Regulations constituting the Gaelic Place of Worship in Aberdeen*, for example, regulation VIII ensured that only Gaelic speakers had a say in who ministered to them.[27] Despite such close management and the close connections between at least a section of the Highland communities that it hints at, there were disputes within what we may call this institutionalised Highland élite. In 1797, for example, in Glasgow's Ingram Street Chapel, a row broke out over the appointment of a successor to the Rev. Angus McIntosh. One party, headed by Malcolm McGilvra, favoured the Rev. John MacLaurin, but the congregation, led by the deacons, preferred the Rev. John Mackenzie, then minister of Aberdeen Gaelic Chapel, a preacher opposed by the MacLaurin faction. MacKenzie was the subject of personal attack over his religious and political fitness for the post: 'it was industriously reported that he was a Democrat, and this report was continued to be propagated in the face of unquestionable evidence to the contrary'. The dispute was not a Highland matter alone: as the MacKenzie faction represented to the managers of the Gaelic Chapel, 'it is well known to the Revd. Presbytery that in the said Election the improper manner by which votes were sought and obtained is the common Topic of conversation in the city of Glasgow'.[28] MacLaurin was elected despite claims that 'the congregation had never been fairly consulted',[29] and it is likely that this fractiousness within the city's Highland community was a significant influence upon the foundation in the following year of the Duke Street Chapel.[30] The observation has also been made of this affair that none of the managers of Ingram Street Gaelic Chapel appeared in support of the petition for a second chapel. The Duke Street congregation had one manufacturer and one merchant amongst its kirk session members, but the remaining office bearers were all from the artisan class, and, in that, they reflected the make-up of the congregation, at least some of whom may have been Highlanders employed at George MacIntosh's nearby Dunchatten dye-works.[31] Social differences were apparent, then, within and between urban Highland chapel populations even at their foundation.

Clear differences existed, too, in the use of Gaelic and English. Edinburgh seems to have been the only Gaelic chapel in which, in the beginning at least, Gaelic alone was used in religious worship. In Aberdeen, the introduction by about 1800 of English in one sabbath service seems to have been agreed upon without recorded dissent: 'and as time wore on English became the predominant medium both in the Sunday services and in the various meetings throughout the week'.[32] In Edinburgh, the circumstances surrounding the earliest use of English and Gaelic in the Gaelic Chapel are illuminating for the light they shed upon the social and linguistic divisions both within the Highland community as a whole and within the groups managing the Chapel. Towards the end of 1779, the Rev. Joseph MacGregor (who had first been employed in Edinburgh as a clerk in an upholstery warehouse and who had taken over Gaelic preaching upon Buchanan's death) conducted catechisms in English for the benefit of the Highland children. The topics discussed were then enlarged upon, in Gaelic, for the benefit of adults. This prompted William Dickson, a Chapel manager, a dyer by trade and an Edinburgh Burgess, to ask why English services could not be given regularly. Dickson was in a position of considerable influence: he owned the ground on which the Chapel was built, was owed £100 by the congregation (a sum loaned to help build the chapel), and, importantly, was a committee member of the Society in Scotland for Propagating Christian Knowledge, an institution greatly concerned with the extension of English as a marker of 'civility' and 'improvement' (see above, page 164). By November 1780, Dickson was using his influence to suggest to the minister that he 'have an afternoon's Diet of Divine [service] in the English Language once in Four Weeks'.[33] Discussion of this issue went back and forth between the minister, representing the Gaelic congregation, and Dickson, speaking on behalf of managers and others who, though not openly hostile to Gaelic, clearly saw English services as an expression of cultural progress. For MacGregor, the introduction of English was 'not consistent with the original Design of the Gaelic Chapel'. For Dickson, 'Such a Modest Deviation from the Gaelic Language . . . could be no Great Detriment to any Member of the Congregation'. The matter dragged on into 1781 before it was agreed to refer the matter to the congregation: 'to Ask of those who paid for Seats if they would incline it'. Unfortunately for our purposes, this seems either never to have been done or not to have been recorded since extant sources make no further mention of the matter.[34] But twenty years later, English was regularly used in Edinburgh Gaelic Chapel, the deacons in 1807 pointing to 'the formation of connections with those . . . who do not understand the Gaelic' and the fact that 'the children of a considerable part of the Congregation having been born and brought up here, are for the most part unacquainted with their parents' "native tongue"' as reasons for the introduction of many Highlanders in the capital into Lowland urban society. At the same time, an additional Gaelic service was introduced to mollify those who opposed the use of English services: 'to satisfy such among us as do not understand the English, but who scarcely make up a tenth part of the Congregation'.[35]

It may be, as Dickson hinted in 1780 and as the deacons confirmed in 1807, that Edinburgh's Highland population was not wholly Gaelic-speaking, even although religious worship was much preferred in that language, and that some could understand church services in English. Evidence for Gaelic chapels other than Edinburgh's supports this assertion. In Aberdeen, English and Gaelic services, given at different times on Sundays, had a single end in view:

> The minister conducts the service in the Gaelic tongue in the forenoon, and in the English language in the afternoon of the Sabbath day. This plan has been found to be attended with good effects, as it tends to convey religious instruction to the relatives and children of the members of the congregation who frequent the chapel, but are unacquainted with the English tongue.[36]

To judge from the records of the Gaelic Society Aberdeen, as the managers of the Aberdeen Gaelic Chapel termed themselves, Gaelic and English services were given from the outset.[37] The minister, who had been elected by 'those who understand the Gaelic language, and have possessed seats in the chapel during twelve months previous to the election', considered this use of the two languages for the edification of all', and the local presbytery deemed it 'expedient'.[38]

In Greenock, the assistant in the town's Mid Parish Kirk had given occasional Gaelic services in the Star Hotel in Broad Close since the early 1780s. In 1792, a Gaelic Chapel was opened in the town: the eleven petitioners for its establishment were all prominent in the local population.[39] They spoke on behalf of Greenock's Gaelic population:

> We are just now Erecting a house for divine service . . . for the edification of those who do not understand the English language . . . the worship to be alternately in Gaelic and English as a great many of the Inhabitants of this large and populous Place do not understand the English so as to receive Instructions from Sermons in that language. This building we have undertaken from the sole View of promoting the religious instruction of that Class of the inhabitants.[40]

Gaelic was used because 'many of their fellow citizens do not understand the English language', English because 'the Gaelic Chapell Committee' and the presbytery held that it was a means to promote religious instruction and social improvement.[41] Local opponents of the earlier use of Gaelic were assuaged in their opposition to the chapel upon learning that English would also be used, as a means to social advancement.[42] Duke Street Chapel in Glasgow was, for the same reasons,

English and Gaelic from the outset: 'according to the word of God and the standards of the national Church'. Chapel minutes also hint at the differing linguistic capacity amongst members of the congregation, a fact which demanded both languages: 'the Gospel shall be preached one half of the day in Gaelic and the other half in english in order that both parents and Children and Husbands and Wives may have an opportunity of hearing it in Language which they understand'.[43]

Such evidence suggests that from their foundation or shortly afterwards these chapels, directed in their policies of operation by the presbytery, petitioners and managers, acted to establish Gaelic in one social setting, that of church worship, whilst simultaneously offering a means to promote an understanding of English. As well as highlighting linguistic divisions *within* the Highland populations, this also suggests that, influenced as they were by chapel managers and others within their ranks, urban Gaelic communities were, to some extent, complicit in their own anglicisation. Indeed, this evidence illustrates that, in a particular context admittedly, the terms 'Gaelic speaker' and 'Highland-born' or 'Highlander' should not always be deemed equivalent. For some within these congregations, Gaelic was probably used only in the course of the chapel service even as, over time, such people more commonly attended English language worship as a marker of social status. For others, Gaelic worship was greatly preferred and was the language of daily conversation with other Highlanders as, at the same time, the English language became more and more familiar to them. These questions are explored further below with regard to Glasgow's Gaelic chapels in the 1830s.

The chapels also had a cultural function as a source of poor relief for destitute Highlanders, either permanently resident or, as was the case in Edinburgh in the 1780s, impoverished temporary harvest migrants (see above, page 64). But not all permanently resident Highlanders could receive support. Only Highlanders attached to the congregation and paying seat rents were eligible. As the minutes of the Edinburgh Gaelic Chapel for 20 May 1791 record:

> No person shall be supleyed [*sic*] from the collection of the Chapel but such as were formerly members of the Same that is to say who had Seats and payd for them and that if a Deacon Shall Supley any that are not thus entitled to it must be out of his own pocket and the members who have any benefit from the chaple must onley be when in Seike Bed.[44]

It is unclear if this social distinction underlying the Edinburgh Chapel's charitable principles was always strictly adhered to, was continued long into the nineteenth century or was followed by other bodies, but it is further evidence, nevertheless, of differences within the city's Highland population as, too, it confirms a shared concern amongst Highlanders there. The Chapel Minutes for 17 February 1801, for example, certainly indicate the concern to help the less fortunate amongst Edinburgh's Highlanders, but only if they were chapel-goers:

> A Member reported that one of the Brethren had given a Supply of Money to a poor person not belonging to the Congregation, it was requested of the Deacons to be very cautious in bestowing Charity on any without examining minutely into their circumstances, and also to recognise them to be Members of the chapel in the event of any of the brethren to trespass again in this respect it is unanimously agreed that the person so transgressing shall refund the money so given.[45]

Earlier Minutes of 27 August 1789 record how 'various persons in distress and poor widows of the Congregation were mentioned by the Bretheren [sic] and ordered to be Supplied with a small Matter to each from the Collections', a directive that came at a time when only £19 8s. 11d was available for such purposes: £10 12s 9d went to the poor of the congregation and to Highlanders in the city's Royal Infirmary.[46] Such sums were insignificant in comparison with those paid by some better-off Highlanders on behalf of particular groups within the congregation. In 1786 and 1787, plans were being discussed in Edinburgh to enlarge the chapel from its original seating for 800 persons: it was enlarged to hold 1,100 persons by 1776 and, by 1790, further plans were drawn up to enlarge the building to hold 1,800 persons.[47] Several wealthy individuals promised support for these schemes. Amongst them was Colonel Murray-MacGregor of the East Indies who donated 'Fifty Pounds Sterling towards enlarging the Present House or Erecting another'. He also used his position to support his own clan in Edinburgh:

> In the meantime I agree to allow the Interest of the Money viz. fifty shillings yearly for a suitable Number of Seats for my Clan in the Chapel on condition That the Managers of the Chapel will set apart a front seat – with others behind it – for my family and Clan – on the forepart of which you will be so good as to have the Arms of the Family painted and the Words *MacGregor of MacGregor* in a conspicuous part of the Seats allotted for the Clan in order that they may distinctly know where to sit.

Other Highland chapel-goers were occasionally allowed to use these seats: 'As there may not perhaps be enough of the name in Edin. to occupy the seats I do not mean to exclude others from using them the preference is exclusively to be given to my own people – When there is not enough of them you will be so good as to use your Discretion in granting permission to others to use the Seats'.[48]

These social distinctions within Edinburgh's Highland community in the late eighteenth century were based on wealth and kin, and, in the case of the Chapel's policy toward the Highland poor, on membership of the Gaelic congregation rather than a shared sentiment derived simply from being Highland-born. Religious divisions also under scored the general category 'urban Highlander'. In Glasgow and in Edinburgh, Catholic Highland Chapels were established in the later 1700s (Figure 6.1). For some Catholics, the fact that industrialists in Glasgow like David Dale were now prepared to support them in the form of employment and funds for a chapel was remarkable given recent anti-Catholic sentiment: 'who would have thought that those who a dozen of years ago burnt our houses & Chappels would in so short a time think of building chappells for us themselves'.[49] What is remarkable in the case of Edinburgh's Catholic Highland community is that when their chapel in Blackfriars Wynd was burnt in the city's anti-Catholic riots of 1779, the incumbent priest, Robert Menzies, accused the City Guard not only of being negligent in not stopping the mob but of taking a leading role in the associated looting:[50] Edinburgh's City Guard was then almost entirely made up of Highlanders. As one contemporary noted in 1779, they 'seem to preserve the purity of their native Gaelic tongue so that few of the citizens understand or are understood by them'.[51]

There is no doubt that Gaelic chapels provided a focus of sorts for the urban Highland populations from the later eighteenth century. But we should not see in them a straightforward manifestation of urban Gaelic migrant culture. Their origin through subscription from amongst the mass of Highland-born city residents clearly points to a common purpose in providing religious service in a language most preferred and which alone some could understand. Yet the facts of their foundation and constituent management reveal social differences within and between the respective Gaelic congregations and suggest that for some presbyterial and civil authorities, what mattered was not the Highland nature of the institution but provision of religious worship for a particular section of the local urban population. Such provision was linked with the moral improvement of civil society, and it is for this reason that Gaelic, as the only language many could understand, and then English, was introduced in religious services in each of these chapels. Chapels acted as sources of charitable support, albeit in restricted ways, for urban Highlanders. But as the size of the urban Highland populations increased during the nineteenth century, Gaelic chapel authorities faced not just the problems of non-attendance from local Highlanders, but also how best to manage the chapel at all given the social and linguistic differences within the Highland communities.

172

Distinctions in class, language and patterns of worship: the example of Glasgow's Gaelic Chapels in the 1830s

Glasgow's two Gaelic chapels in Ingram Street and in Duke Street were insufficient to meet the needs of the continuing 'very great influx of Highlanders' into the city during the nineteenth century. In 1811, a petition was advanced to use a vacated church in Buchan Street in Glasgow's Gorbals because 'a considerable proportion of the people in Gorbals are Highlanders who best understand and are most attached to the Gaelic language'. Further, the petitioners noted that many of such people had applied for but not got seats in Ingram Street or Duke Street Chapels.[52] In 1813, the Kirkfield (Gorbals) Gaelic Chapel was opened for the benefit of Gaelic speakers in Glasgow's south side. The Kirkfield Chapel ceased as a Gaelic chapel in 1824 during the petition for another Gaelic Chapel in Glasgow, in Hope Street, chiefly because it had been created as a chapel-of-ease, and not a specifically Gaelic chapel.[53] Hope Street Gaelic Chapel (also known as West Gaelic Chapel) ostensibly had its origin in claims from the intending congregation that their hoped-for chapel would be for Argyllshire Highlanders in the city, a group whose Gaelic dialect was not catered for in the existing churches where the preachers were all northern Highlanders. The petitioners claimed that 'the difference between the dialects of the West and North Highlands is so great that the natives of the one frequently do not understand at all the language spoken in the other'.[54] There is some evidence to support this claim, at least in respect of a perceived difference within Glasgow's Highland population in the 1830s between 'northern' and 'western' Highlanders (see below, page 178). But as MacDonald has shown, the real reason for the foundation of Hope Street lay in disputes within the Duke Street Gaelic congregation over ministerial appointments there, not in differences over dialect. As MacDonald also notes, Glasgow's existing Gaelic congregations were uniformly opposed to a fourth Gaelic chapel: each had unlet sittings and mounting debts and much to lose from spreading the potential chapel-going population too thinly across the city.[55]

The petition for Hope Street claimed that 'at a moderate computation the number of inhabitants in Glasgow and the suburbs who were born in the Highlands is not less than 30,000'.[56] The Glasgow statistician, James Cleland, could not, however, confirm this figure, noting in a letter of December 1823 that he could not give 'the necessary information respecting the numbers of Highlanders in this city and suburbs with any accuracy' and that he had himself tried, 'but was obliged to give up the idea from the difficulty of finding out who could and could not receive instruction in the English language'.[57] In 1835, however, the three Gaelic churches undertook to enumerate all the Gaelic speakers in Glasgow, an enumeration itself part of a survey of the extent of their *quoad sacra* areas of responsibility within the city. This survey, or 'Gaelic Census' as it was known at the time, provides important insight into Glasgow's Gaelic chapels and the city's Highland community. The original returns do not survive: we are told only of volumes, prepared by the three ministers of the Gaelic chapels, that contained:

> The names of all the individuals of the adult [Highland] population in Glasgow, the parishes in the Highlands where they were born, the trade and occupation which they follow in Glasgow, the street and lands in which they reside, the number of their families under and above ten years of age, the churches which they profess to attend, according to their own statements, and also the number of seats which they occupy [in the respective Gaelic chapel].

The result of this enquiry was that:

> There are 22,509 native Highlanders in Glasgow, including all descriptions of persons. Of that number 5,336 are under 10 years of age; 2,529 have seats in churches where the English is preached. 3,102 attend the three Gaelic churches, and 11,522 adult persons have no seat in any church, and these make up the entire number stated. It will be found from these lists, that 1,529 who attend the churches in which English is preached, are of the wealthier portion of the community as may be expected. It will be seen that they are merchants, and people in the respectable walks of society, who have prospered in life and trade, and that the greater proportion of the 11,522 having no seats, will be found to be labourers at public works, employed as operatives and labourers. This is the result of the census we have taken.[58]

The difference in total for the Highland migrant population in Glasgow of 22,509 persons (in 1835–36) and the 14,959 enumerated in 1851 (see Table 4.2 and page 89 above) is easily accounted for and hints at a crucial distinction underlying Highland migrant identity in the city. The former totals enumerated all those 'resident within 3 or 4 miles of the city' *who were able to speak the Gaelic language*. For the purposes of the three ministers managing the Gaelic Census, ability in Gaelic, rather than the fact of Highland birth, qualified one as Highland: 'Many of the persons included in the above 22,509 were born in Glasgow, and most of them could speak English, but all of them were able to speak Gaelic. Many who had been born in the Highlands, spoke it imperfectly, some of them not at all'. Although the enumerators and their assistants confined themselves 'to those who are *bona fide* native Highlanders, of whom many attend

English, as well as Gaelic Churches', they included Glasgow-born Gaelic speakers in the Highland population because 'they have been educated at firesides where the Gaelic only is spoken from morning to nights; and some of them are the best speakers of Gaelic, and the most zealous Highlanders'. English speakers were omitted: the enumerators 'were directed to exclude every person born of a Highland family in the Lowlands, and speaking English. I could specify [testified one Lachlan McLean on 26 March 1836] one or two families, out of which they have taken one and left five'. Superintendents corrected returns when, as McLean said, 'there were [Gaelic-speaking] people left in particular instances that I knew'.[59] Such differences in language (and see also pages 204–226 below) were the basis of social distinctions dependent upon age, personal preference and social class.

In all three chapels both Gaelic and English services were held. In Duke Street: 'The attendance is smallest in the forenoon when Gaelic is spoken, as children who understand it imperfectly attend the afternoon service only, which is in English'. Elsewhere, Gaelic services were not as well attended 'owing to the circumstance that the parents themselves prefer the Gaelic service, and their children do not'. The Rev. McColl, a Gaelic missionary employed in St Columba's parish, was asked if 'children born in Glasgow of Highland parents, and bred up in the knowledge of Gaelic and English, would . . . be inclined, in after life, to go to a Gaelic church'. His answer – 'Yes, because a Gaelic sermon will make a far greater impression on those who understand the Gaelic language' – points in one sense to a deliberate and widespread preference for Gaelic in religious worship. In another sense, however, it is directly contradicted by the evidence of those who observed how Lowland-born children of Gaelic-speaking Highlanders were often only partly fluent in Gaelic, even when that language was used in daily conversation by their parents at home. Further, in each chapel Gaelic was much preferred in religious worship by 'the labouring classes', English by 'the wealthier section of the population'. This point is made again and again in the course of the Gaelic Census. There was what the Rev. Dr. Norman McLeod of the West Gaelic Church considered 'a great desire among . . . the working poor to have service in their native language'. This choice was born partly of a belief in the superior oratorical and symbolic power of Gaelic sermons over English: 'It is a feeling of nature, which, like the mountain torrent, not only moves, but sweeps everything before it'. It was partly, too, the result of relative inability in English amongst Glasgow's Highland working class. Lachlan McLean noted how 'a great proportion of them can do little or no business whatever in the English language'. This meant that he and other bilingual Highlanders in similar positions within the Highland

and chapel-going community had to assist those who spoke Gaelic only or predominantly: 'I have myself got Highlanders into situations, warehouses, and shops, the masters of whom took them chiefly, if not altogether, because they could talk Gaelic, to those who could not talk English to their masters'.[60]

What is crucially important is the fact that Gaelic services for the Highland working class could only be given *at all* in Glasgow's three Gaelic chapels because of the provision of English-language services for the better-off Highland migrant population. The answer to this seeming paradox lies in the seat rents, those charges levied by church managers to permit an individual a certain position in church. Seat rents, in nineteenth-century Glasgow and in all other towns, separated congregations by ability to pay:[61] the evidence of Colonel Murray-MacGregor in Edinburgh's Gaelic Chapel in the 1780s certainly illustrates how wealth separated seats. In Glasgow's Gaelic chapels in the 1830s, seat rents paid by the wealthy Highlanders to attend English-language services were much higher than those paid by labouring Highlanders attending Gaelic services in the same building. In some cases, seat rents for Gaelic services were not paid at all because of the poverty of the Highland population. Many were said to be 'deterred from coming to the public worship by want of proper clothing', and because, in McLeod's words, Highlanders were 'extremely averse to the system of seat-rents . . . they never heard of it till they came to Glasgow'.[62] Such poverty and prior cultural circumstance threatened the very existence of the Gaelic chapels. For McLeod:

> The chief obstacle to the prosperity of the Gaelic churches is the practice of having sermons in the two languages in the same day, which he thinks to be necessary, as those who understand Gaelic only are of the working classes, and unable to maintain a church exclusively for their own use; and that therefore an English service must be performed once a day, to induce the wealthier Highlanders who understand the English to take seats in the church . . . If a church exclusively for Gaelic were set on foot, there would be a lower standard of fashion as to dress, and an attendance of the working classes in their working dresses . . . But without an endowment . . . the latter could not be upheld, as, partly from their extreme aversion to the system of seat-rents, to which they had not been accustomed before coming to Glasgow, no adequate revenue from that source could be expected.[63]

In Duke Street Gaelic Chapel the question of seat rents – a matter of prior experience and of poverty – was likewise crucial:

> This church has of late years been upheld chiefly by the attachment and liberality of a very few individuals . . . We have enough of accommodation for the paying Gaelic population of Glasgow, but there is a subordinate

Gaelic population, either unable to pay, or that, owing to various circum-stances, have been so much out of the habit of attending public worship that they are now too careless about it . . . The Highlanders have not, in their earlier days, been accustomed to pay any seat-rents, and . . . the very idea of paying seat-rents is abhorrent to their nature, and the privileges they formerly enjoyed.[64]

And so also in the West Gaelic Church, poverty and aversion to seat rents meant that whole Highland families could not attend Gaelic services: 'They do not take a sufficient number of sittings for the accommodation of their families, seldom renting more than one for the husband and wife, and several grown up children of ten or twelve years of age'.[65]

The final Report to the Commissioners of Religious Instruction offered a summary of the circumstances of the Gaelic population in these three Gaelic places of worship in Glasgow:

Of the whole Gaelic population above ten years of age being 17,173, it was stated that 1738 held seats in churches connected with the establishment where English is preached; that 3102 attended the three Gaelic established churches; that 791, holding 558 sittings, attended churches not connected with the establishment, leaving 11,522 persons above ten years having no sittings in any place of worship. Among those 11,522 persons having no sittings, were included 116 Catholics. The 2529 persons having sittings in the churches where English is preached, consist of merchants, and people of the wealthier classes. The greater proportion of the 11,522 having no sittings, consisted of operatives and labourers. Dr. McLeod was not prepared to say, but that some of them spoke English, and perhaps in ordinary matters, as good English as Lowlanders, but considered, that as an entire people, they were incapable of deriving benefit except from preach-ing in the Gaelic language.[66]

Given these facts, we should be wary of uncritically assuming the urban Highland population to be a unified migrant 'community'. For one thing, Glasgow's Highland population was not the same as either the Gaelic-speaking or the chapel-going population there. Further, the poverty of the majority of Glasgow's Gaelic population ensured the continued existence of English-language services within Gaelic chapels. Maintaining Gaelic services *and* being financially secure were not possible, and this fact has to be acknowledged in understanding the varied nature of Glasgow's High-land and Gaelic migrants. During the course of the survey of Glasgow's Gaelic population, the Rev. Dr. Norman McLeod was asked 'What effect would it have on the funds of the Gaelic churches, were the Gaelic language banished, and preaching in the English language adopted?'. 'Much depends', he replied, 'on the individual clergymen, and their acceptableness in either the one language or the other, but in general, I hesitate not to say, that while it would have a most ruinous effect as to the spiritual interest of the Highlanders, it would have a most beneficial effect as to the funds of the churches. My colleague Mr. Rose [of Duke Street Gaelic Chapel] will answer that question; he has informed me that it would add L.200 a-year to the funds of his church if that principle were adopted'.[67] Social distinctions of language, wealth and occupation were, for McLeod, also underlain by differences in migrant origin: 'The wealthier part of the population, in general, are from the districts of the Highlands near the low country, where they have had the advantages of schools, with the exception of Ross-shire, at an earlier period than other districts of the Highlands. The poorer class, and by far the greater proportion of the Highland population, are from the islands, and the western coast of Argyleshire, and Inverness-shire'.[68] Although this perception bears only the most general relationship to what we know of migration patterns to Glasgow by 1851 (see above, pages 89–93), it lends some credence to the claims of petitioners in Hope Street in the 1820s.

It is an inescapable conclusion, however, that whatever notions of cultural identity were fostered by these three chapels, monetary inequalities served to split and separate the city's Gaelic congregations. Certainly, the shared fact of being Highland-born or speaking Gaelic in Glasgow in the mid-1830s could still prompt support from one's fellows, especially for a lucky few amongst the very poorest of the city's Highlanders. The Rev. Dr. McLeod allowed such poor access to his Gaelic services without charging them seat rent: 'In my own congregation I have a correct list of those who are poor, *whom we accommodate with seats without asking them to pay rent* [author's emphasis] . . . their number is upwards of ninety'.[69] But more commonly, being brought together on the Sabbath for worship in a language over 11,000 labouring Highlanders preferred depended upon having the money to pay the seat rent and buy appropriate clothing: even then, the fact of attendance was, we might suppose, no simple means to a cultural identity with wealthier Highlanders from other parts of the Highlands who sat in better seats, lived elsewhere in the city and understood English-language services. What compounded such divisions within Glasgow's urban Highland population was the fact that, from the middle years of the nineteenth century especially, and not just in Glasgow, many never attended Gaelic chapels or services at all.

The urban Gaelic ministry and the problem of 'Highland home heathenism'
Throughout the course of the 1835–36 survey of Glasgow's Gaelic chapels, witnesses testified to the large numbers of Highlanders who

never attended services and, indeed, were almost 'invisible' to the eyes of the outside world: as one noted, 'The other poor classes, unless we look after them from charity and kindness, may live and die here without any body asking a question'.[70] In Glasgow as elsewhere, the fact that so many migrant Highlanders went without religious supervision was indicative of what, in 1860, the Rev. Duncan MacGregor of Hope Street Gaelic Church termed 'a mass of Highland home heathenism'.[71] The non-attendance at religious services of large numbers of the urban poor is, in this context, further evidence that Gaelic chapels did not provide a central focus for all migrant Highlanders in Lowland cities and illustrative, too, of the problems faced by the incumbent Gaelic clergy in coping with what was seen by many as the spiritual destitution of the urban Highlander.

The overall provision of Gaelic church accommodation in Glasgow was little affected by the 1843 Disruption although all bar the St Columba's congregation under the Rev. Dr. Norman McLeod moved to the Free Church.[72] In 1844 the Free Church of Scotland Assembly appointed a Gaelic Committee to assist the development of weak congregations, and, from 1849, as the Highland Committee, this body was responsible for promoting religious attendance amongst migrant Highlanders in the Lowlands. In Glasgow, its work was paralleled by the Presbytery of Glasgow Committee on Highland Evangelization, begun in 1855, and sometimes termed the Glasgow Home Highland Mission, whose purpose was 'to evangelise the masses of Highlanders in the public means of grace'.[73] In Glasgow and in other towns, the work of such bodies was urban mission outreach. In Glasgow, for example, although the city's Highland population was said by Norman McLeod in 1836 to be 'dispersed', he knew the districts in which Highlanders congregated: 'The Bromielaw [*sic*] and a few of the streets that branch off from the Bromielaw . . . Towards Tennant's works, and the public works at Bridgeton, they are found assembled in great numbers'.[74] Patterns of relative residential concentration (and see also above, pages 151–154) remained constant enough by 1856 for the Free Church to divide the city into three mission areas: Cowcaddens to the north, Broomielaw and Anderston in the west, and the south side. By mid-1857, Gaelic urban missionaries had visited 3,770 Highland families in total and were alarmed to discover that 3,200 of them were 'not in any way connected with any church'.[75] In some respects, of course, such visitation did put the Church authorities in touch with ordinary Highlanders in their homes, but it was unable to do anything much about the scale of the problem. As MacGregor noted in 1860: 'It [the Free Church Gaelic Home Mission] has benefited isolated individuals . . . but it has made no impression on the mass with which we have to deal'.[76] He concentrated his missionary efforts in the north of Glasgow, given what he saw as the greatest potential for a new congregation, and by October 1861 about 500 people were recorded as attending Gaelic worship in a public hall in Cowcaddens with a further 120 families indicating their desire for sittings in any new church should one be established. All worshippers were of 'the lapsed classes'.[77] This, the most successful of the city's Gaelic missions, became MacDonald Memorial Church, the name given by MacGregor in honour of the Rev. John MacDonald of Ferintosh. Yet even here, in a congregation drawn from a section of the less well-off Highlanders, the language used in services suggests that the congregation may not have been as strongly Gaelic as was claimed. As early as 1865, the most popular service on the Sabbath, the afternoon service, was made the English-language service and from 1868, the Presbytery of Glasgow sought to suppress MacDonald Memorial as a Gaelic charge since many of the congregation, although Highland-born or of Highland parents, appeared totally unacquainted with Gaelic. Its status as a Gaelic church was not formally discontinued until 1902.[78]

The more general picture for Gaelic missions throughout urban Scotland was likewise one of failure: a failure to reach many Highlanders with the word of God either in church or at home, but, in many cases, a failure even to know who such persons were or where they lived. In Dundee's Gaelic church, a list of communicants drawn up on 23 November 1859 enumerated 308 communicants on the roll, declared as 'the correct list of the Communicants now belonging to the congregation'.[79] But in the church's minute book for the same date, concern was expressed about the presence of Highlanders in Dundee 'resident in town and suburbs, who have fallen into a neglect of the means of all' and were not receiving any spiritual ministration. A mission committee established to visit and enumerate these people found at least 40 Highland families scattered throughout the town who knew and spoke Gaelic but, principally for reasons of poverty, never attended the Gaelic Chapel.[80] In Perth, where the records of St Stephen's Gaelic Chapel between 1856 and 1865 allow us to know the differences between the number of people listed in the congregation and the actual number of seats taken at any service, it is likely that only about 10 to 20 per cent of the town's Highland population attended the Gaelic Chapel in this period and did so at a time when Gaelic was anyway less and less frequently used as a language of worship.[81] In Edinburgh, the Gaelic Chapel managers had divided up the city into five 'missionary' districts from January 1836, as part of discussions concerning their *quoad sacra* delimitation. All the elders were charged 'to pay particular attention to visiting all the Highland families in their districts especially the Sick'.[82] In 1855, the visitors enlisted to work in each of the districts were exhorted not only 'to keep the present Congregation together, but also to exert themselves to the utmost to gain new members and increase the numbers as well as to impress upon every one whom they have influence to do the same'.[83] Kirk session minutes for the period 1856–1863 certainly indicate the admission of new communicants, but, to judge from their address and from what little we know of their occupation, many of those admitted to the Gaelic chapel seem to have been amongst Edinburgh's better-off rather than the sought-after urban Highland working class in the city.[84] MacGregor still thought the problem extensive in 1860: 'two-thirds of the young men coming from the Highlands to Edinburgh . . . join no church; if they go to the Gaelic Church, they do not settle – they wander from one church to another, till at last they go to no church – they fall into bad company – they sink into an early grave'.[85] In Greenock likewise, commentators spoke in 1855 of 'the neglected spiritual condition . . . of the major portion of the Highlanders in Greenock', and in 1871 the minister and kirk session of the town's Gaelic Church spoke of how they had been 'long impressed with the difficulty or impossibility of maintaining in the minds of young Highlanders, both male and female, coming to Greenock, for employment, the habits of their youth in attending religious worship, and it has been very often found that persons who at home were regular church-goers have here fallen into the practice of being only occasional worshippers where they have not abandoned the practice of their youth altogether'.[86]

Even allowing for the poverty of statistics on the actual extent of 'Highland home heathenism' and the inflation of the problem by Gaelic ministers and others, it is clear by the middle years of the nineteenth century that Gaelic churches and chapels did not have full congregations, that large numbers of urban Highlanders went without regular religious worship in any form, and that urban Gaelic missions were largely a failure. Why should this be so? Church historians and others have generally explained low levels of church attendance amongst Scotland's urban populations as a combination of a lack of accessible church accommodation, an inability or unwillingness to pay seat rents, lack of suitable clothing, the fact of free sittings which, whilst in principle welcome, carried a social stigma, and inadequate pastoral visitations.[87] All these are important in regard to the urban Highlander, with, to judge from the evidence given to those enumerating Glasgow's Highlanders in 1835–36, the aversion to seat rents and the lack of proper dress the most commonly cited reasons. The 'most frequent excuse' given to Free Church Gaelic missionaries during their visitations to about 1,000 non-church-going mostly Gaelic-speaking families in Glasgow in 1861 was that the lack of suitable clothing prevented them attending church: only when it was made clear to the mass of non-attending Highlanders that working clothes were acceptable was missionary work at all successful.[88] In Glasgow, the Free Church urban congregations in particular faced a shortage of Gaelic clergy in the 1850s and all Gaelic churches had a shortage of suitable persons from within their own kirk sessions to act as city missionaries. Gaelic churches were never wealthy establishments: the fact that many operated with debts restricted their capacity to recruit and pay urban missionaries. An additional problem peculiar to the Gaelic congregations was the fact that numbers of Highlanders moved in and out of cities and within cities on a regular basis, dictated by the rhythms of local labour markets and the demands of harvest and fishing seasons at home. Such mobility meant that many potential congregationalists were not inclined to join a Gaelic charge: certainly, ministers both of the Church of Scotland and of the Free Church in Glasgow noted that migrants who were going to join a congregation did so soon after arrival and those who settled for any length of time without so joining were very unlikely ever to join. Even the relocation of the churches seems not to have made a difference: the Gorbals Gaelic congregation moved to Oswald Street in Broomielaw in 1847, for example, moving again in 1893 to Kingston, south of the Clyde, to become Tradeston Gaelic Free Church, and several missions moved within those parts of the city recognised as having large numbers of Highlanders.[89] The evidence would suggest, too, that it was the lower working-class Highlanders who were most reluctant or unable to join a Gaelic congregation although we should recognise differences within this general picture. Female Highland domestic servants, for example, were often expected to attend church worship, most favouring the Gaelic services: 'There is no class of Highlanders in Glasgow who attend church, and take more seats in the church in proportion than the servant girls of the Highland population'.[90] Other types of employment – distillery work, for example, harbour and porterage and police work – often kept men from Sabbath worship. Many Highlanders simply stayed at home: as MacGregor noted, 'many of them spend the Sabbath sitting in their houses, or visiting their friends, or wandering the streets, without the least idea that they are sinning against the Lord on the Sabbath'.[91] In 1904, at the opening of new premises for the St. Columba's congregation, a speaker commented upon 'the lapsing from church attendance on the part of the Highlanders in Glasgow, saying that there were as many Highlanders to be found under the Bridge in Argyll Street [a popular Highlanders' meeting place under the railway bridge, known colloquially as 'the Hielandman's Umbrella'] on Sundays as would provide for our five congregations'.[92]

These questions of infrequent religious observance, spiritual destitution and the 'statistical invisibility' of the urban poor were, of course, not unique to migrant Highlanders. What we can discern about the extent and cause of 'Highland home heathenism' in Glasgow and other towns is owing to men like the Rev. Dr. Norman McLeod and the Rev. Duncan MacGregor who were 'social explorers' for the urban Highland populations in ways men like Charles Booth, Andrew Mearns and others were in enumerating, describing and improving the lot of the nineteenth-century urban poor elsewhere.[93] The issue was one of poverty, spiritual and worldly, not simply a question of being an urban Highlander. The picture we are afforded of that section of the population, however, perhaps particularly of Glasgow, is of a social polarisation within the urban Highland population. On the one hand was a well-off relatively less Gaelic-speaking section of the population who could afford to and did attend church regularly. On the other was the mass of Highland-born, many of whom spoke Gaelic mainly and who certainly preferred Gaelic religious services but whose children less commonly used Gaelic, who either attended church infrequently or not at all. English services within Gaelic chapels were vital to the financial viability and future of these chapels. Chapels provided a focus for philanthropic work amongst some of the urban Highland-born. Some, like Greenock in the the 1850s, organised Gaelic teaching for Highland children as a means to promote a literacy that was then extended through English.[94] More widely, Gaelic continued to be used in at least one service in the Gaelic chapels and mission stations for much of the nineteenth century: the Free Church in particular was concerned enough about the spiritual salvation of Highland migrants to organise Gaelic missions even for temporary migrants working at the harvest or at public works (see Figure 6.2), and did so into the early 1900s even in places as far south as Great Yarmouth and Lowestoft for Gaelic speakers working at the fishing.[95] But more generally, Gaelic chapels promoted that language in one context to people more and more familiar with English in other ways, and to people whose shared sense of being Highland, derived from birthplace or language, was at the same time weakened by the facts of employment, residence in the city, and because they did not go to church.

HIGHLAND SOCIETIES AND URBAN GAELIC CULTURE

In reviewing the changing nature of the Highland Society of Scotland in its shift from cultural concerns to matters of agricultural economy, Black posed the question: 'What, then, is particularly Highland about the Highland Society?'[96] The question might more generally be asked of the many Highland societies and clubs of the eighteenth and nineteenth

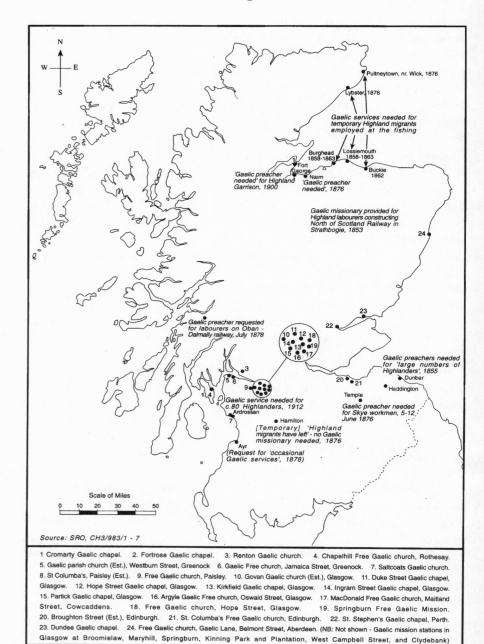

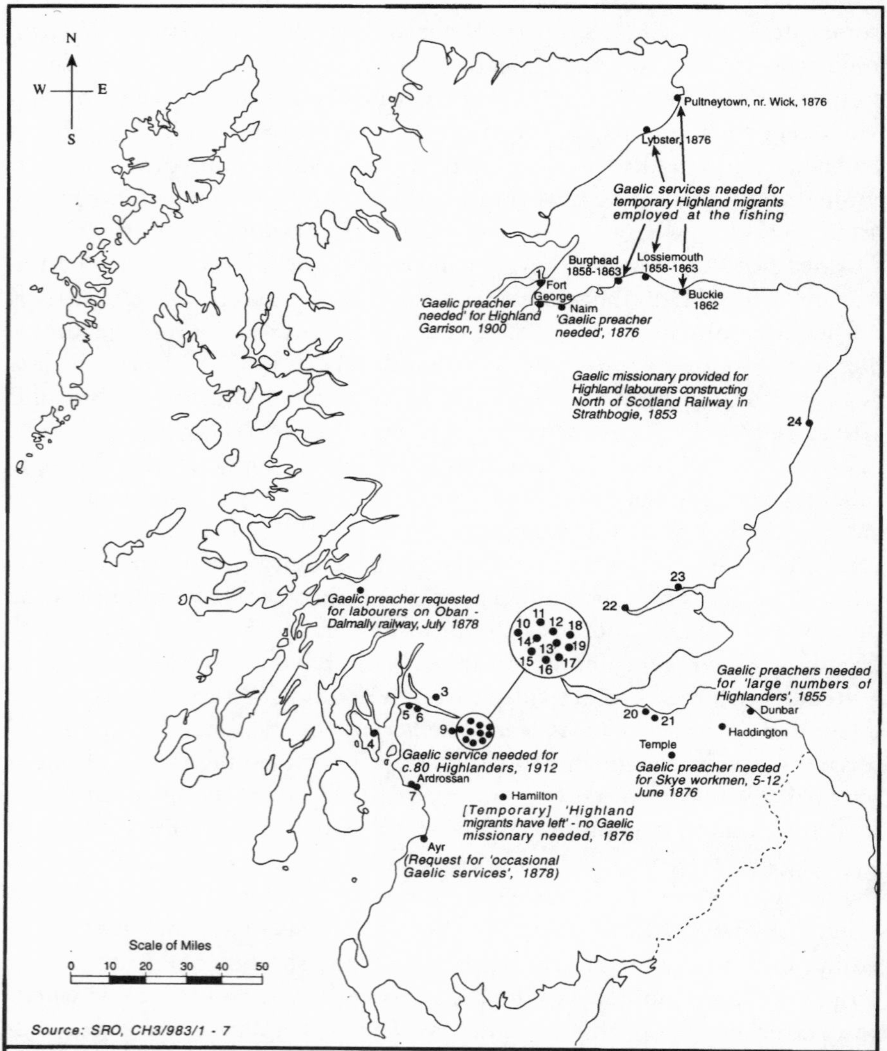
N
W
E
S
Pultneytown, nr. Wick, 1876
Lybster, 1876
Gaelic services needed for temporary Highland migrants employed at the fishing
Burghead 1858-1863
Lossiemouth 1858-1863
1
2
Fort George
Buckie 1862
'Gaelic preacher needed' for Highland Garrison, 1900
Nairn
'Gaelic preacher needed', 1876
Gaelic missionary provided for Highland labourers constructing North of Scotland Railway in Strathbogie, 1853
24
23
22
Gaelic preacher requested for labourers on Oban - Dalmally railway, July 1878
10
11
12
18
14
13
19
15
16
17
3
5
6
9
4
Gaelic service needed for c.80 Highlanders, 1912
Ardrossan
7
Hamilton
[Temporary] 'Highland migrants have left' - no Gaelic missionary needed, 1876
Ayr
(Request for 'occasional Gaelic services', 1878)
Gaelic preachers needed for 'large numbers of Highlanders', 1855
Dunbar
20
21
Haddington
Temple
Gaelic preacher needed for Skye workmen, 5-12 June 1876
Scale of Miles
0 10 20 30 40 50
Source: SRO, CH3/983/1 - 7

1 Cromarty Gaelic chapel. 2. Fortrose Gaelic chapel. 3. Renton Gaelic church. 4. Chapelhill Free Gaelic church, Rothesay. 5. Gaelic parish church (Est.), Westburn Street, Greenock 6. Gaelic Free church, Jamaica Street, Greenock. 7. Saltcoats Gaelic church. 8. St Columba's, Paisley (Est.). 9. Free Gaelic church, Paisley. 10. Govan Gaelic church (Est.), Glasgow. 11. Duke Street Gaelic chapel, Glasgow. 12. Hope Street Gaelic chapel, Glasgow. 13. Kirkfield Gaelic chapel, Glasgow. 14. Ingram Street Gaelic chapel, Glasgow. 15. Partick Gaelic chapel, Glasgow. 16. Argyle Gaelic Free church, Oswald Street, Glasgow. 17. MacDonald Free Gaelic church, Maitland Street, Cowcaddens. 18. Free Gaelic church, Hope Street, Glasgow. 19. Springburn Free Gaelic Mission. 20. Broughton Street (Est.), Edinburgh. 21. St. Columba's Free Gaelic church, Edinburgh. 22. St. Stephen's Gaelic chapel, Perth. 23. Dundee Gaelic chapel. 24. Free Gaelic church, Gaelic Lane, Belmont Street, Aberdeen. (NB: Not shown - Gaelic mission stations in Glasgow at Broomielaw, Maryhill, Springburn, Kinning Park and Plantation, West Campbell Street, and Clydebank)

Figure 6.2 *Gaelic chapels in the Lowlands in the late nineteenth century and the recorded location of short-term Free Church Gaelic missionaries in the Lowlands, c.1853–1912*

centuries, especially of urban Highland 'émigré organisations'. Given the evident social and linguistic distinctions within the urban Highland populations, knowing something of how such organisations worked is important in understanding the life of the migrant Highlander. In Glasgow, with the largest concentration of migrant Highlanders, there were numerous Highland societies in this period, many with specific local or regional interests in terms of migrant origin (see Table 6.1 and page 93 above), yet little is known of most of them or of similar bodies in other towns. Several failed to survive long. The two Highland temperance societies, the Fingal Lodge of Good Templars and the Ossian Lodge of Good Templars, the Gaelic Lodge of Free Masons, *Comunn Tir nam Beann*, the Caledonian Catholic Association, the St Rollox and Springburn Highland Association, the Skye Vigilance Committee, the Ardnamurchan, Morven and Sunart Society, the Coll Association, the Northern Counties Association, the Appin Association and the Lochgilphead and Lochfyne Association were not listed in the 1919–1920 *Glasgow Highland and Clan Association Directory*, for example, and must be presumed to have formally ceased by then.[97] Many were involved in the support of migrant Highlanders from certain parts of the Highlands (see above, page 80). It is possible with regard to some urban Highland societies, however, to know *how* they offered charitable and educational support, that there were social and cultural differences within and between them, and that, by the mid-nineteenth century, there were differences between Highland societies that were so only in name, émigré organisations with a particular interest to serve and those bodies closely involved with the politics of the Highland land question.

Charity, education and social change: the Glasgow Highland Society, 1727 – c.1850

Apart from the monies dispersed by the urban Gaelic ministry in the late seventeenth and early eighteenth centuries, the first evidence of what we might term institutionalised Highland benevolence was the Buchanan Society, begun in Glasgow in 1725, with the purpose of putting boys of that clan to trades.[98] The principal Highland society in the town, certainly in the eighteenth century, was the Glasgow Highland Society, established on 12 January 1727: 'At a friendly meeting of several inhabitants of the city . . . some were born in the Highlands, and others descended from Highlanders'.[99] The basis of their foundation was a shared view amongst such persons that 'there were a great many of that denomination in that place, and that numbers of their children, though found to be of good genius, were yet lost for want of

Table 6.1

PRINCIPAL HIGHLAND AND GAELIC SOCIETIES IN GLASGOW, 1725–c.1919*

Name of Highland/Gaelic Society	Date of Foundation (where known)
Ardnamurchan, Morven and Sunart Association	?
Auxiliary Society of Glasgow for the Support of Gaelic Schools	1812
Buchanan Society	1725
Caledonian Catholic Association	?
Coll Association (*An Comunn Collach*)	*c.*1831
Comunn Gaidhlig Eaglais Chaluim Chill	?
Comunn Gaidhealach Ghlaschu	*c.*1872
Comunn Tir Nam Beann	*c.*1871
Federation of Celtic Societies	1878
Fingal Lodge of Good Templars (*Fardach Finn*)	?
Gaelic Lodge of Free Masons (609)	?
Gaelic Club of Gentlemen	1780
Gaelic Chapel Theological Society	1785
Gaelic Chapel Society of Glasgow (Managers of Ingram Street Gaelic Chapel)	1778
Gaelic Society of Glasgow (*Comunn Gaidhlig Ghlaschu*)	1887
Gairloch and Lochbroom Society	?
Glasgow Appin Society	?
Glasgow Argyllshire Society	1851
Glasgow Caithness Benevolent Association	?
Glasgow Celtic Society	1857
Glasgow Cowal Society	?
Glasgow Highland Association	?
Glasgow Highland Society	1727
Glasgow Inverness-shire Society	?
Glasgow Islay Association (*An Comunn Ileach*)	1862
Glasgow Lewis and Harris Association	1887
Glasgow Lochaber Society	?
Glasgow Perthshire Charitable Society	1834
Glasgow Northern Highland Benevolent Society	1836
Glasgow Skye Association	1865
Glasgow Sutherland Association	1857
Glasgow Ross-shire Association	?
Glasgow University Ossianic Society	1828
Highland Branch of the Glasgow Total Abstinence Society	1841
Highland Strangers' Friendly Society	1814
Highland Welcome Club	1892
Jura Association	*c.*1895
Kintyre Club	1825
Lewis Association	1876
Lochgilphead and Lochfyne Association	*c.*1862
Mid-Argyll Association (*An Comunn Dail-Riadach*)	?
Mull and Iona Association (*Comunn Mhuile agus Ithe*)	1866
North Uist and Barra Association	?
Northern Counties Association	*c.*1863
Ossian Lodge of Good Templars	?
Oban and Lorn Association	*c.*1894
Skye Vigilance Committee	1881
St Rollox and Springburn Highland Association	1885
Tiree Association (*An Comunn Tirisdeach*)	1865
Uist and Barra Association	1890

* Not including clan societies

From J. Strang, *Glasgow and its Clubs* (Glasgow, 1856); *Glasgow Highland and Clan Association Directory 1919–1920* (Glasgow, 1920); *The Highlander* 30 November 1878, *Oban Times*.

education'. A fund was established to educate Highland boys and put them to trades:

> And that the sons of such, who are entered and received members of the Society, being Highlanders, or descended from Highlanders, be in the first place preferred upon application, provided the father be a member four years before such application; and failing of such, those born in the Highlands, or descended from, and branches of Highlanders, whether in this city or country, without distinction, and for other charitable and laudable ends; at the direction of the Managers of the said fund.[100]

We have already seen that most members of the Glasgow Highland Society, within Glasgow, elsewhere in Scotland and further afield, were merchants, manufacturers and amongst the better-off urban Highland-born (see Table 5.1). Membership fees in excess of twenty shillings together with additional outgoings reinforced the social exclusiveness of Society membership. Such established urban Highlanders, commercially successful sometimes on an international scale yet with a shared sense of responsibility to less well-off Highlanders locally, chiefly directed the 'charitable and laudable ends' of the Society towards integrating Highland children into English-speaking Lowland society. This was done through apprenticeships and education. Such schemes were not undertaken out of any dislike of Gaelic or rejection of Highland origin – far from it, as the sentiments expressed at foundation show – but because both schemes, schooling in English particularly, were seen as means to social progress.

If a note of 1787 that the Society was in a position to apprentice 20 boys a year is taken as representative of the numbers indentured since 1727, perhaps as many as 1,200 boys aged between 12 and 15 benefited in that period and a further 1,500 by 1861. Apprenticeship occurred after an education that largely sought to promote English and which was conducted in close association with the city's Gaelic chapels. In 1835, Norman McLeod reported thus of the connections between the Society, its educational practices and his own Gaelic chapel:

> The boys after a certain number of years at school are apprenticed to trades, and have the benefit of instruction at night in the school; and the girls are taught English reading, writing, arithmetic – the simple branches of it – the branches of female industry – they are prepared for being respectable servant-maids. A certain number of the boys and girls receive clothes. The education is given in English. We accommodate from 80 to 100 of the older boys, of those who are further advanced, in my church in the afternoon, and these seats are occupied by poor Highlanders in the forenoon.[101]

His evidence in 1843 to the Poor Law Commissioners documents in detail these institutional charitable and educational connections:

> There is a Highland society which was instituted in Glasgow about 110 years ago, by certain patriotic individuals connected with this city . . . It was looked after with great care, and we have an income now of from 1200*l*. to 1400*l*. a year from property. We apply to every man we have access to, from whatever quarter, and induce him to to become a member of the society. The sum paid is 2*l*. That society is become very popular in Glasgow. We built schoolhouses at a cost of 4000*l*. a year ago. We educate 600 children, taking the most destitute orphans. We send about fifty boys every year to trade. We indenture and superintend them at their trades. We clothe them for three years after they have been three years in the schools. We clothe about eighty young girls, many of them orphans, and we educate them for servants, teaching them washing, knitting, sewing, and altogether there are about 600 children, with four excellent teachers. Besides that, Mr McLachlan, a native of the Highlands, who went to India and made a fortune, left a large sum of money (I cannot state the precise sum) for the establishment of a free school in Glasgow for the children of native Highlanders; and in that school there is something approaching to from 300 to 400 pupils; but altogether we can educate about 1000 children; and confining myself to children of the poorest class, I don't think there is a child whose parents are from the Highlands in Glasgow, that need want education. . . .
>
> Practically, do you find that through your own exertions and those of other parties, that the Highland population in Glasgow do take advantage of the provisions for the education of children? – They are exceedingly ardent after it. We are obliged to reject a good number, but on the ground that the parents can educate the children themselves, and that we confine ourselves invariably to the poorer classes. . . . The result is most gratifying. The children are not only educated, but we have a visiting committee (gentlemen who are most enthusiastic in the cause), and they visit all the boys after they have entered on their apprenticeships. Every complaint against a master, or *vice versa*, is examined. There is a most minute superintendence with regard to the conduct of the young people.[102]

Apart from the key role of public-spirited individuals in founding and operating Highland societies, several other features are noteworthy. The Society's policy informing education and its close links with the Gaelic chapels may help explain the preference for English services amongst children attending Glasgow's Gaelic chapels. Indeed, the Society may have acted to reinforce a gendered division of labour amongst the Highland young in ways which could explain the attendance patterns of Highland-born female domestic servants in the Gaelic chapels. Unlike many Highlanders amongst the urban poor, the Highland child benefiting from this educational or apprenticeship scheme seems to have been carefully watched lest he or she stray from the path of moral improvement. Perhaps most interestingly, Highland parents were keen for their children to receive such education and assistance, even if it meant, as it so clearly did here, a decline in use of Gaelic in some social contexts. In this context anyway, Highland philanthropy was as concerned with the integration of the young into English-speaking society as it was with maintaining a sense of identity amongst persons of like background, perhaps even more so.

Some bodies fulfilled both functions. In Glasgow, for example, the Gaelic Society of Gentlemen, known also as the Gaelic Club of Gentlemen, had been founded in 1780. In their amended constitution of 1798, it was decreed 'That every Candidate must be a Member of the Glasgow Highland Society'; analysis of the membership lists of that body, of the Glasgow Highland Society and of the management committees of the Gaelic chapels reveals considerable cross-membership, with men such as George McIntosh of the Dunchatten works as first President of the Gaelic Club of Gentlemen.[103] One of their rules at foundation stated:

> That no one can be a Candidate, unless he possesses one or other of the following qualifications: speaks the Gaelic Language; is a native of the Highlands; is descended of Highland Parents; has Landed Property in the Highlands; is married to a Highland Lady; has served his Majesty in a Highland Regiment; or is otherwise connected with, or particularly interested in, the Highlands.[104]

The club shared the use of the Black Bull Inn at the west end of Glasgow's Argyll Street with the Glasgow Highland Society: this inn, much used by Highland drovers to the city, was enlarged by the latter body in 1758 as a base for its operations. The Gaelic Club of Gentlemen met there monthly. Whilst this particular society did establish a fund for the relief of distressed Highlanders, it is clear from its minute books in the early nineteenth century both that the initial Gaelic qualification was soon dispensed with and that it served more as a gentlemen's dining club than as a charitable institution for the relief of destitute Highlanders.[105] Yet at the same time some of its members were involved with the Celtic Dispensary and with the Highland Strangers' Friendly Society, for example, which, between 1814 and cessation for lack of funds in 1842, provided for poor Highlanders in the city with no legal claim to poor relief.

With what is known of the Glasgow Highland Society in this period, and recognising connections in membership with other bodies in the city, we can with some certainty suggest that it acted as a charitable and educational organisation, as a social focus for the better-off male High-lander and a means to personal contact for members of an urban Highland 'elite' of Gaelic ministers, prominent industrialists and military men. The Society certainly assisted many Highland children. But there is no evidence that it, or other comparable bodies in other towns, acted to maintain either a Highland identity or the Gaelic language for all or even the majority of urban Highlanders.

'Making believe to be Highlanders' or agencies for political reform?: Highland societies and the condition of the Highlands in the later nineteenth century

In a letter to the Honorary Secretary of the Highland Society of London in 1871, J. F. Campbell, the collector of Gaelic folktales, declined the invitation to become a director, noting that 'This is a remnant of the ancient dining clubs with a good deal of drink . . . those who frequent the dinners chiefly are not the genuine article but Londoners making believe to be Highlanders'.[106]

In urban Scotland, the activities of several nineteenth-century Celtic and Highland societies likewise suggest an interest more in the 'imagined Highlands' than in assisting Highlanders in Scottish cities or in under-standing the dramatic changes then affecting Highland society. The Edinburgh Celtic Society, begun in 1820 by Sir Walter Scott and David Stewart of Garth, confined itself to awarding book prizes to Highland boys in the city furthest advanced in reading and writing English. Both men were hugely influential in establishing the cult of 'Highlandism' – the idea of a glorious past, a valorous people in a wilderness landscape, creating a national myth out of Highland history – and did so both through their own writings and, in 1822, by orchestrating the arrival in Edinburgh of George IV. What one modern historian has seen as 'the King's Jaunt', a 'Plaided Panorama', established in the contemporary imagination a particular, if almost wholly erroneous, view of the High-lands and of the Highlander that ignored the circumstances affecting ordinary Highlanders within their native parishes or in Scotland's cities: 'No laments were heard – or none beyond the bounds of the *Gaidheal-tachd* – for the evictions, the burnings and the white-sailed ships that were emptying the glens while the men who profited from this Diaspora formed their Highland societies and solemnly debated the correct hang of a kilt and the exact drape of a plaid'.[107] Although these issues pre-date 1822, Prebble is broadly correct in placing the emphasis he does upon 'the King's Jaunt' and upon the significance of Sir Walter Scott as Master of Ceremonies for the King's visit in 1822: 'Scotland could not be the same again once it was over. A bogus tartan caricature of itself had been drawn and accepted, even by those who mocked it, and it would develop in perspective and colour'.[108] Further affirmation of the importance of the 'imagined Highlands' came also with Queen Victoria's purchase of Balmoral in 1848, the artistic representation of the region by men like Landseer, MacCulloch, and, later, the photographs of George Washington Wilson and others, and, not least, because the Highlands became a recreational arena for botanists, tourists, geologists, mountaineers and stalkers all 'bagging' Nature in particular ways.[109]

It is hardly surprising, then, that by the middle years of the nineteenth century a number of Highland societies and Gaelic associations in the urban Lowlands were concerned more with sustaining particular myths about the region than with the material circumstances of peoples' lives in the region, or with philanthropy for the urban Highland poor. Yet we should be wary of establishing absolute distinctions between or even within Highland societies, both because many had dual or multiple functions and because membership characteristics clearly reveal divisions of class and status within the urban Highland populations. In Dundee, for example, numerous Highland organisations were established in the town during the nineteenth century as the town's Highland population increased, the first (excluding the Gaelic Chapel managers) being the Dundee Highland Society in 1814. The chief object of this body was 'the preservation of the dress and antiquities of the ancient Caledonians, also for Raising a fund for relieving distressed Highlanders at a distance from their native homes and such other Benevolent purposes the Society may deem proper'.[110] The Dundee Ancient Caledonian Society, begun in February 1822, likewise had a dual aim: 'the preservation of the dress and several of the antiquities of the ancient Caledonians . . . and to afford relief to its members when necessity required'.[111] The membership records of the Dundee Highland Society show that several committee members were on the board of management of Dundee's Auxiliary Gaelic School Society, the town's only Highland educational establishment, and that the Society was always short of funds. It was formally wound up in 1868, at which time a new body, the Dundee Gaelic Club, was established. This body organised a Highland Ball in Dundee on 4 April 1871, and a Grand Highland Festival in April 1873. From April 1878, 'purely Gaelic soirees' were held in Thorburn's Hall in Dundee's Wellgate 'with a most respectable company of true Highlanders, all of whom appeared to appreciate the programme, which was rendered from beginning to end in Gaelic'.[112] Such events – and there were many then as now throughout urban Scotland – were attended more by the better-off amongst the local Highland population, however, and by persons with a particular, rather

Romantic, sense of the part played by the Highlands in Scotland's history, and not by the mass of urban Highlanders. Even where we can determine a society's purpose to be support of working-class Highlanders from particular districts, as in the short-lived Lewis Association in Glasgow, for example, membership figures fluctuated in relation to city wage rates and circumstances in the home parishes. During 1879, a year of economic hardship generally, the Association noted:

> The last year has been an exceptionally severe one on the working classes, on whom the Society is mainly dependent. Consequently, a considerable number of the oldest and most useful Members had either to go home to Lewis or seek employment elsewhere. Even a good number of those residing in the city have been so situated as to be unable to pay the qualifying fee, [2s/6d (12p)], and thus could not keep up their connection with the Society.[113]

In contrast, the membership of the Glasgow Skye Association and the Lewis and Harris Association increased greatly in the later 1890s as a result of recruitment campaigns amongst Highlanders from those areas resident in the city.[114]

At the same time, it is clear that many Lowland-based Highland societies, in the later nineteenth century especially, were actively engaged in contemporary Highland affairs. In his inaugural address of 7 October 1880 to the Perth Gaelic Society, John Stuart Blackie, Professor of Greek at Edinburgh University and much involved with establishing the Chair of Celtic Languages at that University through the support of migrant Highlanders,[115] claimed that Gaelic and Highland clubs and associations had a role to do 'something towards the preservation and maintenance of a race of genuine Highlanders in the Highlands', to campaign for radical reform of the land laws and to work for the modernisation of Highland agricultural practices.[116] Mackenzie has shown how John Murdoch, the radical editor of *The Highlander* newspaper and political commentator, urged Glasgow's Highlanders at an annual gathering of *Comunn Gaidhealach Ghlaschu* to speak out against landlordism and depopulation in the Highlands: 'The voice of the country must be raised to protest against it and especially the voice of our Highlanders and countrymen driven to large cities must there give forth a sound which can neither be mistaken nor resisted, demanding the consideration of our legislature to the state and condition of our rural population'.[117] The Skye Vigilance Committee in Glasgow was active in support of the Valtos crofters on Skye in 1881, the organisation having been expressly founded to support the tenantry in its rural protest. The Committee was also active in support of crofters at Braes and played a leading role in organising meetings in Glasgow in 1882 and 1883 in support of crofters' rights.[118] Mackenzie has also recorded, however, an unwillingness on the part of some bodies – the Glasgow Skye Association, and the Lewis and Harris Association – to campaign for Highland land law reform in their native parishes, both because such bodies feared that identification with radical causes might diminish their income from the many landlords who were the societies' patrons, and because such bodies did not see themselves as having a political function.[119]

CONCLUSION

Even allowing for the incomplete and varied nature of the source material and for the statistical invisibility of many within the urban Highland population, it is clear that Gaelic chapels and Highland societies did not offer a means to a unified 'migrant culture'. That they did not do so was because of differences within and between the institutions themselves, because of particular and different policies of management, and, chiefly, because the very term 'urban Highlander' has itself been shown to be underlain by differences of geography, class, social aspiration and language.

Yet Gaelic congregations and certain émigré organisations were important sites for reinforcing in limited ways a sense of Highland identity. The formalisation of Gaelic worship in Gaelic chapels and churches from the later eighteenth century and throughout the nineteenth century certainly secured the use of Gaelic in one particular context in urban Scotland. Migrants from certain parts of the Highlands or with a particular affiliation – being poor in the Highland Strangers' Friendly Society in 1830s Glasgow or a pauper in Edinburgh's Gaelic congregation – shared a common experience of sorts with some other Highlanders. But such experiences were also shared with many other non-Highlanders. And because the Gaelic-speaking congregations were drawn from the less wealthy Highland-born, and because seat rents were both unusual and unaffordable, Gaelic congregations were seldom full. Even from the foundation of Gaelic chapels, English services were also given. There are several reasons why this was so: the cultural importance attached to English within contemporary society; the key management role of chapel committees; increasing familiarity with the English language amongst the Highland-born population, especially amongst the children; and, chiefly, because seat rents payable on English services – which had the effect of bringing the better-off Highlander to worship – ensured the viability of Gaelic chapels. Many of the chapel ministers, kirk elders, session clerks and others either administrating the Gaelic congregations or employed on their behalf to record the state of the urban Highland poor were also leading members of Highland societies and associations. The picture we are afforded, then, is of social divisions based on class and status *within* populations otherwise sharing broadly similar patterns of migrant origin and, to some extent, language.

The charitable and philanthropic functions of these institutions seem to have had only limited effect. This was either because of institutional policy, as in the case of poor support for Edinburgh's Gaelic-chapel going population in the late eighteenth century, or – more commonly by the mid-nineteenth century – because many migrant Highlanders could not be reached. The spiritual questions raised by the extent of 'Highland home heathenism' in Scotland's cities by the 1860s were paralleled in a material sense in the many urban Highlanders who were not members of Highland societies because they could not afford to be, because their membership had lapsed as trade slumped or because, for a period, they were moving elsewhere within the city, within the Lowlands or even returning to the Highlands. It is tempting to suggest a four fold typology of Highland societies: charitable bodies; émigré organisations serving Highlanders from a particular district or clan; bodies dominated by an interest in Highland culture (however understood); and societies actively engaged in Highland affairs. But, in truth, many societies had several functions. And within their membership and amongst the many Highland-born non-members, it is clear that differences in language mean we should be careful about the uncritical use, as equivalents, of the terms 'urban Highlander' and 'Gaelic speaker'.

NOTES

1. SRO, CH 1/2/46, ff.253–277.
2. Ibid; see also Ian R. MacDonald, *Glasgow's Gaelic Churches: Highland religion in an urban setting 1690–1995* (Edinburgh, 1995), pp.7–10.
3. Ian R. MacDonald, 'The beginning of Gaelic preaching in Scotland's cities', *Northern Scotland 9*, 1989, pp.45–52.
4. *Acts of the General Assembly of the Church of Scotland*, XVII, 1698, p.276; IX, 1699, p.282; XVI, 1699, pp.287–288.
5. Charles W. J. Withers, *Gaelic in Scotland: the geographical history of a language, 1698–1981* (Edinburgh, 1984), pp.35–6; *Acts of the General Assembly of the Church of Scotland*, IX, 1708, pp. 248–9.
6. SRO, CH 1/2/30/4, f.304.
7. MacDonald, 'The beginning of Gaelic preaching', p.46.
8. W. Sime, *History of the Church and Parish of St Cuthbert or West Kirk of Edinburgh* (Edinburgh, 1829), p.115; G. Lorimer, *The Days of Neil McVicar* (Edinburgh, 1926), p.14. I am grateful to Ian MacDonald for the reference to Lorimer.
9. SRO, CH 2/546/8, f.96; SRO, CH 1/3/18, f.230.

10. Withers, *Gaelic in Scotland*, pp.116–181.
11. *Scots Magazine*, XXVIII (July 1766), p.343.
12. Withers, *Gaelic in Scotland*, pp.162–7.
13. MacDonald's *Glasgow's Gaelic Churches* offers a good account of the minister-ial and denominational history of Gaelic congregations in that city without detailing much of the contemporary social context; the definitive account of all Scottish church ministers and their charges remains Hew Scott (ed.), *Fasti Ecclesiae Scoticanae* (Edinburgh, 1915–1961), 9 volumes.
14. Scott, *Fasti*, Vol. 7, pp.7–8.
15. L. MacBean, *Buchanan, the sacred bard of the Scottish Highlands* (London, 1919), p.24.
16. *Scots Magazine*, XXVIII (1766), p.341.
17. *The Scheme of Erection of the Charitable Highland Society in Glasgow* (Glas-gow, 1787), pp.30–1.
18. SRO, CH 2/766/1, f.32.
19. W. Kennedy, *Annals of Aberdeen* (Aberdeen, 1818), II, pp.187–8.
20. *Ibid.*, p.188; W. Gammie, *The Churches of Aberdeen* (Aberdeen, 1909), p.188.
21. MacDonald, *Glasgow's Gaelic Churches*, p.9.
22. SRO, CH 1/171/1, f.153.
23. SRO, CH 1/171/2, ff.159–160.
24. A. MacWilliam, 'The Glasgow Mission, 1792–1799', *The Innes Review* 4 (1953), pp.84–91; C. Johnson, 'Secular clergy of the Lowland district 1732–1829', *The Innes Review*, 34 (1983), pp.66–87.
25. SRO, CH 1/171/2, f.159.
26. SRO, CH 1/171/2, f.163; J. Cleland, *Enumeration of the Inhabitants of the City of Glasgow* (Glasgow, 1820), p.33.
27. *Extract of Regulations, by the General Assembly, for the Gaelic Chapel of Aberdeen* (Aberdeen, 1820), pp.3–6, 9.
28. SRO, CH 2/171/2, ff.149–150; SRO, CH 2/171/15, ff.148–151.
29. SRO, CH 2/171/2, f.149; SRO, CH 2/171/15, f.149.
30. MacDonald, 'The beginning of Gaelic preaching', p.50.
31. SRO, CH 2/171/15, f.168; MacDonald, *Glasgow's Gaelic Churches*, pp.12–14.
32. G. M. Fraser, 'The Gaelic in Aberdeen', *Aberdeen Press and Journal*, 16 June 1924.
33. SRO, CH 2/766/1, f.2.
34. SRO, CH 2/766/1 and CH 2/766/2 (Minute Books of the Records of Deacon Court of Gaelic Chapel, Edinburgh, 1769–1780, 1780–1799, respectively); for a fuller account of the denominational history of the Gaelic congregation in Edinburgh, see W. Reid and J. Hume, *Edinburgh Gaelic Chapel 1769–1969* (Edinburgh, 1969), a pamphlet prepared for the Kirk Session of the Highland Church to mark its bicentenary.
35. SRO, GD.95.1.6, ff.346–7; interestingly, there is no discussion of this matter within the Minute Books of Edinburgh's Gaelic Chapel at this time [post-1780], perhaps because the Chapel authorities seem to have been preoccupied with the poor condition of the building and, chiefly with difficulties in the appointment of the next minister: SRO, CH2/766/3, ff.18–46, 56–63.
36. Kennedy, *Annals of Aberdeen*, pp.188–9.
37. This is clear from the manuscript 'Record of Gaelic Society of Aberdeen [Minutes of Managers of Aberdeen Gaelic Chapel], Minute 1, p.1, 1 July

1796 and Minute 4, p.3 21 October 1796'. I am indebted to Ian MacDonald for faciliting my access to this source material in his possession. G. M. Fraser in his 'The Gaelic Church of Aberdeen' states (without offering justification) that Gaelic only was used in services at the outset, a claim which must now be regarded as false.

38. *Extract of Regulations*, p.11.
39. SRO, CH 2/294/12, ff.115–6.
40. SRO, CH 2/294/12, f.116.
41. SRO, CH 2/294/12, ff.134–6.
42. Greenock Town Council Records, 20 October 1783.
43. SRO, CH 2/171/2, ff.159–160.
44. SRO, CH 2/766/1, f.46.
45. SRO, CH 2/766/3, ff.4–5.
46. SRO, CH 2/766/1, ff.48–9.
47. SRO, CH 2/766/1, f.40; CH 2/766/3, ff.56–9.
48. SRO, CH 2/766/1, f.31.
49. Scottish Catholic Archives, BL 4/67, f.4 (Mr. Thomson (Rome), to Bishop Hay (Edinburgh), 24 March 1792).
50. W. J. Anderson, 'The Edinburgh Highland Chapel and the Rev. Robert Menzies', *The Innes Review*, 17 (1966), p.197. For a full discussion of the Lowland vicariate and the Catholic Gaelic congregations in this period, see C. Johnson, 'Secular clergy of the Lowland district 1732–1829' and her *Developments in the Roman Catholic Church in Scotland* (Edinburgh, 1983), pp. 22–4, 130–160, 219–230.
51. William Creech, the Edinburgh printer, in *Letters Appended to H. Arnot, The History of Edinburgh* (Edinburgh, 1779), p.56.
52. SRO, CH 2/171/16, f.313.
53. For a fuller story of the Kirkfields (Gorbals) Gaelic Chapel 1813–1834, see MacDonald, *Glasgow's Gaelic Churches*, pp.17–24.
54. SRO, CH 16/3/1/1, Minutes of the Managers of Hope Street Gaelic Chapel, Petition of March 1823.
55. MacDonald, *Glasgow's Gaelic Churches*, pp.20–23.
56. SRO, CH 16/3/1/1, Minutes of the Managers of Hope Street Gaelic Chapel, Petition of March 1823.
57. SRO, CH 16/3/1/1, Letter from Mr Cleland to Mr McGeorge, 24 December 1823.
58. BPP, *Second Report of the Commissioners of Religious Instruction, Scotland*, 1837–38, XXXII, p.459. The detailed evidence in this *Report* appears in the Appendices, although some brief mention is made of the Gaelic chapels in the text. The evidence relating to the two chapels appears in Appendix II as follows: for Duke Street on pp.32–36; for St. Columba's on pp.60–64; and for West Gaelic Church on pp.168–172 respectively. In Appendix III, the pages covered for the three chapels are pp.101–7, 179–98, and 529–533 respectively. In the following notes, this evidence is referenced as *Report of the Commissioners*, with the Appendix and page number(s) following.
59. *Report of the Commissioners*, Appendix III, p.503.
60. *Report of the Commissioners*, Appendix II, p.189.
61. C. G. Brown, 'The costs of pew-renting: church management, church-going and social class in nineteenth-century Glasgow', *Journal of Ecclesiastical History*

38:3 (1987), pp.347–361; A. D. Gilbert, *Religion and Society in Industrial England: churches, chapels and social change, 1740–1914* (London, 1976), pp.69–93; K. S. Inglis, *Churches and the Working Classes in Victorian England* (London, 1963), pp.48–57, 96–7, 105–8, 129–30; H. McLeod, *Class and Religion in the late Victorian City* (Oxford, 1974), pp.1–22.

62. *Report of the Commissioners*, Appendix II, p.119.
63. *Report of the Commissioners*, Appendix III, p.421.
64. *Ibid.*
65. *Report of the Commissioners*, Appendix III, pp.421–2.
66. *Report of the Commissioners*, Appendix III, pp.117–8.
67. *Report of the Commissioners*, Appendix III, p.505.
68. *Ibid.*
69. BPP, *Poor Law Inquiry Commission for Scotland*, 1844, XXI, p.642 5 May 1843.
70. *Ibid.*
71. D. McGregor, *The Necessity of Applying the Territorial System to the Gaelic Non-Church Goers of Glasgow* (Glasgow, 1860), p.3.
72. Ian MacDonald, *Glasgow's Gaelic Churches*, pp.30–44.
73. J. Smyth in the *Scottish Guardian*, 12 June 1857; MacDonald, *Glasgow's Gaelic Churches*, pp.46–7.
74. *Report of the Commissioners*, Appendix III, p.501.
75. J. Smyth in the *Scottish Guardian*, 12 June 1857.
76. *Scottish Guardian*, 7 June 1860, 2 August 1860, 19 September 1861, 3 October 1861.
77. *Scottish Guardian*, 7 February 1861.
78. On the MacDonald Memorial Gaelic Church, Cowcaddens, see MacDonald, *Glasgow's Gaelic Churches*, pp.47–52.
79. SRO, CH 3/322/2, f.50 23 November 1859.
80. SRO, CH 3/322/2, ff.50–52, ff.181–82.
81. This is apparent in the place of birth of the ministers – increasingly non-Highland men by the latter part of the century – and by manuscript records relating to the Gaelic Chapel in Perth: Sandeman Library Perth, MS B.59.28, f.183.
82. SRO, CH 2/766/3, f.127 19 January 1836.
83. SRO, CH 2/766/4, ff.19–20 2 January 1855.
84. SRO, CH 2/766/4, *et seq*; for example, the list of persons admitted, drawn up on 12 May 1863, enumerating persons who had not hitherto been admitted in the period 1856–1863, can be correlated with the 1861 census enumerators' books for Edinburgh. Most were from the skilled manual trades, with several domestic and general servants and only one pauper, James Donaldson, then resident at the West Church Poorhouse.
85. McGregor, *The Necessity of Applying the Territorial System to the Gaelic Non-Church Goers of Glasgow*, p.4.
86. *Greenock Advertiser*, 16 March 1855, 23 November 1871.
87. Brown, *op.cit*; Gilbert, *op.cit*; Inglis, *op.cit*; McLeod, *op.cit*.
88. *Scottish Guardian*, 7 June 1861.
89. MacDonald, *Glasgow's Gaelic Churches*, p.72.
90. *Report of the Commissioners*, Appendix III, p.506.
91. *Scottish Guardian*, 7 June 1860.
92. J. C. MacGregor, *The History of St Columba Parish Church* (Glasgow, 1935), p.37.
93. See, for example, P. Keating (ed.), *Into Unknown England 1866–1913: selections from the social explorers* (Manchester, 1976).

94. *Greenock Advertiser*, 25 April 1854.
95. SRO, CH 3/983/1 – 3, *passim*.
96. R. I. Black, 'The Gaelic Academy: the cultural commitment of the Highland Society of Scotland', *Scottish Gaelic Studies*, 14 (2) (1986), p.1.
97. J. Mackenzie, 'The Highland Community in Glasgow in the Nineteenth Century', (unpublished Ph.D. thesis, University of Stirling, 1987), p.296.
98. G. Eyre-Todd, *History of Glasgow* (Glasgow, 1937), III, pp. 201–2.
99. *The Scheme of Erection of the Charitable Highland Society in Glasgow* (Glasgow, 1787), p.3.
100. *Ibid.*, p.4.
101. *Report of the Commissioners*, Appendix III, p.182.
102. BPP, *Poor Law Inquiry Commission for Scotland*, 1844, XXI, p.649, 5 May 1843.
103. Glasgow City Council (Mitchell Library, Archives), TD 746/1, 7 March 1798.
104. *Ibid.*, TD 746/1, 7 March 1780.
105. *Ibid.*, TD 746/1, 7 March 1780; 12 December 1798.
106. This appears in a letter from Campbell to Ramsay, 6 February 1871, attached to the 1869 list of members of the Highland Society of London.
107. J. Prebble, *The King's Jaunt: George IV in Scotland, 1822* (London, 1988), p.365; on 'Highlandism' more generally, see Charles Withers, 'The historical creation of the Scottish Highlands', in I. Donnachie and C. Whatley (eds.), *The Manufacture of Scottish History* (Edinburgh, 1992), pp.143–156; R. Clyde, *The Image of the Highlander 1745–1822* (East Linton, 1995); M. Chapman, *The Gaelic Vision in Scottish Culture* (Beckenham, 1978); P. Womack, *Improvement and Romance: constructing the myth of the Highlands* (London, 1989); T. M. Devine, *Clanship to Crofters' War: the social transformation of the Scottish Highlands* (Manchester, 1994), pp. 84–99. It is tempting to see parallels between 'Highlandism' and the ways in which the Highlands and Highlanders were imaginatively constructed and represented in the minds of outsiders, and Edward Said's stimulating discussion of the ways in which 'the East' has been portrayed by Western authorities: see his *Orientalism* (London, 1978).
108. Prebble, *The King's Jaunt*, p. 364.
109. Withers, 'The historical creation of the Scottish Highlands', *passim*.
110. Dundee Central Library, MS 273 (5).
111. Dundee Central Library, MS 118 (2).
112. Dundee Central Library, MS 368 (10), ff.3–4.
113. *Third Annual Report of the Lewis Association* (Glasgow, 1879), p.5.
114. Mackenzie, 'The Highland Community in Glasgow in the Nineteenth Century', pp.311–312.
115. W. Gillies, 'A Century of Gaelic Scholarship', in W. Gillies (ed.), *Gaelic and Scotland: alba agus a'ghaidhlig* (Edinburgh, 1989), pp.3–21.
116. The Gaelic Society of Inverness has a distinguished record in this respect: M.A.MacDonald, 'History of the Gaelic Society of Inverness', *Transactions of the Gaelic Society of Inverness*, XLVII (1971), pp.1–25.
117. Mackenzie, 'The Highland Community in Glasgow in the Nineteenth Century', p.327.
118. *Oban Times*, 21 May 1881, 18 June 1881, 13 May 1882, 20 January 1883.
119. Mackenzie, 'The Highland Community in Glasgow in the Nineteenth Century', pp.335–337.

CHAPTER 7

Gaelic Language use
in the Urban Lowlands

Understanding in detail how many persons spoke Gaelic in the urban Lowlands is not possible until the later nineteenth century and, even then, is almost entirely restricted to the Census evidence available decennially from 1881. This is unfortunate since, as previous chapters have shown, Gaelic speakers were permanently resident there from at least the 1690s and, from 1851, migration paths from the Highlands can be determined at parish level. We know that the 1835–36 'Gaelic census' in Glasgow enumerated at least 22,509 *Gaelic speakers* in and around the city (see above, page 86), and that there were 11 Gaelic language periodicals produced in that city between 1803 and 1892.[1] Gaelic language services continued in most Lowland Gaelic chapels throughout the nineteenth century, and there is every reason to suppose that both amongst those who attended and those who could not, Gaelic was spoken at home and in the workplace. But only from 1881, and, reliably, from 1891, is it possible systematically to link migration patterns to language ability, and to know the numbers of persons in urban Scotland either speaking Gaelic only or Gaelic and English. Census statistics are, however, just that: enumerated totals give almost no clue either as to *how* Gaelic was used, of the particular social contexts – the *domain* – in which it was employed, or of the processes determining its use, particularly behind what we might term here generational language change: the fact that many city-born children of Gaelic-speaking Highland-born migrants were, over time, less and less familiar with Gaelic.

Despite such limitations, there is much that can be determined from the Census, principally from its unpublished form in the enumerators' books, about the patterns of Gaelic use in the urban Lowlands, and analysis of such material forms the greater part of this chapter. What is also true, however, is that the Gaelic language was less and less commonly spoken within the *Gaidhealtachd* itself during the eighteenth and nineteenth centuries, in some domains less than others. Temporary and seasonal circulatory migration had the effect of introducing English into the Gaelic parishes, and of familiarising persons, migrants and others, who otherwise spoke Gaelic predominantly if not entirely, with English words and phrases (see above, page 78). Further, the Gaelic language was considered by many a barrier to civilisation and social improvement, and knowing how and to whom it was spoken in urban Scotland is not directly to understand the contemporary context that attached to its use, either amongst the speakers themselves or amongst the more numerous English-speaking populations. An editorial in the *Greenock Advertiser* on 11 June 1852 – a town then with 4,243 Highland-born persons (1 in 9 of the total population: Table 4.1) – certainly had no doubts in this respect:

> We believe that this jaw-breaking tongue is one bar to Highland ameliora-tion and renders our countrymen belonging to the Highland districts foreigners to their fellow-citizens. Older Highlanders regard it as a very expressive vehicle for devout sentiment, but how can this be considering the poverty of the language. . . . It is a matter of great consequence to have English taught universally to the rising Celts, who, in many, if not most cases will require to leave their native hills and villages for scenes of exertion. Indeed, it would be a great matter to have Gaelic extinguished altogether as a spoken language. There is no use for it in the world, and it stands in the way of the well-doing and well-being of those whose only principal language it unfortunately happens to be.

As previously noted, the view that having Gaelic as one's language upon arrival as an urban migrant was likely to hinder employment opportu-nities was certainly held by the Poor Law Commissioners in the 1840s (see above, page 133). To understand the strength and use of Gaelic in the urban Lowlands in the later nineteenth century we must recognise this broader context in which Gaelic and its speakers were set.

GAELIC'S DECLINING USE IN THE HIGHLANDS, C.1700–1900

The detailed history of Gaelic's position within the Highlands has been documented elsewhere:[2] only the broad outlines are presented here. To judge from source listings of *c.*1698, 1765 and 1806 which defined the then boundaries of the Gaelic-speaking parishes, Gaelic was spoken through-out the Highland region, predominantly so in the more isolated north and west mainland and island parishes. Contemporary reports on the state of the language in the 'Old' *Statistical Account* (1791–1799) allow under-standing of the social position of Gaelic within individual parishes. Even in what were adjudged by contemporaries to be strongly Gaelic-speaking parishes, and especially in the 'border' parishes between the largely Gaelic-speaking north and west and the English-speaking south and east, much of the population understood and used English for some social purposes. Of the Aberdeenshire Highland parish of Crathie and Braemar in 1795, for example, we are told that 'The language generally spoken is

200

the Gaelic. Most of the people, however, understand so much of the English, as to be able to transact ordinary business with their neighbours of the low country'.[3] What we know of the southern Argyllshire parish of Dunoon in 1792 is illustrative of the general picture in what it suggests of the patterns of language use and of the processes of language change in one language-border parish:

> The language of the parish is changing much, from the coming-in of low-country tenants, from the constant intercourse our people have with their neighbours, but above all, from our schools, particularly those established by the Society for Propagating Christian Knowledge. Hence the English or Scottish language is universally spoke, by almost all ages, sexes. But the Gaelic is still the natural tongue with them, their firseside language, and the language of their devotions. They now begin, however, to attend public worship in English as well as Erse, which 30 years ago they did not do.[4]

By the mid-nineteenth century, detailed reports in the *New Statistical Account* (1831–1845) make it possible to chart the ebbing away of Gaelic along the border and its decline within hitherto more strongly Gaelic-speaking parishes, and, where comparative parochial accounts exist for the 1790s, to document the nature of the retreat. For Comrie parish in Perthshire in 1794, for example, it was the case that:

> The common language of the people is Gaelic. All the natives understand it; but many, especially the old, do not understand the English well. All the young people can speak English; but in order to acquire it, they must go to service in the Low Country.[5]

By 1837, the language situation in the parish was much changed:

> The English language is generally spoken, and has gained ground greatly within the last forty years. At present, scarcely a fourth part of the congregation attend on the afternoon Gaelic service, whereas forty years ago, the attendance on English was very limited.[6]

Such language shift between Gaelic and English, involving as it did differentiation by age and social domain, is partly to be explained with reference to those processes of agricultural and social transformation we have already noted (see Chapter 2), and was also the result of temporary migration, such movement itself influenced by much greater facility of movement from the northern and western Highlands to the 'Low Country' by the nineteenth century than in previous years. In general, the in-migration of English speakers as a consequence of changes in Highland agriculture occurred earlier and was more widespread along the *Gaidhealtachd* border parishes and in the farming Highlands than in the north and west. In the crofting districts, even admitting that seasonal and temporary migration there was crucial to the maintenance of crofting and a source of anglicisation amongst the younger returning migrants, Gaelic remained the predominant language. Migration and permanent re-location to the urban Lowlands, leading to loss of population, were more important agencies behind the decline of the language. The most important agency of language decline was the school.

The association of Gaelic with backwardness and of English with authority and civility was clearly expressed in policies of educational authorities from at least the early eighteenth century. The most important agency in this respect was the Society in Scotland for Propagating Christian Knowledge, established in 1709. The role of the SSPCK in determining the fortunes of Gaelic through education is crucial for three reasons. Firstly, before 1766, and effectively until 1825, Gaelic was to all intents and purposes prohibited as a medium of use and instruction within its schools. From 1825, Gaelic was only allowed as a means of comprehending English. Secondly, the SSPCK did much to engender a view among Gaelic speakers themselves that education was synonymous with anglicisation: to advance in life, it was argued and believed, one had to understand and speak English. This view has been shown to have had age-related consequences insofar as it manifested itself in the attitudes of Gaelic-speaking parents to their children. Sacred worship in Gaelic was acceptable, but English as the language of worldy progress should be learned as soon as practicable. Thirdly, the location of SSPCK schools has revealed a close correspondence between the spread of English through schools and the changing fortunes of Gaelic within the Gaidhealtachd. Most SSPCK schools between 1709 and 1854 were located in Highlands border parishes: south and west Argyll, central Perthshire, and in the eastern districts of Inverness-shire and Ross and Cromarty. Few SSPCK schools were established in the north and west Highlands and islands.[7] From the early nineteenth century, the efforts of the SSPCK were complemented by the work of the Gaelic Schools Society, chiefly that of the Edinburgh Society for the Support of Gaelic Schools, established in 1811. Gaelic schools were established on the ambulatory principle, moving, sometimes within the larger parishes to a different part of the parish, at the end of the school year, and were much more heavily concentrated in the north and west Highland parishes. The teaching method employed was reading the scriptures in Gaelic and, largely for this reason, the schools were known in Gaelic as *Sgoilean Chriosd* (Schools of Christ). Gaelic schools certainly strengthened the Highlanders' deep feeling for Gaelic as a spiritual language. Given that reading the scriptures in Gaelic was the only teaching method and that religious texts were fairly widely available, this attachment resulted simply from being taught to read the word of God in their native language. The result was a close relationship between Gaelic literacy, the use of Gaelic as a language of religious worship, religious revivalism and, indeed, evangelicalism. But Gaelic schools were also directly responsible for promoting comprehension and usage of English and intended to do so from the outset. This seeming paradox is simply explained. The policy of teaching Gaelic scripture reading was strictly adhered to. This policy had the effect of stimulating a desire for knowledge, a desire which could only be met through English: 'Besides we are satisfied [noted the Edinburgh Gaelic School Society in its first *Annual Report*] 'that the reading of the Gaelic will implant the desire of knowledge, as well as improve the understanding; and thus you [the schoolteachers] insure both the extension and use of the English language'.[8] The extension of literacy in Gaelic and the reinforcement of that language as the preferred spiritual medium thus went hand-in-hand with the spread of English.

Of course, even in the smaller Highland parishes and where it was possible to locate and operate schools, not all the potential school going population attended. We know that boys predominated over girls; that the demands of agricultural labour often took precedence over schooling; and that the shortage of texts and lack of funds to pay teachers, most without formal training, were persistent handicaps. Schools were important agencies of language change, but they were not so in isolation. Nor should we see the decline of Gaelic as a simple 'retreat' north-westwards of a *Gaidhealtachd* in which Gaelic was uniformly spoken and common in all social domains. Contact with the Lowlands meant that English was particularly in use, notably in towns, marketplaces and quaysides, as the language of trade and of commerce, especially amongst younger males, before it was common in other areas of daily life. Gaelic was widely used for all social purposes throughout the north-west Highlands by the time of the 1901 Census, and was still spoken by native speakers in language – border parishes in upland Perthshire and Aberdeenshire, for example, as late as the 1950s.[9] But elsewhere by the turn of the twentieth century, Gaelic was understood and regularly used more by older age groups, notably by women and chiefly in association with the rural economy, than it was by all groups in Highland society. Gaelic was everywhere strongest as the language of religion. Understanding English did not demand its common usage, yet, in the context of what has been documented about Highland-Lowland migration patterns and the diverse nature of urban Gaelic culture, it is important to realise that the urban Highlander did not come from parishes wholly Gaelic in language and move without experience of English and the English way of life. Within the Highlands, using Gaelic at home, in church, at work on the land or at sea was, for many, accompanied by growing anglicisation amongst children, and by hearing more regularly than before the voices of English incomers and tourists. Those trends were paralleled in the urban Lowlands at the same time by gradual shifts from predominantly Gaelic to Gaelic and English-language worship, an evident decline in use of Gaelic amongst the children of Highland-born persons and by increasing familiarity with English amongst the adult Highland migrant population through the jobs they did, however much Gaelic was spoken in the home.

Some insights into the social differences in Gaelic use within an urban context in the past are afforded by the results of an inquiry from the Presbytery of Dunoon into the 'the state of Gaelic in the parish of Rothesay' in November 1834. The inquiry had arisen as a result of popular feeling about the relative lack of Gaelic religious services in Rothesay, Gaelic services having been discontinued in the chapel of ease in 1829 and Gaelic services having taken second place to English in Rothesay parish church. The inquiry sought to determine reaction to a proposal for a separate Gaelic chapel in which worship would be in Gaelic only. In its general purpose, then, the Rothesay inquiry, although on a smaller scale, was motivated by the same concerns as the 1835–36 'Gaelic census' in Glasgow. By the end of November 1834, 52 witnesses, all male, had been interviewed: their responses concerning the patterns of language use in and about the town of Rothesay provide valuable insight into language use in the historic urban *Gaidhealtachd*.[10]

Throughout the town and parish of Rothesay, Gaelic was in many districts only spoken at all as a result of the immigration of Gaelic speakers from elsewhere. Gaelic was quite commonly used only in the north of the island of Bute and most commentators testified that, in their view, the majority of those persons who spoke Gaelic in Rothesay town and parish were incomers, usually in the previous 40–50 years. For example, Archibald MacInroe, a Rothesay magistrate, enumerated the language patterns of 310 persons in one district of the town: 60 persons were noted as 'preferring Gaelic to English' but there were only 25 persons who could not 'converse freely in English', including five children and one adult Gaelic-only speaker. None of these 25 was a native, and most were aged 40 or over and had been resident in the town from anything between 10 and 30 years.[11] Selkirk, writing of the early nineteenth century – just the period when many Gaelic-speaking Highlanders were migrating to Rothesay – notes that many were moving to textile mills and other employment in the town. In Mull, recruitment for the Rothesay mills was intensive[12] (in just the same way as we have seen David Dale and George Macintosh to have operated at the same time, in Barra and east Sutherland respectively: pages 126, 136 above): a fact which may explain the enumeration of several Mull natives amongst the strongly Gaelic-speaking sections of Rothesay's population. More generally, English was widely used as the language of commercial transactions, even though, in many cases, enumerated individuals and families could speak Gaelic and preferred that language in other domains. At the same time, many preferred Gaelic for worship: even some of those who used English in business and spoke it in other walks of life could not benefit from English sermons. One James McConechy, a 70–year-old Rothesay native and farmer at Auchiemore about two miles south-west of Rothesay town since 1787, perhaps epitomised this division: business matters with his factor were in English (McConechy 'understood English tolerably'), yet he did not have enough English to benefit from worship in that language and domestic worship was, as a result, in Gaelic, even though his family of five had virtually no Gaelic.[13] Within the home more generally, considerable variation existed in language use. Most families seem to have spoken English even though Gaelic was both understood and used. Several enumerators noted how one of the chief causes of Gaelic's decline within the previous twenty years was that Gaelic was 'not descending from parents to children'. Few children were recorded as speaking the language in the town, certainly within the family circle, although more did in the landward parts of the parish. This generational shift within the family is exemplified by William McConechy, a 56–year-old native of Rothesay town who noted: 'His parents spoke it, he has a little; his 8 children don't'.[14]

What is also true is that many people, Gaelic speakers amongst them, used the languages they had in the ways they did because of a profound sense that Gaelic was 'a lower class language'. Many of the enumerators and those interviewed made this point. Robert Stewart, for example, a 56–year-old native of Kingarth parish in south Bute, noted of his enumerated district of 50 persons that:

> there is no-one under 30 who understands Gaelic better than English; not aware that any parents in his district are anxious to instruct their children in the use of the Gaelic language; besides the 3 mentioned [persons there who did not 'converse freely in English', of whom two were native to Rothesay], there are those who give their servants orders in Gaelic or talk amongst themselves in Gaelic;- servants referred to are not natives; believes that those throughout the parish who understand the Gaelic better than an English sermon belong generally to the more ignorant and uninstructed part of the population.[15]

Such a view stemmed, it was argued, from Gaelic speakers 'priding themselves in the English tongue' and, in turn, seeing Gaelic as intrinsically socially inferior.

The 1834 Rothesay evidence documents complex patterns of bilingualism, within different parts of the island and town, within given streets and even within families and individuals. Distinct domain differences were apparent in the use of Gaelic and/or English for business, home life, and church worship. The fact that a separate Gaelic chapel was built, in 1836, is testimony to the strength of use and of feeling for Gaelic in one particular context. To judge from congregation figures, perhaps 800–900 persons – about 15 per cent of the parish total – represented the core of the Gaelic population. But this figure was much greater than actual attendance figures. Many Gaelic speakers did not attend, the result, variously, of an attitude to Gaelic as an 'inferior language', poverty, lack of proper Sabbath dress and distance from the chapel. In that regard, the complex patterns of language use in Rothesay in 1834 have much in common with the state of the language in Glasgow at the same time. The evidence of Peter McNab's declaration to the Church Commissioners' inquiries there in March 1836 certainly suggests as much:

> *You had charge of a district in the survey?*
> I had.
> *How did you proceed in your enquiries?*
> I went to every house, and enquired after all who could speak Gaelic, and took down the names of all who could do so. The children that did not understand Gaelic I did not take down at all.
> *How did you proceed afterwards?*
> Some of the children could not speak Gaelic, and I did not take them. I took down the churches they attended, and the sittings they held.
> *Did you enquire where the children were born?*
> I did.
> *Did you find many children speaking Gaelic who were born in Glasgow?*
> Yes; little was spoken at home but Gaelic. When the father spoke English I did not take down the children, because they did not speak Gaelic.
> *Did you ask any of the families if they had been long in Glasgow?*
> I did; most of them.
> *What was the general answer?*
> Most of them had been in it for several years. Indeed I met with very few Highlanders newcomers into Glasgow. Most of those who have been several years in Glasgow talk English now and then, but they talk Gaelic in their families.
> *Is the English they talk about their every-day business affairs, or could they carry on a conversation in it?*

The English they talk is generally about their business affairs, and some of them are not very good at it; but always when at home they speak Gaelic.[16]

We should be wary, however, despite these close parallels, of simply assuming the Rothesay evidence was typical of the patterns of language use in other and larger Lowland towns. What it and McNab's evidence does afford is an indication of the complexity of language use 'behind' the enumerated statistics.

GAELIC SPEAKING IN THE URBAN LOWLANDS, 1881–1901: THE CENSUS EVIDENCE

The Census of Scotland first enumerated ability in Gaelic in 1881. Table 7.1 shows the numbers of persons recorded as Gaelic speaking within each of the study towns here from 1881 to 1901. In each of these Census years, urban-resident Gaelic speakers represented a significant

Table 7.1
NUMBERS OF GAELIC SPEAKERS IN SCOTLAND'S PRINCIPAL TOWNS AND CITIES, 1881–1901[*]

| Town/city | Numbers of Gaelic speakers and as a percentage of urban population | | |
	1881	1891[(†)]	1901[(‡)]
Aberdeen	150 (0.14)	660 (0.52)	712 (0.46)
Dundee	237 (0.16)	733 (0.47)	736 (0.45)
Edinburgh	1,724 (0.75)	4,781 (1.81)	4,604 (1.45)
Glasgow	7,451 (1.52)	17,978 (2.73)	18,517 (2.43)
Greenock	2,838 (4.44)	3,191 (5.03)	2,607 (3.82)
Paisley	376 (0.67)	992 (1.49)	977 (1.23)
Perth	391 (1.35)	800 (2.67)	789 (2.40)
Stirling	94 (0.58)	499 (2.97)	432 (2.34)

* From *Census of Scotland*
† Total Gaelic-speaking population
‡ Total Gaelic-speaking population aged 3 years and above

proportion of the total Gaelic-speaking population of Scotland: in 1881, for example, in a total Gaelic-speaking population of 231,594 persons (about 6.8 per cent of the total population), there were 10,513 Gaelic speakers enumerated in Lanarkshire alone (the majority in Glasgow City), a further 5,190 in Renfrewshire and 2,142 in Midlothian.[17] Given the numbers speaking Gaelic in the urban Lowlands by the late nineteenth century, it is possible to consider Gaelic's geography as a whole within

Scotland as a three fold division: between the still strongly Gaelic north and west Highlands – a sort of 'true Highlands' or *'Fior Ghaidhealtachd'* – and an 'urban *Gaidhealtachd'*, with the rest of the country having relatively or very low levels of Gaelic speaking – what some have seen as a *'Breac-Gaidhealtachd'* or 'Lesser *Gaidhealtachd'*.[18] In general terms, this is true, but we must for several reasons be cautious over the nature of the Census evidence on language.

The enumeration of Scotland's Gaelic-speaking population in 1881 was based upon answers to a question about speaking Gaelic 'habitually'.[19] Interpretation of this term in particular caused great difficulty given the complex ways in which the language was actually used, and, in reviewing the extent of under-counting in the Census, the Gaelic Society of Inverness considered that many Gaelic-speakers had been omitted, especially in the urban Lowlands, 'on account of the misleading character of the phrase . . . "habitual" speakers of Gaelic'.[20] The problem was compounded by the fact that, elsewhere in the 1881 Census, reference is made to plans to enumerate those said either to be 'Gaelic speaking' or in the habit of 'making colloquial use of the Gaelic language'.[21] One contemporary commentator reckoned the total number omitted as a result of these difficulties to be about 5,000 persons:[22] the actual figure may have been higher but will now never be known.

The 1881 Census is not the only one to present problems to later researchers. That of 1891 distinguished between ability in Gaelic only, and Gaelic and English, and, unlike 1881, required that householders themselves and not enumerators complete the forms. From 1901, and in all censuses thereafter, only persons three years old and over were enumerated. In many parts of the north-west Highlands especially, this had the effect of omitting many young, largely Gaelic-speaking children who had not yet begun formal schooling. Commissions of Education on Uist in the early 1900s considered, for example, that the real number of persons not having Gaelic was probably 174 persons, not the 740 given in the Census returns. And on Lewis at the same time, 860 people rather than the listed 3,031 should have been classed as non-Gaelic speakers.[23] There is no way to know the extent to which such differences in enumeration were evident throughout Scotland.

Given the difficulties with the 1881 Census, the 1891 Census must be regarded as the first reliable indication of numbers of Gaelic speakers in Scotland. For our purposes here, the 1891 evidence is additionally important in that the original enumerators' returns are open for study, and it is possible, therefore, to relate ability in Gaelic to place of birth, to occupation and to determine the age and sex characteristics of the Gaelic-speaking populations in the urban Lowlands.[24]

Gaelic speaking in the urban Lowlands in 1891 at town level:
Aberdeen, Dundee, Perth and Stirling

To illustrate these issues, enumerators' returns for four Lowland towns have been examined in detail. The volume of material and the time taken in analysis precluded attention to the returns for Glasgow, Edinburgh, Paisley, and Greenock: parish-based samples from the first two mentioned towns are, however, discussed below. What follows discusses three related themes for each of the sample towns: the numbers speaking Gaelic according to the printed Census volumes and the manuscript enumerators' books; the age and sex structure of the Gaelic-speaking and Highland-born population; and the places of origin of the Gaelic population in each town.

Aberdeen in 1891 had a Highland-born population of 1,257 persons (Table 4.4), the great majority of whom had moved, from 1851 and before, and throughout the period 1851–1891, from the north-eastern Highland parishes (cf. Figures 4.12, 4.20, 4.21). Aberdeen had an enumerated resident total of 660 Gaelic speakers in 1891, a figure given in both the published census volumes and in the unpublished enumerators' books. These figures should not be taken as meaning, however, that about half of the Highland-born population in Aberdeen spoke Gaelic. Of the 660 enumerated Gaelic speakers in the town, only 514 were *Highland-born* as here defined (40.8 per cent of the town's Highland-born population), since, as we shall see, the difference of 146 persons was made up by persons who were Gaelic speakers but not Highlanders. Assessment of the age and sex structure of the Highland-born Gaelic-speaking population reveals that, as a whole, more males were enumerated as Gaelic speakers than females – 275 male Gaelic speakers to 239 female – but, within certain age-ranges of Gaelic speaker, more females than males spoke Gaelic. Table 7.2 shows the numbers of Highland-born Gaelic-speaking persons in Aberdeen in 1891 in each age group, and that number, distinguished by sex, expressed as a percentage of the total Gaelic-speaking population in the town. The right hand columns, also distinguished by sex, show the Gaelic-speaking population in each age group as a percentage of the total Highland-born population in that group. This form of data analysis and presentation allows us to know, then, the numerical strength of Gaelic, by sex, within different age groups and to know what proportion of the Highland-born population within given age groups was Gaelic-speaking. For example, there were 20 female Gaelic speakers in Aberdeen in 1891 between the ages of 45 and 49. These 20 women represented a little over 8 per cent of the entire female Gaelic-speaking population in the town and exactly 40 per cent of all Highland-born women in that age range. Put another way, fewer than half of all Highland-born women in their late 40s spoke Gaelic or, at least, were

Table 7.2

NUMBERS OF HIGHLAND-BORN GAELIC SPEAKERS IN ABERDEEN,
1891, BY AGE AND SEX*

Age cohort	Numbers of Gaelic speakers in group		Percentage of Gaelic-speaking population		Percentage of total Highland population	
	Male	Female	Male	Female	Male	Female
0–4	1	1	0.36	0.42	9.09	6.66
5–9	–	5	–	2.09	–	20.00
10–14	3	1	1.09	0.42	12.00	3.12
15–19	17	8	6.18	3.34	39.53	26.66
20–24	30	15	10.90	6.27	54.54	26.78
25–29	18	19	6.54	7.94	43.90	33.92
30–34	16	24	5.84	10.04	32.66	45.28
35–39	29	30	10.55	12.57	52.72	53.57
40–44	16	30	5.84	12.57	43.24	60.00
45–49	25	20	9.09	8.36	48.07	40.00
50–54	26	14	9.45	5.85	57.77	29.78
55–59	22	15	8.00	6.27	62.85	33.33
60–64	24	20	8.72	8.36	52.17	58.82
65–69	22	14	8.00	5.85	53.65	38.88
70–74	13	11	4.72	4.63	48.14	44.00
75–79	6	7	2.18	2.92	33.33	46.66
80–84	7	1	2.54	0.42	58.33	25.00
85–89	–	2	–	0.84	–	66.66
90–94	–	2	–	0.84	–	100.00
95–99	–	–	–	–	–	–
100+	–	–	–	–	–	–
TOTALS	275	239	100.00	100.00		

*From the *Census of Scotland*, Enumerators' books.

enumerated as speaking it. Similarly, the two Highland-born women who were aged between 90 and 94 – the only urban Highlanders of that age range in Aberdeen in 1891 – were both Gaelic speakers. The 30 male Gaelic speakers between the ages of 20 and 24 represented 10.9 per cent of all Highland-born males in the town. Further, only 44.14 per cent of the male Highland-born population were Gaelic speakers (275 persons out of a Highland-born male total of 623). For females, the figure is 37.69 per cent (239 of 634 Highland women). There is no evidence to suggest here that the older age ranges of the Highland-born population were more strongly Gaelic-speaking than the younger sections of the population. In only seven age ranges for Highland men and in only five for Highland women was Gaelic spoken by more than 50 per cent of the Highland-born population. There were no Gaelic-only speakers in Aberdeen in 1891.

Almost one in four Gaelic speakers in Aberdeen in 1891 was born outwith the Highlands as here defined. The great majority of these non-Highland-born Gaelic speakers were born elsewhere in Scotland, with a handful born furth of Scotland (Table 7.3). Four trends are discernible from analysis of the places of origin of the non-Highland-born Gaelic-speaking population, for Aberdeen and for the other towns in this study, trends which can be related to what we know about Highland-Lowland migration and the strength of Gaelic in Scotland as a whole at this time.

Table 7.3

PLACE OF ORIGIN AND NUMBERS OF NON-HIGHLAND-BORN GAELIC SPEAKERS IN ABERDEEN, 1891*

Elsewhere in Scotland

Aberdeen	30	Forgue	1	New Machar	1
Aberdeenshire	1	Fraserburgh	1	New Mills	1
Abernethy (Moray)	1	Garlieston	1	Old Aberdeen	2
Alves	1	Garvock	1	Old Machar	3
Ardclach	5	Glasgow	2	Ordiquhill	1
Ballater	2	Glenmuick, Tullich		Perth	2
Ballindalloch	1	and Glengairn	2	Pluscarden	1
Banffshire	3	Grange (Banff)	1	Port of Monteith	1
Birse	1	Grantown	2	Stirling	2
Caithness	1	Halkirk	4	Thurso	2
Cluny	1	Huntly	1	Tomintoul	3
Corsiehill	1	Inverallen	1	Wick	3
Crathie and Braemar	14	Kildrummy	2		
Crimond	1	Kincardine O'Neil	1		
Cullen	1	Kinloss	1		
Duthel	1	Kirkmichael (Banff)	3		
Dunnet	2	Lonmay	1		
Dyke	1	Lybster	2		
Edinburgh	4	Meikle Logie	1		
Elgin	3	Methlick	1		
Fife	1	Nairn	2		

TOTAL <u>129</u>

Not in Scotland

America	1	Ireland	6
England	8		
Hull	2		

TOTAL <u>17</u>

*From the *Census of Scotland*, Enumerators' books.

Firstly, the totals given for towns such as Aberdeen itself and Old Aberdeen, Stirling and Glasgow in Table 7.3 most commonly represent the birthplace of children of Gaelic-speaking Highland-born parents whose pattern of out-movement was characterised by a series of stages or steps, moving between several places, before settling in Aberdeen by 1891. As we have already seen, the journey from Highlands to Lowlands should not be conceived of as immediate and direct (cf. Figure 3.3 and see pages 61–83). Since, for many Highland-born adults, the move south and formal enumeration in the enumerators' returns or poor house register involved intermediate moves over a period of time, it is reasonable to suggest that these totals indicate the transmission of Gaelic down the generations and, possibly, within the family from Gaelic-speaking Highland-born parents to their Lowland-born children, and, to an extent, may include the adoption of Gaelic by the marriage partner of a Gaelic husband or wife. Among the 30 Gaelic-speaking persons born in Aberdeen, for example, many were Aberdeen-born Gaelic-speaking children of Gaelic-speaking Highland-born Aberdonians with a handful of Gaelicspeaking Aberdeen-born wives and husbands of Highland-born Gaelicspeaking partners.

Secondly, the relatively large numbers of persons from parishes like Crathie and Braemar and, to a lesser extent, Glenmuick, Tullich and Glengairn, and Ardclach is an indication of the in-movement into Aberdeen of persons from parishes still quite strongly Gaelic but whose actual total numbers speaking the language represented less than 25 per cent of the total parish population and, therefore, are not Highland as here defined. Crathie and Braemar, for example, had a Gaelic-speaking population of 284 persons in 1891, 20.7 per cent of the total parish population, and in Kirkmichael (Banff) 248 people out of a parish population of 1,043 spoke Gaelic (23.7 per cent of the total). Fifty years earlier, Gaelic had been much stronger but English increasingly common in what were by the 1891 Census language border parishes. In Crathie and Braemar in 1842, for example, we are told that 'The Gaelic language is very generally spoken throughout the whole parish, and, during the summer months, is used in conducting part of the public worship, both at Crathie and Braemar. There are, however, very few, if any of the inhabitants, who are not so well acquainted with the English language as to be able to converse and transact business in it, when necessary'.[25] In Kirkmichael at the same date, the position was similar: 'The language generally spoken is the Gaelic, but it has decreased very considerably within the last forty years. There is not an individual between twelve and forty years who cannot speak English. They all read English, and there are many of the rising generation who cannot speak Gaelic'.[26] The resident Gaelic population of Aberdeen was thus made up in part of Gaelic speakers who had migrated from what may perhaps be called the *Gaidhealtachd* 'margin', and this feature will be shown to hold for other Lowland towns, albeit from other 'marginal' parishes.

Thirdly, it is possible to suggest that the presence of American-born or English-born Gaelic speakers is an indication of the return to Scotland of

Gaelic-speaking emigrants or of their children, or children born to Highlanders whose Highland-Lowland migration path in the nineteenth century, like that of Catherine McAllister between 1871 and 1890 (see Figure 3.3), took them beyond Scotland. Both Hull-born Gaelic speakers, for example, were the children of Highland-born Gaelic-speaking parents.

Finally, the enumeration of Irish-born persons as speakers of Gaelic *may* indicate ability in Irish, not Scottish Gaelic. The Census asked only for information on 'Gaelic only' or 'Gaelic and English' without explicit reference to its being *Scottish* Gaelic. It is possible, then, that such individuals rightly enumerated themselves as Gaelic speakers although what they had was Irish. This issue is discussed further below.

Dundee's Highland-born population in 1891 totalled 1,277 persons, 525 males and 752 females, an imbalance that probably had much to do with the occupational demands and sexual division of labour within Dundee's textile industries in the nineteenth century, a major employer of Highland-born. The great majority of Dundee's Highlanders, by 1891 and throughout the nineteenth century, had migrated from Highland Perthshire parishes, eastern Inverness-shire and Easter Ross (cf. Figures 4.10, 4.11 and 4.18). Unlike Aberdeen, however, the Census evidence on the numbers of Gaelic speakers in the town varies between the published and unpublished returns. The published printed volumes give a figure of 733 Gaelic speakers in Dundee.[27] The unpublished manuscript enumerators' books give a total of 760 persons. There is no easy explanation to account for this difference: no boundary changes have occurred; we must assume the enumerators' books to be accurate and the activities of the enumerators to have covered all persons within prescribed enumeration districts.[28] Whatever the *cause*, the *fact* of the difference is undeniable. Since the enumerators' books may be presumed more accurate given the door-to-door procedures of collection and the personal knowledge of the enumerators, the enumerators' books figure of 760 has been taken here as the 'actual' Gaelic-speaking population in Dundee.

Within this total, 555 persons were Highland-born Gaelic speakers; that is, only 43.46 per cent of the total Highland-born population of Dundee in 1891 were Gaelic speakers. Assessment by age and sex of the Highland-born Gaelic-speaking population shows that Gaelic was more commonly spoken by (or, properly, numerically more prevalent amongst) women than men (Table 7.4). For women, the 315 Highland-born Gaelic speakers represented 41.8 per cent of the Highland-born female population. In general, what Table 7.4 shows is that Gaelic was most commonly known by adults within the working age ranges, was more commonly known by men than women within most individual age groups as well as

Table 7.4

NUMBERS OF HIGHLAND-BORN GAELIC SPEAKERS IN DUNDEE, 1891, BY AGE AND SEX*

Age cohort	Numbers of Gaelic speakers in group		Percentage of Gaelic-speaking population		Percentage of total Highland population	
	Male	Female	Male	Female	Male	Female
0–4	1	1	0.41	0.31	14.28	9.09
5–9	1	1	0.41	0.31	9.09	8.33
10–14	2	1	0.82	0.31	10.52	4.76
15–19	2	11	0.82	3.48	8.00	26.1
20–24	19	25	7.91	7.92	40.40	55.5
25–29	22	35	9.16	11.09	56.41	42.16
30–34	23	37	9.58	11.74	50.00	48.05
35–39	13	30	5.41	9.52	30.20	44.10
40–44	21	36	8.75	11.42	40.38	54.50
45–49	28	31	11.66	9.84	63.63	41.89
50–54	27	32	11.25	10.15	60.00	45.00
55–59	16	21	6.66	6.66	41.00	42.00
60–64	21	16	8.75	5.07	50.00	38.00
65–69	18	8	7.70	2.53	64.20	25.80
70–74	13	15	5.41	11.11	72.70	46.80
75–79	5	9	2.08	2.85	55.50	45.00
80–84	5	3	2.08	0.95	55.50	75.00
85–89	2	3	0.82	0.95	100.00	100.00
90–94	1	–	0.41	–	100.00	–
95–99	–	–	–	–	–	–
100+	–	–	–	–	–	–
TOTALS	240	315	100.00	100.00		

* From the *Census of Scotland*, Enumerators' books.

in overall total, and, as for Aberdeen, there is no evidence to suggest an increased prevalence in Gaelic towards the upper age ranges. Dundee had a non-Highland-born Gaelic-speaking population in 1891 of 205 persons, of whom 150 were born elsewhere in Scotland (Table 7.5): persons from still quite strongly Gaelic-speaking but 'marginal' parishes such as Crathie and Braemar; and Gaelic-speaking Lowland-born children of Highland-born parents and others, probably returning migrants.

Broadly similar trends are apparent for Perth and for Stirling in 1891.[29] Perth's Highland-born population of 1,117 persons in 1891 (Table 4.4) – 469 males and 653 females – has been shown to have come predominantly from north-west Highland Perthshire (cf. Figures 4.9 and 4.17). As with Dundee, Perth had an enumerated Gaelic-speaking population total in the

Table 7.5

PLACE OF ORIGIN AND NUMBERS OF NON-HIGHLAND-BORN GAELIC SPEAKERS IN DUNDEE, 1891

Elsewhere in Scotland

Aberdeen	7	Dunning	1	Monifeith	1
Aberdeenshire	1	Edinburgh	4	Morayshire	1
Aberdour (Banff)	1	Forfar	1	Murroes	1
Alyth	2	Forres	3	Nairn	4
Amulree	1	Foyers	1	Newtyle	2
Arbroath	2	Glasgow	4	Perth	11
Auchterarder	1	Grantown	1	Perthshire	16
Auchtermuchty	1	Greenock	7	Redgorton	1
Auldearn	1	Halkirk	2	Renfrewshire	2
Bendochy	1	Kincardineshire	3	St. Ninians	1
Blairgowrie	1	Kirkcaldy	1	Stonehaven	2
Boat of Garten	1	Kirkmichael (Banff)	6	Stonehouse	1
Caputh	2	Kirriemuir	1	Strathtummel	1
Claverhouse	1	Laurencekirk	1	Thurso	1
Carmichael	1	Longforgan	1	Tomintoul	7
Carthie and Braemar	4	Lundie	1	Wick	1
Dumbartonshire	1	Mains	2		
Dundee	25	Meigle	1		

TOTAL 150

Not in Scotland

Canada	1	Manchester	1
England	3	Montgomery	1
Ireland	49		

TOTAL 55

*From the *Census of Scotland*, Enumerators' books.

published printed returns different from that resulting from assessment of the unpublished enumerators' returns, figures of 800 and 815 respectively. Of the 815 'actual' Gaelic-speaking population in the town, 595 persons were Highland-born Gaelic speakers (53.26 per cent of the total Highland-born population in Perth). Of this total, 240 were males and 355 females. Across most individual age groups, Gaelic was spoken more by women than by men and more Gaelic speakers are enumerated within the adult working age ranges than in either younger or older age groups. In Perth, the non-Highland-born Gaelic-speaking population of 220 persons in 1891 was made up of 89 Scots-born and 131 others, of whom all bar two persons (both Canadian) were born in Ireland. In Stirling's relatively small Highland-born population in 1891 of 376 persons, 155 were males, 221 females, and Gaelic was spoken by only 229 persons from within the total Highland population (60.9 per cent of the total Highland population). As for Dundee and Perth, there is for Stirling a difference between the published volumes and the enumerators' books in the given totals for the Gaelic-speaking population. In Stirling, however, the published volumes give the greater figure – 499 persons – as against the 482 derived from analysis of the unpublished returns. In contrast to the other towns discussed here, the non-Highland-born Gaelic-speaking population was larger than those Gaelic speakers claiming Highland birth. As for Dundee, Perth and Aberdeen, these were people from partially Gaelic parishes on the language border, or from overseas, or who were the Lowland-born children of Highland-born Gaelic speakers. What is noteworthy about Stirling, however, is the presence of 150 persons of Irish birth enumerated as Gaelic speakers. There is no reason to suppose on the evidence presented in the Census and given the question asked by the enumerators that such persons did not speak *Scottish* Gaelic. Yet, there is every reason to suppose that these 150 individuals, or a propor-tion of that total, did *not* speak Scottish Gaelic and were enumerated on their facility in Irish. In several cases in Stirling (but not for the three other towns here), there is evidence of Highland-born wives, enumerated as Gaelic speakers (and one Lowland-born Gaelic-speaking wife), married to Irish-born Gaelic-speaking husbands. In itself, of course, this provides no indication of what, exactly, was the 'Gaelic' they spoke – Scottish Gaelic or Irish – and it is certainly not a guide as to how the language was used for various social purposes by such persons. But what it may point to as a matter of language use in the urban Lowlands is the adoption of Gaelic by one marital partner with no other prior cultural connections with either the Highlands or with Scottish Gaelic, but with connections with 'Gaelic' through an Irish husband. It is certainly the case in Green-ock that the enumerators were confused by the actual patterns of language use amongst 'Gaelic-speaking' households: Lobban recorded about 100 persons there in 1891 who were Irish-born yet listed as Gaelic speakers.[30]

In summary, it is clear that the Gaelic-speaking proportion of the Highland-born population of the four towns varied between 40 per cent (in Aberdeen) to 60 per cent (in Stirling) and that there were marked differences within and between these towns in the proportions of the male- and of the female-Highland-born populations speaking Gaelic (Table 7.6). This evidence numerically illustrates the important difference between the terms urban *Highlander* and urban *Gaelic speaker* since, for these four towns anyway, two things are clear: far from all Highland-born persons spoke Gaelic or, at least, were enumerated as having any knowledge of that language, and many Gaelic speakers were not High-land-born. It may be that the relative numerical strength of Gaelic in each of the towns is a reflection of the relative prevalence of Gaelic in the parishes of origin in the *Gaidhealtachd*. But we must remember that the 1891 Census provides only a static image of a dynamic process and that

Table 7.6

GAELIC SPEAKING IN URBAN LOWLAND SCOTLAND, 1891:
THE EXAMPLES OF ABERDEEN, DUNDEE, PERTH AND STIRLING

	ABERDEEN	DUNDEE	PERTH	STIRLING
Total urban population	124,943	155,985	19,919	16,776
Total Highland-born population (as here defined) and as % of total population	1,257 (1.00)	1,277 (0.81)	1,117 (5.60)	376 (2.24)
Total Gaelic-speaking population, from				
(a): Published Census volumes	660	733	800	499
(b): Enumerators' books	660	760	815	482
(c): (b) as % total urban population	0.52	0.48	4.09	2.87
Total Highland-born Gaelic-speaking population (from b above) and as % of total Highland-born	514 40.89	555 43.46	595 53.26	229 60.9
Total non-Highland-born Gaelic-speaking population and as % of total Gaelic-speaking population (from b above)	146 22.12	205 26.97	220 26.99	253 52.48
Male Gaelic speakers as % of total male Highland-born	44.14	45.17	53.09	58.06
Female Gaelic speakers as % of total female Highland-born	37.69	41.88	54.36	62.89

*From *Census of Scotland* 1891 and Enumerators' books.

many Highland migrants would have arrived well before that date, from parishes then more strongly Gaelic-speaking than in 1891. It is possible to suggest that Aberdeen's Highland-born population was less strongly Gaelic-speaking than Stirling's, for example, because Aberdeen was drawing upon Highland parishes less strongly Gaelic, particularly around the eastern seaboard of Ross and Cromarty and Inverness-shire, including Inverness parish and town. This does not explain, however, why Dundee and Perth, which both drew upon similar source areas, should have the differences they do in relative strength of Gaelic speaking within the Highland-born population. Questions to do with age at arrival within the Highland-born migrant population, and, crucially, with age *at departure* from the Highland parishes have, therefore, important implications for our understanding of language use within the Gaelic-speaking Highland-born populations in the urban Lowlands. If, for example, those Gaelic-speaking Highlanders in the older age ranges had recently migrated to one of these towns from quite strongly Gaelic parishes, it is reasonable to suppose they would keep their language and profess ability in it on the enumerators' forms. In contrast, if a large number of the Gaelic-speaking Highlanders in the older age groups had been resident for a length of time in the urban Lowlands, it is legitimate to claim a degree of language maintenance amongst such people and to argue for both the maintenance of Gaelic amongst sections of the 'long stay' migrant population and for continual reinforcement of the Gaelic-speaking population through the in-movement at any one moment of 'new' migrant Gaelic speakers. As we have seen, known age-at-arrival statistics show only great variation with little sound basis for generalisation, and, given the evidence for step-wise migration and the nature of some temporary Highland-Lowland mobility, we should not necessarily assume known age at arrival to be indicative of age at departure from the Highland parish. Overall, migration in the first half of the nineteenth century and before seems to have involved the younger age ranges with older persons participating more commonly by the later 1800s (see above, pages 66, 124). In relation to patterns of language use amongst Gaelic-speaking urban Highlanders, it is possible to argue, then, for processes of continued but fluctuating 'language reinforcement' in urban Gaelic-speaking, rather than for processes of direct 'language maintenance' amongst a younger but aging resident Gaelic-speaking population. The evidence relating to a stated decline of Gaelic amongst the Lowland-born children of Gaelic-speaking Highland-born parents would lend this hypothesis support (see above, and page 168). It is probable, however, that both processes were at work. Migrants, young economically active adults, moving from then strongly Gaelic-speaking parishes in the 1780s and 1790s, would have been just those persons for whom Gaelic chapels were erected and Gaelic services given. Their children, less commonly using Gaelic as the officers of Edinburgh Gaelic Chapel noted in 1807, would perhaps have known and used more Gaelic more commonly than the next generation, as, for example, the enumerators in Rothesay and in Glasgow in the mid-1830s reported. At the same time, Gaelic was being reinforced through the continued in-migration of persons from the Gaelic-speaking districts, albeit that such persons were, for reasons we have explored above, more familar with English in their native parishes than their migrant counterparts had been generations before. The Census does not, however, tell us when an individual left his or her native parish. For the two Gaelic-speaking women in their 90s in Aberdeen in 1891, for example (Table 7.2), we cannot know if they had migrated from their respective parishes of birth (Inverness, Dingwall) as young women, aged about 20 in the

1820s when Gaelic was still predominantly spoken in both places and, arguably, they would be more likely to know Gaelic and to speak it, or if they had moved only late in life from parishes that, during their lifetime, became more and more English-speaking, a trend which they did not themselves share for whatever reasons.

Further, it is impossible to know the extent of what may be called 'language transmission' from Census evidence alone: either the transmission of Gaelic from Highland-born Gaelic-speaking parents to their Lowland-born children or from a Gaelic-speaking to a non-Gaelic marriage partner, or, indeed, the learning of Gaelic in any town by persons not of Highland birth and with no previous connection with the language, the region, or even with Scotland. This is important since if it is the case that we must be careful to distinguish between urban Highlander and urban Gaelic speaker, so, too, the Census shows not all Gaelic speakers to have been Highlanders or, indeed, Scots. Two principal categories may be identified here: non-Highland-born, but Scottish-born, Gaelic speakers; and foreign-born enumerated speakers of Scottish Gaelic, in which category Irish-born Gaelic speakers represented the largest proportion. As noted, numbers in the first category (cf. Tables 7.3 and 7.5) include persons from parishes still quite strongly Gaelic but outwith the Highlands as here defined. The only Gaelic-only speaker in Dundee in 1891, for example – a 91–year-old man from Tomintoul – fell into that category. In the second category, it is not easy to know in detail the place of origin of the Irish-born in these towns since, for the majority, the 'where born' evidence in the enumerators' books lists only 'Ireland'. Many Irish in urban Scotland came from the north and north-west, from Donegal, Tyrone, Antrim and County Down, with relatively few from southern Ireland (although Dundee had several Irish families from Queen's County).[31] Irish was still commonly spoken in parts of north and west Ireland during the nineteenth century: by between 50 and 80 per cent of the population of parts of Donegal, for example, though by less than 10 per cent in parts of Country Antrim.[32] This is not proof, however, that what the Irish-born Gaelic speakers enumerated in these four towns were actually speaking or knew was Irish and not Scottish Gaelic. But the fact that so many Irish-born persons were enumerated as 'Gaelic speaking' may suggest that the published Census figures on Scottish Gaelic which have hitherto been taken as *accurate* totals of Scottish Gaelic speakers may not only not be accurate enumerations, but may also include numbers of persons with ability in Irish rather than *Scottish* Gaelic.

Given what we have noted of parish-level variations in patterns of Highland-Lowland migration to the larger towns of Glasgow and Edinburgh (see above, pages 92, 100), and in order to be able to relate language use more closely to occupation, similar questions can be posed at the parish scale.

Gaelic speaking in the urban Lowlands in 1891 at parish level: Partick parish, Glasgow, and St. Giles' parish, Edinburgh
The majority of the 3,456 Highlanders resident in Partick parish in 1891 had come from Argyll, with smaller proportions from the eastern parts of Ross and Cromarty and Inverness-shire together with several parishes from the north-west Highlands (cf. Figure 4.14). The total number of Gaelic speakers in Partick in 1891 according to the printed Census returns – 1,230 persons – represented about 6.8 per cent of the total Gaelic-speaking population within Glasgow City at that date. It is clear that Partick was a strongly 'Gaelic' part of the city. Following the methodology outlined above, it is possible to determine that, of this total number, 1,778 persons (51.45 per cent of the total Highland-born population) were enumerated as speaking Gaelic, with many more women than men professing ability in the language (Table 7.7). In terms of the strength of Gaelic speaking, by sex, within the Highland-born population, there was relatively little difference between male and female Gaelic speakers in Partick (59 per cent to 61 per cent, respectively). These proportions were significantly higher, however, than for the Highland-born Gaelic-speaking populations of Aberdeen, Dundee and Perth and broadly comparable with those of Stirling (cf. Table 7.6). In terms of age-range variation by sex in the relative strength of Gaelic speaking in Partick, it is interesting to note that amongst the much larger numbers of Highland-born Gaelic-speaking women, almost half of the overall total were between 20 and 34 years – in the younger working age-range – while, for men, Gaelic seems to have been spoken by roughly only one in ten Highland-born men across a much broader age range, between 20 and 49 years old (Table 7.8). Of the 321 persons who were enumerated as Gaelic speakers but who were not Highland-born, the greater part were Glasgow-born and Partick-born Gaelic-speaking children and, as for other towns we have considered in the context, by Irish-born individuals (Table 7.9).

It is difficult to know how far these circumstances to do with the relative strengh of Gaelic in Partick in 1891 are either applicable to other parishes in Glasgow then, or transferable over time. Knowing that, in 1891, about 60 per cent of the Highland migrants in the parish spoke Gaelic gives a numerical precision to earlier evidence about the relative strength of Gaelic in Glasgow, but, for the reasons discussed above as we have seen in connection with the 1835–36 'Gaelic census', we cannot be sure that such a proportion held true over time. Analysis at parish level

Table 7.7
GAELIC SPEAKING IN PARTICK PARISH, GLASGOW, 1891*

	Total Population	Male	Female
Total urban population	50,463	22,899	27,564
Total Highland-born population (as here defined)	3,456	1,063	2,393
and as % of total population	6.85	4.64	8.68
Total Gaelic-speaking population, from			
(a): Published Census volumes	1,230	(†)	(†)
(b): Enumerators' books	2,099	630	1,469
(c): (b) as % total urban population	4.16	2.75	5.33
Total Highland-born Gaelic-speaking population	1,778	488	1,290
and as % of total Highland-born	51.45	45.91	53.91
Total non-Highland-born Gaelic-speaking population	321	144	177
and as % of total Gaelic-speaking population	15.30	22.86	12.05
Male Gaelic speakers as % of total male Highland-born	59.27		
Female Gaelic speakers as % of total female Highland-born	61.39		

* From *Census of Scotland* and Enumerators' books.
(†) Not given in published *Census* by gender.

does make it possible, however, to link the fact of Gaelic speaking to occupational information and to say something about Gaelic language ability within families and households, particularly where persons were enumerated as 'Gaelic only' speakers. Partick's Gaelic-speaking Highland-born in 1891 were employed across a range of occupations with the majority in the middling ranks of society and in manual occupations. Thus, the presence of two surgeons, three church ministers, and one 'merchant clothier' amongst the male Highland-born Gaelic speakers in the parish was balanced by the large numbers of Highland women employed as 'cook', 'domestic servant', 'housemaid', and 'tablemaid' (246, 302, 161 and 92 persons respectively), and the handfuls of men employed in ship-building and related trades (143 persons), in metal-working (36), and the 27 'general labourers'. It is possible, of course, that Gaelic was spoken as the language of daily conversation by such persons, perhaps particularly where the nature of the job – like ship building and factory labour – brought people together in groups. The sheer diversity of

Table 7.8

AGE AND SEX STRUCTURE OF THE HIGHLAND-BORN GAELIC-SPEAKING
POPULATION IN PARTICK PARISH, GLASGOW, 1891*

Age group	Male No. in group	Percentage of Highland male Gaelic-speaking population	Female No. in group	Percentage of Highland female Gaelic-speaking population	Total population in group
0–4	1	0.21	3	0.23	4
5–9	1	0.21	4	0.31	5
10–14	7	1.43	10	0.78	17
15–19	29	5.94	85	6.59	114
20–24	64	13.12	304	23.57	371
25–29	62	12.70	302	23.41	364
30–34	50	10.25	154	11.94	204
35–39	52	10.65	100	7.75	152
40–44	53	10.86	90	6.98	143
45–49	51	10.45	63	4.88	114
50–54	34	6.97	54	4.19	88
55–59	22	4.51	34	2.64	56
60–64	28	5.74	27	2.09	55
65–69	17	3.48	30	2.33	47
70–74	3	0.61	19	1.47	22
75–79	7	1.43	5	0.39	12
80–84	5	1.02	5	0.39	10
85–89	2	0.41	–	–	2
90–94	–	–	1	0.08	1
95–99	–	–	–	–	–
100+	–	–	–	–	–
Totals	488	100.00	1,290	100.00	1,778

* From Enumerators' books.

occupation followed, however, together with the relative överall strength of Gaelic in Partick and in Glasgow as a whole in 1891 (cf. Tables 7.1 and 7.7) and the fact that all bar a few were returned as Gaelic *and English* speakers means that Gaelic cannot have been their only means of discourse.

Fifteen persons were enumerated as speaking Gaelic only in Partick in 1891, seven men and eight women. From the enumerators' returns in relation to household and family structure, we can speculate for them, and for many Highlanders speaking Gaelic and English, how Gaelic was used amongst city residents. Two of the seven male Gaelic-only speakers were Alan and John McFadden, aged 29 and 18 respectively, from Coll, both lodgers at 49 Dumbarton Road, in a lodging house shared with three other lodgers, two of whom also spoke Gaelic and English. Alan

Table 7.9

PLACE OF ORIGIN AND NUMBERS OF NON-HIGHLAND-BORN GAELIC SPEAKERS IN PARTICK PARISH, GLASGOW, 1891*

Elsewhere in Scotland

Aberdeenshire	2	'Lanark, Glasgow'	110
Ayrshire	10	'Lanark, Partick'	31
Dumbartonshire	7	Perthshire	49
Edinburgh	6	Stirlingshire	6
Fife	1	Orkney	1
Forfarshire	3		
Kincardineshire	1		
Kirkcudbright	1	TOTAL	252

Not in Scotland

East Indies	1	West Indies	1
England	3		
Ireland	63		
Glamorgan	1	TOTAL	69

*From *Census of Scotland* and Enumerators' books.

McFadden was a dock labourer; his namesake (and, probably, brother) was listed as a miller. Assuming the returns in respect of their being 'Gaelic only' speakers to be correct, how are we to envisage their use of language? In the household, we can clearly imagine that Gaelic would have been used to the other Gaelic-speaking lodgers (a 52–year-old Bute man and his four-year-old Glasgow-born daughter). It is possible, given the many Highland men then employed as dock workers in Glasgow (see page 143 above), that Alan McFadden would have been able to use Gaelic almost entirely in the workplace. But we must assume, too, that he and other purportedly 'monoglot' Gaels would have become more and more familiar with English, even if they did not use it themselves. The same patterns and the same difficulties must be presumed to hold for the case of the small household of three Gaelic-only speakers in 7 Anderson Street in 1891: Alexander Stewart, 29, a shipyard labourer from Foss in Perthshire, his 31–year-old wife, Flora, from Benbecula, and their 26–year-old visitor, Annie McLellan, also from Benbecula, employed as a domestic servant. Of other examples, it is possible to see evidence of a generational shift in languages, at least in recorded *ability* in language if not in actual speech patterns. In one residence at 89 North Street, for example, the head of household and his wife, Donald and Maggie McKay, 80 and 75 years old respectively, were both Gaelic-only speakers from Uig on Lewis, and were unemployed, having formerly been a general labourer and a domestic servant. Also present in the household were Mary McKay, their 10–year-old granddaughter born in Lanarkshire and given as a scholar, and John Chalmers, aged 18, also from Lewis, a seaman. Both young people spoke Gaelic and English. For the latter two, school-work and the nature of employment would certainly have made English the dominant daily language; familial and geographical ties would have made Gaelic the language of the home. But in the Islay-born Mutter family of 2 Ashgrove Terrace, where all six enumerated children – the oldest 16, the youngest 9 – spoke Gaelic and English, as did their parents, the use of language in the family and beyond the home would have been very varied.[33]

Similar complexities underlie the use of Gaelic amongst the 616 Gaelic speakers in Edinburgh's St Giles' parish in 1891. Of this total, 492 persons were Highland-born Gaelic speakers and Figure 7.1 shows the migration patterns of these Gaelic-speaking Highland migrants. Broadly, these migration patterns mirror those for Edinburgh as a whole and for Leith in the mid-nineteenth century (cf. Figures 4.6, 4.7 and 4.8), and the relatively large number of Highlanders from the Highland parishes in Sutherland and in Caithness noted in 1851 (Table 4.3) is repeated in 1891 and shown to be from two parishes in particular. In contrast with Partick, however, Gaelic speaking in St Giles' was largely dominated by men, the result of numbers of Highland-born students lodging near the University (25 in all), and, chiefly, of the 73 soldiers resident in the parish who were garrisoned in Edinburgh Castle. As with the other examples, a high proportion of the non-Highland-born Gaelic-speaking population were from Ireland. By the later nineteenth century, many of the Highland parishes from which these young men had come to study or soldier were much less strongly Gaelic than would have been true for their older migrant counterparts: all members of both groups were recorded as Gaelic and English speakers. Colm Rankin, a 26–year-old Gaelic-only speaker from Fortingall and boot cleaner in the Imperial Hotel in Market Street would certainly have found life difficult in his job if he had really had no English, but in the parish more widely, and in the city as a whole, English was known and, we must presume, used by all age groups within the Highland-born Gaelic population.

CONCLUSION

This chapter has illustrated that 'behind' what we know of the patterns of Highland-Lowland migration and of the varied use of Gaelic in Lowland Gaelic chapels lay very complex patterns of Gaelic language use. Over time, as Highlanders moved south, they were doing so from a region less and less strongly Gaelic. Gaelic use within the native Highland parishes and within the communities making up the urban *Gaidhealtachd* varied

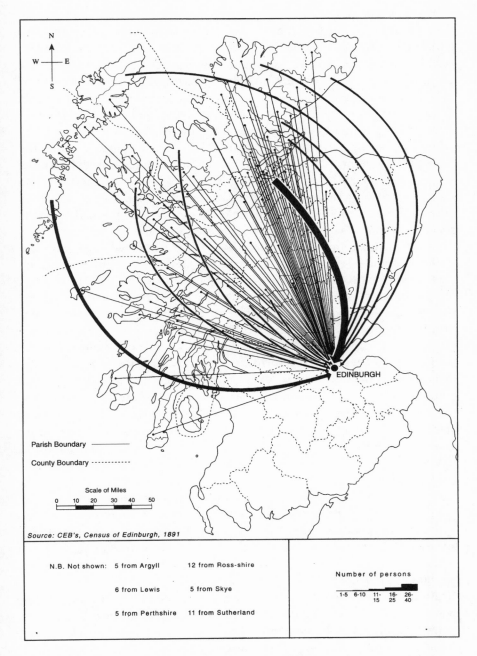

Parish Boundary ——————

County Boundary - - - - - - - - -

Scale of Miles

0   10   20   30   40   50

Source: CEB's, Census of Edinburgh, 1891

EDINBURGH

N.B. Not shown: 5 from Argyll   12 from Ross-shire

6 from Lewis   5 from Skye

5 from Perthshire   11 from Sutherland

Number of persons

1-5   6-10   11-   16-   26-
               15   25   40

Figure 7.1   *The migration of Highland-born Gaelic speakers to St Giles'*
parish, Edinburgh, 1891

by age, social domain and sex, and may even, given the distinctive nature of the migration patterns we have seen, have been reflected in dialectal variations in Gaelic speaking by Highland migrants within and between certain towns. Schools in the Highlands were important sites for the promotion of English and may have prompted migration, notably amongst the young. As one commentator noted of the Highlanders arriving in Glasgow in the 1840s, or, at least, of those arriving aged between 16 and 22, ('at which a great number of them come to Glasgow'), 'those taught in our schools in the Highlands are more disposed to come to Glasgow than those who are not taught, so that a great proportion can read; indeed, I know of very few of those who come to Glasgow to look for service and employment who cannot read, except those advanced in life'.[34] Not all urban Highland-born were Gaelic speakers. Many of those enumerated as Gaelic speakers in the urban Lowlands were not Scots-born.

Amongst those varying proportions in the urban Lowlands who were both Highland-born and Gaelic-speaking, Gaelic was spoken more by persons within the working age ranges – from about 20–24 to 60–64 years of age – than by persons either younger or older, but variations existed within this general picture according to the demographic and occupational structures of the urban Highland Gaelic-speaking populations in individual towns and parishes. At the family and household level, the 1891 Census enumerators' returns do list several Highland-born families or household members for whom each individual is recorded as Gaelic- (and English-) speaking, with, for one or two, an elderly Gaelic-only relative or a visitor professing ability only in Gaelic. But the most commonly occurring feature was the enumeration as Gaelic-speaking of one or both Highland-born parents with non-Gaelic-speaking children, followed by Gaelic heads of household, with one or more fellow householders, often from the same parish, recorded as speaking Gaelic. The part-Highland, part-Gaelic family or household was more common than either entirely Gaelic-speaking, wholly Highland-born families, or families and households where the eldest child and/or lodgers spoke Gaelic together with one or both parents. There is every reason to suppose Gaelic was spoken in the workplace but it was more commonly used in the home, as a language of spiritual devotion and of private communication. *Exactly* how it was used is not determinable from the Census evidence alone, and the complexity of individual usage patterns makes generalisation a hazardous affair. For many Gaels amongst the urban Highland populations, knowing Gaelic and actually using it, given the cultural status attaching to that language and to English, were very different things.[35] And given the numbers of Irish persons enumerated as Gaelic speakers, we ought to treat the Census itself with caution.

NOTES

1. M. Maclean, *The Literature of the Celts* (Glasgow, 1926), p.45 lists the following: *Ros-Roine* (1803); *An Teachdaire Gaidhealach* (1829–31); *An Teachdaire Ur Gaidhealach* (1835–36); *Cuairtear nan Gleann* (1840–43); *An Fhianuis* (1845–50, 1893); *Eaglais Shaor n h'Alba* (1875–93); *A Bheithir Bheuma* (1845); *Teachdaire nan Gaidheal* (1844); *Caraid nan Gael* (1844); *Fear Tathaich* (1848–50); and *Bratach n Firinn* (1873–74). This is to say nothing of the many English-language newspapers deliberately aimed at the urban Highlander (e.g., *The Glasgow Highlander*, which ran only for 1873) and those newspapers and broadsheets which aimed to capture contemporary interest in Celtic artistic and literary matters or actively to campaign for land reform such as John Murdoch's short-lived but influential *The Highlander*.

2. This is discussed in Charles Withers, *Gaelic in Scotland, 1698–1981: the geographical history of a language* (Edinburgh, 1984); Kenneth MacKinnon, *The Lion's Tongue* (Inverness, 1974); V. E. Durkacz, *The Decline of the Celtic Languages* (Edinburgh, 1983).

3. Sir John Sinclair (ed.), *Statistical Account of Scotland* (Edinburgh, 1791–99), 1795, XIV, p.343.

4. *OSA*, (1792), II, p.389.

5. *OSA*, (1794), XI, p.186.

6. John Low (ed.), *New Statistical Account of Scotland* (Edinburgh, 1831–45), 1838, Vol. 10, p.586.

7. On the question of the SSPCK and the evolution of its policies and the changing location of its schools etc, see V. E. Durkacz, 'The source of the language problem in Scottish education, 1688–1709', *Scottish Historical Review*, LVII (1978), pp. 28–39; D. J. Withrington, 'The SSPCK and Highland schools in the mid-eighteenth century', *Scottish Historical Review*, XLI (1962), pp. 88–99; Withers, *Gaelic in Scotland*, pp.120–137.

8. *Gaelic Schools Society Annual Report* (Edinburgh, 1811), Laws and regulations of the Society, Regulation IX.

9. M. Ó. Murchú, *East Perthshire Gaelic: social history, phonology, texts and lexicon* (Dublin, 1989), pp.3–7, 21–28.

10. The Rothesay survey material is contained in SRO, CH 2/111/9, ff.58–144. This extensive folio record has been much abbreviated here. A full summary of the principal evidence is presented in Charles Withers, 'A population observed: Gaelic speakers in Rothesay and the Isle of Bute in 1834', *Scottish Gaelic Studies*, XIV (II) (1986), pp.102–122.

11. SRO, CH 2/111/9, f.89.

12. Selkirk, Earl of, *Observations on the Present State of the Highlands of Scotland with a view of the causes and probable consequences of Emigration* (Edinburgh, 1806), p.xxxvii.

13. SRO, CH 2/111/9, f.109.

14. SRO, CH 2/111/9, f.93.

15. SRO CH 2/111/9, f.82.

16. BPP, *Second Report of the Commissioners of Religious Instruction, Scotland*, 1837–38, XXXII, p.194.

17. BPP, *Census of Scotland* (1881), Appendix, Table XII.

18. J. L. Campbell, *Gaelic in Scottish Education and Life* (Edinburgh, 1950),

pp.21–25; K. M. MacKinnon, *Gaelic in Scotland, 1971: some sociological and demographic considerations of the Census Report for Gaelic* (Hatfield, 1975), pp.15–19.

19. BPP, *Census of Scotland* (1881), I (l), p.iv.
20. See the discussions in the *Transactions of the Gaelic Society of Inverness* (1880–1883), X, p.59.
21. BPP, *Census of Scotland* (1881), I (l), p.iv.
22. C. Fraser-Mackintosh, 'The Gaelic Census of the counties of Inverness, Ross, and Sutherland', *Celtic Magazine* (1881), VI, pp.438–441.
23. On this point, see M. K. Macleod, 'The interaction of Scottish education developments and socio-economic factors on Gaelic education in Gaelic-speaking areas, with particular reference to the period 1872–1918' (unpublished Ph.D. thesis, University of Edinburgh, 1981), p.134.
24. The Census of Scotland enumerators' books are under a 100–year restriction, and, thus, those for 1891 are the first reliable available ones. The release to scholars of the enumerators' returns for the 1901 Census (from January 2001) will represent an important opportunity for further detailed study on Gaelic's geography, both in and of itself and in comparison with that evidence for 1891 presented here.
25. *NSA*, (1842), 12, p.651.
26. *NSA*, (1842), 13, p.303.
27. The published printed returns are given in BPP, *Census of Scotland*, 1891, XCIV, p.141.
28. In each of the four towns studied here, there were no boundary changes occurring which might explain the difference in recorded numbers between the published and unpublished forms of the 1891 Census. Like the censuses for 1861, 1871 and 1881, the 1891 Census was conducted on a house-to-house basis. In the 1891 census, we are told that each enumerator 'left at each dwelling-house within his district a Schedule . . . for the occupier or occupiers thereof, to be filled up by the same'. These schedules were then collected by the enumerators who 'copied all the particulars into the Enumeration Books, which, together with the schedules and other documents, were handed to the Local Registrars, who, after revising the work of the Enumerators, prepared Summaries of each District'. These summaries and the material on which they were based were sent to the sheriffs of the counties and to the chief magistrates of Scotland's eight principal towns, just those towns studied here, 'and, after being examined and approved by them, were forwarded to the Registrar General in Edinburgh' for printing and eventual publication (BPP, *Census of Scotland*, 1891, (1892), XCIV, p.ix). In this procedure, there are four stages at which errors in the numbers of Gaelic speakers may have occurred: first, at initial completion by the occupier; second, at the copying by the enumerator of the collected schedules into the enumerators' books; third, at the 'revising of the work' by the local registrars; and, lastly, at the final examination and approval of the forms by sheriffs and magistrates. Errors are most likely to have been made in transcription at stages two and three above, or, perhaps most likely, in original completion of the schedule by the occupants, although enumerators were required to check the returns insofar as they could. The original schedules no longer survive, so it is impossible to know for sure, but it is possible that the role and local knowledge of the enumerators played an important part in the actual numbers included

within any given qualitative category such as ability to speak Gaelic only or Gaelic and English, but this does not itself explain the numerical discrepancy between different forms of the same data. Enumerators and later census officials made a 'tally mark' across an individual's entry, the usual proof that they have been counted, checked and made ready to enter into the returns to be printed and published.

29. The detailed returns for Perth and Stirling, not presented here, are to be found in Charles Withers, 'Gaelic speaking in urban Lowland Scotland: the evidence of the 1891 Census', *Scottish Gaelic Studies*, 1990 (XVI), pp.115–148.
30. R. D. Lobban, 'The migration of Highlanders into Lowland Scotland, c.1750–1890, with particular reference to Greenock' (unpublished Ph.D., University of Edinburgh, 1969), p.288.
31. J. Handley, *The Irish in Scotland, 1798–1845* (Cork, 1945).
32. B. O Cuiv, *Irish Dialects and Irish-speaking Districts* (Dublin, 1971); R. Hindley, *The Death of the Irish Language* (London, 1991).
33. This information is derived from analysis of the Census enumerators' books for these parishes.
34. BPP, *First Report from the Select Committee on Emigration, Scotland* (1841), VI, p.119.
35. One such illustration of a complexity in language use being determined by the social context attaching to Gaelic appears in *The Highlander* for 10 February 1877. A speaker at the 1877 meeting of the Tiree Association in Glasgow, at pains to ensure his fellow-Highlanders used Gaelic in the city, recounted the tale of two young women from Tiree who were determined not to be stigmatised through their use of Gaelic: 'After they came to Glasgow . . . it was agreed they were not to talk Gaelic because the people would see they were Highland. When they met, the one said to the other 'How was you today?' 'Och', said Jean, 'she's very, she's very'.

CHAPTER 8

Conclusion

Mary Campbell, born in Dunoon, was an 18 year-old nurserymaid when she met the poet Robert Burns in Ayr in May 1786. Burns' brief encounter with his 'Highland Mary' could hardly have been longer: Mary Campbell died in Greenock in October of the same year, having lived and worked in Campbeltown between times.[1] Such circumstances, excepting perhaps the early death, illustrate several of the more general issues discussed in this book: Highland-Lowland migration, with an indication that the move from birthplace to recorded destination was neither direct nor permanent, and an occupation in the urban Lowlands which, we may speculate, allowed the despatch home of money useful to the Highland economy. Despite such a fleeting appearance on the historical stage, Mary Campbell is better known to us, however, than many of those Highland-born in Scotland coping with the reality of social transformation, migration and urban life in the eighteenth and nineteenth centuries. What motivated her move from Dunoon may not, of course, have been the same for others elsewhere and at other times and one must be cautious about generalising upon the aggregate experience from individual circumstances. There is, nevertheless, much that can be said in review of the characteristics of Highland-Lowland population movement, and of the nature of urban Gaelic culture.

THE PATTERNS AND NATURE OF HIGHLAND-LOWLAND MIGRATION

The first detailed picture of Highland-Lowland permanent migration is provided by the Census data for 1851. For that date, we can document at the level of individual supplying parishes the ways in which Highland migration to the Lowlands drew from discrete, but not mutually exclusive, parts of the Highlands. The south-west and west-central Highlands and southern Hebridean island parishes were the principal source areas for the western Lowland towns of Greenock, Paisley, and, notably, Glasgow, with longer-distance movement to all three places from the parishes of the north and west Highlands (cf. Figures 4.1 – 4.5). Edinburgh and Leith drew chiefly from the central and north-eastern Highlands with relatively large numbers from east Sutherland, while the great majority of Highland migrants to Dundee and Perth came from

230

Highland Perthshire and the east-central Highlands (cf. Figures 4.6 – 4.10). Stirling drew its relatively small Highland population mainly from north-east Argyll and south-west Highland Perthshire (Figure 4.13). Aberdeen's Highland migrants were drawn from the eastern parishes of Ross and Cromarty and Inverness-shire with relatively few from the north and west Highlands (Figure 4.12).

These more particular geographies of Highland-Lowland migration within that overall displacement that characterised Scotland in the second half of the nineteenth century (Table 2.3) are also apparent in the evidence of the 1891 Census. What is additionally clear by the latter date is the way in which a larger proportion of Highland migration was from the more distant north and west Highlands and Islands parishes than had been the case in 1851. It is clear for both dates that Highland-Lowland migration was made up not just of persistent patterns of rural out-movement, but also of similarly persistent migration from Highland towns and villages. Notable in this respect was migration from Campbeltown, Inveraray, Fort William and Oban to Glasgow, Greenock and Paisley in 1851; from Inverness and Dingwall to Edinburgh and Leith in 1851 (Leith also having relatively large numbers from Campbeltown: cf. Figure 4.8); and, perhaps most strikingly, the large numbers moving from Inverness and the smaller Highland towns and villages of Cromarty, Dingwall and Tain to Aberdeen, Dundee and Perth. Further, particular parishes within the predominantly rural Highlands were the source of relatively large numbers of migrants for certain towns: Portree and Sleat parishes to Greenock in 1851, for example (Figure 4.3); the eastern seaboard parishes of Sutherland and Caithness to Edinburgh in 1851 (Figure 4.6); and, for both 1851 and 1891, movement from the northernmost Skye parish of Kilmuir to Dundee (cf. Figures 4.10 and 4.18).

Although they provide a detailed picture at parish level of the geography of Highland-Lowland migration, the maps based on analysis of the Census material of 1851 and 1891 must, for several reasons, be treated with caution. The pictures we are given for both 1851 and 1891 do not record migration in those years, but for a period of time preceding the date of enumeration. For each of the towns whose Highland migration areas have been established for these respective dates, the migration patterns incorporate, then, the experiences of the oldest Highland-born, and those of the youngest. For the former, this *may* record a move undertaken over ninety years or more before enumeration: for the latter, movement must have been recent and part of a family move. It is likely, given the non-Census evidence examined here, that the regional geography of Highland-Lowland migration documented for the middle and later nineteenth century was apparent throughout the second half of the nineteenth century and that, in all probability, it held for the period from about 1820, at least for Dundee (cf. Figures 4.11, 4.15 and 4.16). And since the evidence in any one of these aggregate pictures embraces the 'life-time' migration of people who were born in the 1770s or, in the case of the Highland-born in Dundee's burial registers, in the 1740s, it is possible that the geography of Highland migration so clearly established here at the parish scale for 1851 holds also for at least the later decades of the eighteenth century, if not also from the 1750s. This claim would find support, for Greenock at least, from Lobban's assessment, using surnames and analysis of the parochial registers, of the birthplace of Highland men employed in the herring fishing based in that town which showed the vast majority in the early and mid-1700s to have come from the mainland and island parishes of south and west Argyll.[2] And the above chapters have documented the case of several individuals for the years before 1851 – for example, Norman Maclean born in North Uist in 1806 but a pauper in Glasgow in 1865 (Figure 3.3), or Alexander Forbes, Inverness-born but resident in Dundee from 1792 (page 101 above) – whose individual circumstances for earlier dates support the certain general evidence of later periods. Whilst we can with some confidence record the pattern of migration from the mid-nineteenth century onwards, it must remain the case that the earlier we get before 1851, the less certain we can be in detail of the geography of Highland-Lowland migration. Further, and for all supposed direct lifetime movement, it is clear that the experience of migration was of a move that was neither direct, nor, indeed, permanent.

The patterns of 'permanent' migration to the urban Lowlands were underlain by circuits of temporary and seasonal mobility, notably from the crofting parishes of the north and west. For some persons from these parishes (like the Waternish crofter in East Lothian: page 68), migration to the rural Lowlands was the custom of a lifetime. For others, it was a short-term expedient prompted by harvest failure, a decline in local fish stocks or a need for cash income. We know, too, that many persons often took several years to move south and did so either after having lived elsewhere in the Highlands, often in the nearest village or small town, or, even, after having lived elsewhere in Britain (see, for example, the case of 19-year-old Catherine McAllister claiming poor relief in Glasgow's Barony Parish in 1890 whose migration from Tarbert in Argyll involved two previous visits to that city as well as short stays in four other places, including Liverpool: Figure 3.3). Our understanding is complicated still further by the fact of the periodic residence in the Lowlands of Highlanders whose job either presupposed a short-term stay (at harvest labour or the east-coast fishing industry), or whose urban employment was often accompanied by considerable mobility (for women, for example, the position of domestic servant: consider, as a well-documented case, the experience of Christine Johnston in and around Glasgow between 1819 and 1852: Figure 5.2). For these individuals, as for Burns' Mary Campbell, we know that age at arrival was relatively young, and, therefore, that age at departure from their native parish was likewise young. If, in general, it is the case that most migrants before the middle years of the nineteenth century were young and single, we must also allow that much later migration was either as a family or of older, even elderly, adults. Further, for many persons, either as adult individuals or as members of a family, the move to the urban Lowlands was in stages and took years. Migration was, literally for some, the experience of a lifetime.

In explaining the geography and the nature of Highland-Lowland migration, we should not suppose the Highlands and the Lowlands separate regions whose integration into a national economy occurred only after the events of 1745–46 and later related moves to 'improvement'. Both regions were closely connected socially and economically long before then: in terms of temporary mobility of harvest labour from the mid-seventeenth century, in the movement of grain and livestock; in local systems of fishing, notably in southern sea lochs; in the ways in which Highlanders would move south temporarily to escape epidemic disease or the effects of a poor harvest; and, in some parts of the Highland-Lowland borders, by enduringly local marriage patterns. Highland-Lowland migration was prompted, then, not by the political circumstances of the eighteenth century, but by the accelerated nature of social and economic change that followed, and, from the early 1800s, by the increasingly rapid transformation of both the farming Highlands and, later, the crofting Highlands of the north and west. Temporary migration from the Highlands was a means to maintain a way of life in the Highlands and that it was not simply a consequence of agrarian change in either the farming or the crofting districts. Such movement, as with permanent migration, was affected by the changing relationships within the Highlands between the facts of economy and of demography: those of prices, rents and money income on the one hand, and, on the other, the number of people in relation to the resource base. Three broad phases have been noted in the connections between prices, rents and monetary income after about 1750: an expansive phase from 1750 to 1815, a period of decline and monetary collapse from 1815 to 1850, and a period of relative improvements in rentals and a rise in prices between 1850 and 1882 (see above, pages 35–36). Recognising that related explanation may not apply equally to all parishes, it is possible to suggest that the 'expansive phase' before 1815 was, in the farming Highlands, accompanied by out-migration as a result of farm engrossment – as in the case of Ardchattan and Muckairn in 1792 (see page 124) – whereas, in the crofting districts, the bulk of the population remained on the land, held there by the demands of landlords for kelp production, the widespread use of the potato as a subsistence crop, and, importantly, because of the seasonal rhythms and cash income derived from temporary migration. The return to the Highlands of temporary migrants may have contributed to the local economy but, in association with other exogenous changes, it also helped destabilise economic relationships in Highland parishes. As one commentator noted of Kilmore and Kilbride in Argyll in 1791:

> The excursions made to the Low Country, by the labourers and servants, may account, in a good measure, for *their* advancement in luxury, in dress and in living. These excursions have also made a considerable change on their language, and on their demand for wages, perhaps too little to their own advantage, and certainly not to that of their country.[3](original emphasis).

Migration increased throughout the Highlands after 1815 and, as permanent out-movement from the crofting parishes, was then much more than earlier the consequence of wholesale rural transformation – failure to pay the rent, decline in livestock prices, the collapse of kelp, estate clearance. As crofting became more firmly established, so temporary migration remained crucial to its survival. As Devine has shown, the potato famine was a crucial watershed in these patterns for the north and west Highlands: older persons and heads of household now moved out; parishes hitherto without traditions of labour mobility sent persons south; the time spent away was longer (see page 70). And to those conclusions we may add the fact of increased permanent out-movement of persons from especially destitute parishes, such as Kilmuir and Sleat on Skye, to several Lowland towns, notably to Paisley and Dundee. This particular migration flow was influenced both by the textile work established as a relief measure in those Highland parishes and the importance of that industry in those towns. In the farming Highlands, out-movement continued as a response to agricultural change as it did throughout the relative recovery of prices from the 1850s. People continued to re-locate permanently from the crofting Highlands in the decades after 1850 – as we have seen, more parishes from the farther north and west Highlands and islands were supplying more people by 1891 than earlier in the century – yet the crofters' relative security of the 1860s and 1870s was to a great extent dependent upon the cash income derived from by-employments and seasonal migration to the Lowlands.

Migration also had demographic effects in the Highlands, other than the permanent loss and seasonal draining of population. The out-movement of women in particular created an unbalanced sex ratio which led, in turn, to a rising age at first marriage, decreasing nuptiality and higher rates of age-specific marital fertility. One study of the islanders of Gigha in Argyll has shown, for example, that by the second half of the nineteenth century, no males and few females were married by the age of 25, that between 50 and 75 per cent of men aged between 25 and 50 were bachelors, often fishermen, and that between the ages of 50 and 64, over half remained unmarried. Proportions of single women were likewise high: 25 per cent of all women aged between 25 and 50 were unmarried in both 1851 and in 1861, a figure that rose to over 50 per cent in 1871 and 1881. The necessity for employment off the island necessitated both migration and demanded that marriage, if it was an option at all, was prudently planned. As the local minister noted in 1843, 'young men and women leave home for service at an early period, are absent for years and generally leave for about half the year'.[4] In consequence, the average age at first marriage in the parish by the second half of the nineteenth century was over 31 years of age for men, over 27 years for women, ages which were normal for the Highlands and Islands but almost three years older than the average for Scotland as a whole.[5] The relationships between migration, economy and Highland demography are, perhaps, accentuated in a small island parish like Gigha with its relatively low totals of vital events and almost total reliance upon employment elsewhere, and for these reasons Gigha should not be seen as 'typical' of the Highland experience. But it serves to illustrate that the facts of migration, however motivated, were an integral part of the ways Highlanders lived their lives.

The detailed regional geography of migration documented here is to be explained also by the relative demographic capacity of certain districts and parishes to shed population: this is particularly true for the farming Highlands as a whole and for the concentrations of people in Highland parishes such as Inverness and Campbeltown dominated by a town or large village. It is to be explained, too, by the relative movement of coastal trade and transport – from the western isles, north-west mainland parishes and Argyll to western urban Lowland towns such as Greenock and Glasgow, for example, and from Easter Ross and east Sutherland to Aberdeen, Dundee, Leith and Edinburgh. Industrialists such as George MacIntosh and David Dale influenced some migration south and it is clear from the evidence of the 1834 enquiry in Rothesay that that town and parish had received migrants from Mull in the early nineteenth century as a result of estate re-organisation there. Migrant institutions assisted individuals and families to move and assisted those persons from particular districts or parishes already resident in Lowland towns. For a few, this took the form of assistance to return home. Disease may have prompted some Highland migration, notably in the seventeenth century, and there is certainly evidence of moral judgement upon young Highland migrants returning home with 'the South Country disease'. The following extract relating to Kilmallie parish in 1792 documents something of such circumstances:

> It is a common practice for people to go hence to the low countries, in time of harvest, and return again in the beginning of winter. Within these very few years, a woman of this description came home, infected with a disorder that is a disgrace to human nature. Her father, who had been a stranger to the nature of her complaint, spoke to the minister about her;- and upon his enquiring what her disease was, answered, "I am entirely ignorant of it;-" it is such as I never heard of; neither did you, I am persuaded. – It is some *"low country disorder"*. It cannot be denied, however, but that the army have frequently introduced this same *too fashionable* disease, into Fort William and its neighbourhood.[6] (original emphasis).

By the same token, disease in the cities, or fear of contagion from returning migrants or visitors, restricted movement south. Hearing reports from the south of the cholera epidemic then affecting urban Scotland, the priest on South Uist wrote to his Bishop in Glasgow in May 1832, noting:

> Your Glasgow cholera has frightened us most completely – Not a boat is allowed to leave our shores to the South under pain of virtual banishment. . . . We have preventive guards in every harbour in the island; and unless we recover our senses, and the alarm is subsided by the time your Lordship proposes to visit us, I do not know with what safety you can approach our coast.[7]

Such local influences and circumstances will always underlie what is known about the general patterns and causes of Highland-Lowland migration. It has not proved possible here to document the causes of movement for each parish in the same detail as the numbers moving from particular Highland parishes to given Lowland towns. But the general nature of the 'push' factors has been determined. Particularly in relation to the seasonal circulation of labour, what characterised the Highlands was little different from the movement of rural labour in many countries in Europe, notably those bordering the North Sea. Migration was a commonplace – for many, a way of life – between two regional economies. Permanent migration increased because of major alterations in the nature of economy and society in both Highlands and Lowlands. Increased levels of permanent migration from the later eighteenth century were apparent in the emergence in the urban Lowlands of numerous Highland cultural institutions whose foundation reflected the transformation of Highland life and whose purpose was to assist urban Highlanders make new lives for themselves.

THE MAKING OF URBAN GAELIC CULTURE

In one sense, permanent Highland-Lowland migration and the establishment of institutions like the Glasgow Highland Society extended the Scottish *Gaidhealtachd* in the same ways as the foundation of Highland newspapers in south Australia, for example, or the replication of Highland tenurial patterns by Glengarry emigrants in Upper Canada or the use of Gaelic by Highland congregations in North Carolina until the 1860s all reflected that new global *Gaidhealtachd* being established in consequence of overseas emigration.[8] At the simplest level – that of being Highland-born – it is possible to say that there was, indeed, a new *Gaidhealtachd* being made in the urban Lowlands from at least the early 1700s. But it is quite another thing to suppose that this migrant Highland presence was the result of Highlanders establishing an urban 'migrant culture' based alone on the replication in that context of beliefs and attitudes they had brought with them from 'traditional Highland culture'. For one thing, it is not helpful to consider Highland culture as an absolute and essential 'thing' since, as has been shown, economic conditions differed between districts and over time, Gaelic was not used for all social purposes by all people in the Highlands, and Highland 'culture' depended for some upon familiarity with life beyond that region. For another, this book has shown that the facts of geographical mobility were also ones of occupational change: from crofters to Glaswegian policemen, for example, from the daughter of the house to somebody else's domestic servant, from fisherman-crofter for one part of the year to railway labourer for another part before again being a land worker back home. For such people, as for most urban Highlanders, what we must loosely consider 'migrant culture' was locally made, and in a variety of ways, and was not a matter of bringing with them to the cities 'residual' beliefs from an archetypical culture area. The nature of the evidence presented above, chiefly in Part Three, lends itself to the general conclusion that we ought not to refer to migrant Highland culture in the singular, but to *a diversity of cultures* in which distinctions were based on social status and class, different geographical origins and related institutional affiliation, even perhaps residence, and the use of Gaelic. In this respect, we should note the important distinction between urban Highlander and urban Gaelic speaker since, as has been shown, the two terms were not strictly synonymous.

It is tempting, nevertheless, to see the foundation and continuation of Gaelic chapels in the urban Lowlands as indicative of a separate urban Highland culture or, even, 'sub-culture'. In earlier work, I subscribed to such a view myself.[9] After all, these were institutions largely established *by* Highlanders *for* Highlanders with the intention of providing worship in Gaelic, a language preferred by many and which was, for some, the only language they could understand. Highlanders contributed to the building costs and the salary of Gaelic-speaking ministers, and church authorities were diligent in securing suitable men. Many chapels provided poor relief for destitute Highlanders and congregation members orga-nised the collection of funds amongst local citizenry, either to maintain schools in the Highlands, for example, or to lessen hardship during the potato famine. And, for some, the fact of being a Highland-born, Gaelic-speaking, and chapel-going resident of Glasgow with kin in a particular part of the Highlands no doubt signified an identity of sorts. But closer examination of the role of Gaelic chapels reveals them to have been institutions dealing not with a coherent 'migrant identity' based on shared birthplace and language, but with social difference, diversity and ambivalence *within* the urban Highland populations. Three related sets of evidence, detailed more fully above, support this conclusion. Firstly, it is clear that those persons advancing the funds, securing leases and negotiating with presbyterial authorities saw in these chapels a means to extend civilisation and moral improvement through regular worship rather than maintain Highland identity through the use of Gaelic. The use of Gaelic was designed to extend a desire for social advance that was otherwise synonymous with English only, and it was because of such generally-held cultural sensibilities as well as the particular views of local people, and only lastly because of an increasing familiarity with the language amongst Highlanders and their children, that English services were introduced. Secondly, Gaelic was not alone used in these chapels. Where it was used, it was seen, even by some Highlanders, as a 'second-rate' language, and, as the evidence for Glasgow's Gaelic chapels in the 1830s most notably suggests, it was continued as the language of worship only as a result of the sums received from the seat rents paid by the better-off Highlanders attending English-language services. Knowing and speak-ing Gaelic in the urban Lowlands outwith the confines of the chapel may have tended towards a certain sense of identity, but Gaelic's use in chapels was both cause and effect of marked social differences within the chapel-going migrant populations. Thirdly, it is clear that not all those who wanted to attend Gaelic chapels could attend. The problem of 'Highland Home Heathenism', evident most particularly amongst the less well-off urban Highland populations, was the result, in combination, of an aversion to seat rents, lack of appropriate clothing, and distance from the chapels and churches. These matters are partly to be explained by reference to Highlanders' prior cultural circumstances rather than to any innate beliefs – the fact that seat rents were unknown to most of them – and partly, too, by reference to the local circumstances they encountered upon living in towns and cities: distance from chapel, jobs which demanded work on Sundays, and so on. For these reasons, then, wealth and social status divided the urban Highland-born chapel-going population, however much Gaelic's use as the language of religion was widely preferred or seen by contemporaries as having the greater rhetorical force, or the shared fact of being born in the Highlands or migrants in one close or household all being from the same parish otherwise lent such people an identity. The evidence of increased familiarity with English amongst the Lowland-born children of Highland parents points also to a diversity within the urban Highland populations which is belied in assuming the term 'migrant culture' to be a singular shared thing.

In simple terms, the picture we are afforded from examination of chapel records, for the mid and later nineteenth century especially, is of a social polarisation between the better-off Gaels who could afford to attend services, Gaelic or English, and of larger numbers of non-attending urban Highlanders who remained without regular worship. But urban Highland populations were also divided internally, in terms of affiliation through particular organisations to particular parts of the Highlands if not directly to the parish of one's birth. Such organisations generally shared a similar philanthropic rationale: financial support for fellow Highlanders from that district or island, for example, as well as an interest in the economic condition of one's native parish. But the very fact that there were so many bodies with *particular* loyalties, and that the membership of such bodies was divided along class lines, argues against a *general* Highland identity and further supports the idea of diversity among, rather than a simple polarisation within, the urban Highland-born populations. Given the circulatory nature of much Highland-Lowland migration, it is possible to argue, too, that what such urban migrants would have understood as their 'culture' was determined neither by unswerving adherence to beliefs and practices they brought with them, including using Gaelic, nor by wholesale rejection of such things and adoption of Lowland ways upon city residence. Rather, their culture was an amalgamation of both, a mixing that was itself dependent upon their circulation between two different parts of Scotland and something for which we must admit the possibility of change during migrants' lives as, for example, they married a non-Gaelic speaker, took up a new job, moved to a new part of town. Urban migrant culture was, as a lived experience, then, always 'fluid', ambivalent, shifting. For some, like the 91–year-old Gaelic-only speaker from Tomintoul in Dundee in 1891 (assuming him to be genuinely without any ability in English), getting by would have demanded a reliance upon Gaelic simply not shared by other Highlanders. For others, it is clear that attachment to particular migrant institutions, or membership of a Gaelic church, was central to their place in the city, to helping make sense of their 'new' world whilst retaining connections with their 'old' world. But such practices would not have been – because, for most, they *could* not have been – at the expense of other social relationships made with non-Highland-born or non-Gaelic-speaking in the course of daily life.

The idea of diversity within urban Gaelic culture is evident in what has been shown of the nature of Gaelic speaking in the urban Lowlands. Not all Highland-born spoke Gaelic, at least according to analysis of the 1891 Census, and linguistic divisions were apparent even within the earliest chapel congregations. Not all Gaelic speakers were Highland-born, or, even, born in Scotland, and, given the relatively large numbers of Irish-born enumerated as speaking 'Gaelic' in Scotland's cities in the late nineteenth century, we must, as contemporary commentaries recognised but for different reasons, doubt the accuracy of the Census totals for the numbers of *Scottish* Gaelic speakers. Distinctions by age and sex in the reported ability to speak Gaelic have been noted for the Highland-born population of several towns (see Tables 7.2 and 7.4), and, in general, it has been established that, of the Highland-born population in those places, between about 40 and 60 per cent only spoke Gaelic (Table 7.6). Clearly establishing differences in the use of Gaelic by particular social domains has not been possible: even where we can document reported ability in Gaelic within families or household units, we can only infer the day-to-day usage patterns from, say, a Gaelic-speaking head of household to a Gaelic-speaking relative from the same parish lodging there, or from Highland-born Gaelic-speaking parents to their Gaelic-speaking but city-born children. Most children of Highland and Gaelic parents were also familiar with English, a pattern that is clear for Highland children in early nineteenth-century Edinburgh, for example, in mid-nineteenth-century Glasgow and in several towns, for which there is more systematic documentation, in 1891. At the same time as Gaelic was less commonly spoken by the children of Highland-born Gaelic speakers in urban Scotland, so it was being replaced in the Highlands proper, chiefly through schooling and as a result of the gradual extension of English influences there, but also through returning migrants mixing the two languages together. In general, Gaelic's relative strength in the urban Lowlands was probably maintained more by the continual in-movement of Highlanders who did speak the language and by its regulated use in church and migrant club than as a direct result of transmission down the generations. *How* Gaelic was used differed greatly: a very few migrants would, we may speculate, have had no alternative; some spoke it in chapel and at work whilst others would have used it only within the confines of the home, to close relatives, or in catching up on home news from a newly arrived migrant. Such details are not recoverable from Census statistics.

Migrant identity depended, then, on more than shared place of birth or common use of Gaelic. Identifying Highlanders as migrants by virtue of a particular place of birth is a factually based methodological distinction which, as fact, is not open to interpretation. What I have tried to suggest in this book, however, is that that distinction was itself internally diverse, and, further, that an identity as 'urban Highlander' determined simply from such analytic characteristics may have had little *actual* meaning for such persons themselves, however much it served to distinguish them as migrants in the eyes of contemporaries. For some migrants, a sense of Highland identity may have been maintained precisely *because* they used Gaelic in everyday life in Glasgow's Gallowgate, as, for others nearby, a shared sense of Highlandness was felt *despite* not speaking Gaelic. Some individuals, notably the ministers of urban Gaelic charges, effected a compromise with different sections of the migrant population as, at the same moment, they liaised on their behalf with other sections of society. Men like the Rev. Dr. Norman MacLeod, whose testimonies here have been especially valuable, looked to the lower-class Highlanders in the ways they did because they were amongst the less well-off in Scottish society, not just because they were Highland-born. Urban Highland identity was socially diverse, a class not a mass phenomenon.

A FUTURE AGENDA

No one book can ever reproduce the full range of evidence it rests upon. It may well be that others will dispute the conclusions I have arrived at, and it is certainly feasible that new source material might be found whose analysis would add to the issues explored here. It is possible, if unlikely, that the original volumes of the 1830s Glasgow 'Gaelic Census' survive:[10] data contained there on the occupation, residence and birthplace of Glasgow's Gaelic-speaking population for that period would certainly take further our understanding of several of the issues discussed here. Nor should one book claim to have exhausted the research area or to have offered 'the last word'. I do not do so here. Several related possibilities suggest themselves for further work. They may be enumerated under two headings: different geographical and social scales, and different time periods.

This book advances understanding of the nature and geography of Highland-Lowland migration by, in part, assessing aggregate numbers from Highland parishes in 1851 and in 1891 to particular Lowland towns. This has had the effect of centring the focus of research upon the towns rather than upon the Highlands. Keeping for the sake of consistency the same definition of the Highlands as used here, it would be possible, if time-consuming, to reverse that focus, as it were, and to trace for individual Highland parishes the numbers of migrants in individual towns and urban parishes, and to do so for the intervening years of 1861, 1871 and 1881 in order to establish in greater detail the consistency of the migration patterns established here for the middle and end of the nineteenth century. Levels of migration at the parochial scale could then be related to trends in vital registration in those places and to local economic and social circumstances. There are sufficient pointers here to the local nature of change in given parishes and to the presence of particular organisations. Other, smaller places, such as the north-east-coast fishing villages, which had seasonal influxes of migrants, could also be examined. A complete survey of Glasgow's Highlanders could be undertaken using the 1891 Census. This is to note, then, the possibilities for *informed local studies*, mindful of the criteria of definition, analytical methods and general context established here.

Not enough is known of marriage patterns amongst the urban Highland-born and between such people and 'native' Lowlanders, despite important preliminary work in this direction.[11] More needs to be known in a systematic way of the different levels of reported ability in Gaelic speaking within the family and the household. It should be possible, for example, to identify all Gaelic-speaking lodgers and boarders resident in a particular place in the 1891 Census, and, therefore, to know both by how many temporarily resident persons the number of urban Gaelic speakers was inflated, and where they came from. This is to call for assessment of language use background within *different Highland social units* in towns and cities. Closely related to that question is the extent to which the levels of Irish-born recorded as Gaelic speakers for Aberdeen, Dundee, Perth and Stirling hold true of other Scottish towns. Further, and upon the release to researchers in 2001 of the enumerators' books for 1901, it should be possible to compare the conclusions advanced here with respect to language use in 1891 with those of a decade later. For those persons who resided in the same place over the intervening period, it should be possible to know if some, particularly children, declared themselves as non-Gaelic speakers having earlier reported ability in the language. These and other questions underlie what we might term the *comparative analysis of recorded ability in Gaelic.*

This book effectively ends analysis at 1900, an 'ending' influenced by the date of the most recent detailed Census material on language available to me and for reasons of space and focus. It is quite clear, however, from the continued presence of Highland clubs and societies and from the continued use of Gaelic in church services in several Scottish towns today that the story of the urban Highlander could be brought up to the present. Writing *a history of urban Highlanders after 1900* would demand the use of interviews and other qualitative methodologies and might, indeed, be best done not by the 'external' researcher but by Highlanders themselves as 'native' knowledge could be brought to bear upon an experience they either more recently shared or have memories of relatives doing. Finally, of course, this book has documented and explored differences within and between Highland Scotland and an urban Gaelic Scotland and shown how the two have been intimately connected. But the cultural and historical geography of Gaelic has involved not just the making of that diverse urban *Gaidhealtachd* which has been the subject of study here, but the creation of new *Gaelic geographies overseas* that are 'hidden' within what is known of Highland emigration and the Highlander abroad.

NOTES

1. N. Hill, *The Story of the Old West Kirk of Greenock* (Greenock, 1878), p.84.
2. R. Lobban,'The Migration of Highlanders into Lowland Scotland', unpublished Ph.D. thesis, University of Edinburgh, 1969, see Section 1.
3. *OSA*, 1791–92, XI, p.127.
4. *NSA*, 1843, 7, p.402.
5. M.Storrie, ' "They Go Much from Home": nineteenth-century islanders of Gigha, Scotland', *Scottish Economic and Social History* 16, 1996, pp.92–115; M.Flinn *et al, Scottish Population History* (Cambridge, 1977), p.317.
6. *OSA*, 1792, VIII, p.437.
7. Scottish Catholic Archives, Oban Letters, OL 1/7/12. Letter from John Chisholm, South Uist, to Bishop Scott, Glasgow, 14 May 1833.
8. D. Meyer, *The Highland Scots of North Carolina* (Raleigh, CA., 1963), p.47.
9. I certainly subscribed to an essential place for the Gaelic chapel in earlier work on eighteenth-century Glasgow, but notes of uncertainty about this point can also be traced in more detailed analysis of the Edinburgh Gaelic chapel at the same time: see Charles Withers, 'Highland Clubs and Gaelic Chapels: Glasgow's Gaelic community in the eighteenth century', *Scottish Geographical Magazine* 101, 1985, pp.16–27; and, *idem,* 'Kirk, Club and Culture Change: Gaelic chapels, Highland Societies and the urban Gaelic sub-culture in eighteenth-century Scotland', *Social History* 10, 1985, pp.171–192.
10. I have checked all major manuscript record depositories in Scotland, all copy-

right libraries in Britain, and in the House of Lords' library and archives, and enquired of all relevant Church authorities.

11. MacKenzie offers some analysis to this effect for parts of Glasgow in 1881, noting, in general, that the vast proportion of marriages were taking place after migration and that 'Highlanders were overwhelmingly choosing to marry other Highlanders': J. MacKenzie, 'The Highland Community in Glasgow in the Nineteenth Century', unpublished Ph.D. thesis, University of Stirling, 1987, p.194. How far this would hold for all towns and over time would offer further insight into the relationships *within* Highland populations in given places and, perhaps, *between* Highland parishes and migrants in the Lowlands if, for example, circulatory migration by one partner in order to obtain sufficient income prior to marriage led, in turn, to the mobility of the partner and their permanent residence in the city.

Bibliography

PRIMARY SOURCES

Manuscript sources

Scottish Record Office

Church of Scotland Records

Records of the General Assembly of the Church of Scotland	CH1/1 and CH 1/2
Register Minutes of the Synod of Angus and Mearns	CH 2/12
Register Minutes of the Presbytery of Dunoon	CH2/111
Register Minutes of the Presbytery of Glasgow	CH2/171
Register Minutes of Kingarth Kirk Session	CH2/219
Register Minutes of the Presbytery of Paisley	CH2/294
Register Minutes of Kilmore Kirk Session	CH2/434
Register Minutes of the Synod of Perth	CH2/449
Register Minutes of the Presbytery of Greenock	CH2/517
Register Minutes of the Presbytery of Dumbarton	CH2/546
Register Minutes of the Synod of Argyll	CH2/557
Register Minutes of Edinburgh Gaelic Chapel	CH2/766
Register Minutes of Rothesay Gaelic Chapel	CH2/891
Register Minutes of the Managers of Hope Street Gaelic Chapel	CH16/3

Free Church of Scotland Records

Register Minutes of the Free Synod of Argyll	CH3/26
Register Minutes of the Free Presbytery of Dunoon and Inveraray	CH3/100
Register Minutes of the Deacon's Records, Dundee Free Gaelic Church, Meadowside, Dundee	CH3/322
Register Minutes of Chapelhill Free Gaelic Church, Rothesay	CH3/487
Register Minutes of the Kirk Session of Govan St. Columba's Free Highland Mission	CH3/645
Register Acts of the Assembly of the Free Church	CH3/665
Register Minutes of the Kirk Session of St. Stephen's Free Gaelic Church, Perth	CH3/697
Register Minutes of West United Free Church (St. Matthew's Highlanders' Memorial Church), Glasgow	CH3/972
Register Minutes of the Highlands and Islands Committee	CH3/983
Register Minutes of Glasgow Highlanders' Memorial Church	CH3/992
Register Minutes of the Kirk Session of St. Columba's, Greenock	CH3/1157

Other SRO papers

Report on the Cottar Population of the Lews, 1888	AF67/402
Sheriff Ivory Papers	GD1/36
Campbell of Stonefield Papers	GD14
Marquis of Lothian Muniments	GD40
Seaforth Papers	GD46
Register Minutes of the General Meetings (1708–1878) of the Society in Scotland for Propagating Christian Knowledge	GD95/1
Report of the Committee regarding the Stipend of the Minister of the Gaelic Chapel [Edinburgh]	GD95/14/26
Nomination by the SSPCK in favour of the Rev. Hugh Macleod as Minister of the Gaelic Church in Edinburgh, 20 Sept. 1837	GD95/14/31
Breadalbane Muniments	GD112
Maclaine of Lochbuie Papers	GD174
Lord MacDonald MSS	GD221
Census of the Inhabitants of Blair Drummond Moss, 1814	GD321/1
Highland Destitution Papers	HD1 *et seq*

Manuscript Census Enumerators' Books for 1851 for the towns of Aberdeen, Dundee, Edinburgh, Glasgow, Greenock, Paisley, Perth and Stirling, and for 1891 for Aberdeen, Dundee, Perth and Stirling and for the Glasgow parish of Partick and for St. Giles' parish, Edinburgh

National Library of Scotland

State of Emigration from the Highlands of Scotland, its extent, its causes and proposed remedy	Adv.MS 35.6.18
Sibbald Papers	Adv.MS. 33.5.16
Observations on the North of Scotland, 1796	MS 1034
Letters on Distress in the Highlands, 1837	MS 1054

Central Region Archives

General Register of Poor for Stirling	SB11 (1845–1891)

Dundee Central Library

Dundee Highland Society Papers	MS 55; MS 118; MS 190; MS 273; MS 316; MS 368

Dundee City Archives

Howff Burial Ground Registers
Register of Inmates of Dundee East Poorhouse, 1856–1878

Bibliography

Edinburgh University Library

Report to the Commissioners for Improving fisheries and manufactures in Scotland on the State of Industry and Trade in the Highlands and Islands, 1755 — La. II. 623

Mitchell Library, Glasgow (formerly Strathclyde Regional Archives)

General Register of the Poor for Glasgow, 1845–1891 — D/HEW 10 *et seq* and D/HEW 14 *et seq*

Register of Police — SR22/55

Record of the Gaelic Society in Glasgow (Gaelic Club of Gentlemen), 1780–1936 — TD746

Sandeman Library, Perth

Tibbermore Parochial Board Register of Poor, 1855–1890

General Registers of Poor, Kinnoull Parish, 1845–1890

Records relating to the Gaelic Chapel, May 1795 — MS B.59.28.183

Records relating to the Gaelic Chapel, 1848 — MS PE1/54/5

Scottish Catholic Archives, Edinburgh

Blairs Papers — BL4

Oban Papers — OL1

Printed Primary Sources

Parliamentary Papers

Census of Scotland, 1851, LXXXVIII; 1861, I; 1871, I, II; 1881, I, II; 1891, CVII

Commission of Inquiry into the Condition of Crofters and Cottars in the Highlands and Islands of Scotland, 1884–1885, XXXII–XXXVI

First Report from the Select Committee on Emigration, Scotland, together with the Minutes of Evidence and Appendix, 1841, VI

Fourth Report on the Employment of Children, Young Persons and Women in Agriculture, 1870, XIII

Papers relative to Emigration to the North American Colonies, 1852, XXXIII

Relief of the Distress in Scotland: correspondence, from July 1846 to February 1847, relating to the measures adopted for the relief of the distress in Scotland, 1847, LIII

Report from the Select Committee on Hand-loom Weavers' Petitions, 1834, X

Report of the Central Board for the Relief of Destitution in the Highlands and Islands of Scotland, 1847, LIII

Report of the Poor Law Inquiry Commission for Scotland, 1844, XXVII–XXXVI

Report of the Select Committee on the Health of Towns, 1840, XI

Report on the State of the Irish Poor in Great Britain, 1836, XXIV

247

Report to the Board of Supervision by Sir John McNeill GCB on the Western Highlands and Islands, 1851, XXVI
Second Report of the Commissioners of Religious Instruction, Scotland, 1837–38, XXXII

Reports and Institutions

Address from the Presbytery of Paisley to Friends Interested in the Moral, and Spiritual Welfare of the Highlanders, Residing out of Paisley and within the Bounds of the Presbytery (Paisley, 1816)
Constitution and Rules of the Mull and Iona Association (Glasgow, 1867)
Extract of Regulations by the General Assembly for the Gaelic Chapel of Aberdeen (Aberdeen, 1820)
First Report of the Society in Paisley and its Vicinity for Gaelic Missions to the Highlands and Islands of Scotland (Paisley, 1818)
List of Members of Glasgow Highland Society (Glasgow, 1831)
List of Members of Glasgow Highland Society (Glasgow, 1861)
Rules and Regulations of the Dundee Highland Society (Dundee, 1815, 1824, 1840)
The Scheme of Erection of the Highland Society in Glasgow (Glasgow, 1787)
Third Annual Report of the Lewis Association (Glasgow, 1879)
View of the Scheme of Erection of the Highland Society in Glasgow (Glasgow, 1831)

Unpublished theses consulted

Gauldie, E., 'Scottish bleachfields, 1718–1862', B.Phil., University of Dundee, 1962
Lobban, R., 'The migration of Highlanders into Lowland Scotland (*c*.1750–1890) with particular reference to Greenock', Ph.D., University of Edinburgh, 1969
Mackenzie, J., 'The Highland Community in Glasgow in the Nineteenth Century', Ph.D., University of Stirling, 1987
Macleod, M., 'The interaction of Scottish education developments and socio-economic factors on Gaelic education in Gaelic-speaking areas, with particular reference to the period 1872–1918', Ph.D., University of Edinburgh, 1981
McCleery, A., 'The role of the Highland Development Agency, with particular reference to the work of the Congested Districts Board, 1897–1912', Ph.D., University of Glasgow, 1914
Robertson, I., 'The historical geography of rural social protest in Highland Scotland 1919–1939', Ph.D., University of Bristol, 1995
Sloan, W., 'Aspects of the Assimilation of Highland and Irish Migrants in Glasgow, 1830–1870', M.Phil., University of Strathclyde, 1987

SECONDARY SOURCES

Adam, R., *Sutherland Estate Management* (Edinburgh, 1972)
Agnew, J., 'Liminal travellers: Hebrideans at home and away', *Scotlands* 3, 1996, pp.32–41

——, and Cox, K., 'Urban in-migration in historical perspective: an approach to measurement', *Historical Methods* 12, 1979, pp.145–155

Amit-Talai, V., and Knowles, C. (eds.), *Re-situating Identities: the Politics of Race, Ethnicity and Culture* (Peterborough, Ontario, 1992)

Anderson, B., *Imagined Communities* (London, 1991 edition)

Anderson, J., 'Essay on the present state of the Highlands and Islands of Scotland', *Transactions of the Highland and Agricultural Society of Scotland* II, 1831, pp.16–45

Anderson, M., *Population Change in North-Western Europe, 1750–1850* (London, 1987)

Anderson, W., 'The Edinburgh Highland Chapel and the Rev. Robert Menzies', *The Innes Review* 17, 1966, pp.195–202

Anthony, R., *Herds and Hinds: Farm Labour in Lowland Scotland, 1900–1939* (East Linton, 1997)

Bailyn, B., *Voyagers to the West: Emigration from Britain to America on the Eve of the Revolution* (London, 1987)

Bain, R., 'A Highland industrial pioneer: George Macintosh', *Transactions of the Gaelic Society of Glasgow*, 1939, pp.179–190

Baines, D., *Migration in a Mature Economy: Emigration and Internal Migration in England and Wales, 1861–1900* (Cambridge, 1985)

——, *Emigration from Europe* (London, 1991)

Bauman, Z., *Modernity and Difference* (Oxford, 1991)

Black, R., 'The Gaelic Academy: the cultural commitment of the Highland Society of Scotland', *Scottish Gaelic Studies* 14, 1986, pp.1–38

Blaikie, J., *Illegitimacy, Sex and Society: Northeast Scotland, 1750–1900* (Oxford, 1993)

Bil, A., *The Highland Sheiling* (Edinburgh, 1988)

Boswell, J., *Journal of a Tour of the Hebrides* (Oxford, 1970 edition)

Brown, C., 'The costs of pew-renting: church management, church-going and social class in nineteenth-century Glasgow', *Journal of Ecclesiastical History* 38, 1987, pp.347–361

Campbell, J., *Gaelic in Scottish Education and Life* (Glasgow, 1950 edition)

Canny, N., *Europeans on the Move* (Oxford, 1994)

Carter, I., 'Economic models and the recent history of the Highlands', *Scottish Studies* 15, 1971, pp.99–120

——, 'Marriage patterns and social sectors in Scotland before the eighteenth century', *Scottish Studies* 17, 1973, pp.51–60

——, *Farm Life in Northeast Scotland, 1840–1914* (Edinburgh, 1979)

Cohen, A. (ed.), *Belonging: Identity and Social Organisation in British Rural Cultures* (Manchester, 1982)

The Symbolic Construction of Community (Chichester and London, 1985)

'Owning the nation, and the personal nature of nationalism: locality and the rhetoric of nationhood in Scotland', in Amit-Talai and Knowles, *Re-situating Identities: the Politics of Race, Ethnicity and Culture*, pp.267–282

Chapman, M., *The Gaelic Vision in Scottish Culture* (Beckenham, 1978)

Clark, P., and Souden, D. (eds.), *Migration and Society in Early Modern England* (London, 1987)

Cleland, J., *Enumeration of the Inhabitants of Glasgow* (Glasgow, 1820)

——, *Rise and Progress of the City of Glasgow* (Glasgow, 1832)

Clyde, R., *The Image of the Highlander 1745–1822* (East Linton, 1995)

Connolly, S., Morris, R.J., and Houston, R. (eds.), *Conflict, Identity and Economic Development: Ireland and Scotland 1600–1939* (Lancaster, 1995)

Craig, D., *On the Crofters' Trail: in search of the Clearance Highlanders* (London, 1990)

Cregeen, E., 'The tacksmen and their successors: a study of tenurial reorganisation in Mull, Morvern, and Tiree in the early eighteenth century', *Scottish Studies* 13, 1969, pp.93–114

——, 'The changing role of the House of Argyll in the Scottish Highlands', in Phillipson and Mitchison (eds.), *Scotland in the Age of Improvement* (Edinburgh, 1970), pp.5–23

Cullen, L., 'Incomes, social classes and economic growth in Ireland and Scotland, 1600–1900', in Devine and Dickson (eds.), *Ireland and Scotland, 1600–1850* (Edinburgh, 1983), pp.248–260

——, and Smout, T. C. (eds.), *Comparative Aspects of Scottish and Irish Economic and Social History* (Edinburgh, 1977)

Cummings, A., and Devine, T. (eds.), *Industry, Business and Society in Scotland since 1700* (Edinburgh, 1993)

Dawson, A., Jones, H., Small, A., and Soulsby, J. (eds.), *Scottish Geographical Studies* (St. Andrews, 1993)

Devine, T. M., 'Temporary migration and the Scottish Highlands in the nineteenth century', *Economic History Review* 32, 1979, pp.345–359

——, 'Highland migration to lowland Scotland, 1760–1860', *Scottish Historical Review* LXII, 1983, pp.128–142

——, (ed.), *Farm Servants and Labour in Lowland Scotland, 1770–1914* (Edinburgh, 1984)

——, *The Great Highland Famine* (Edinburgh, 1988)

——, 'The emergence of the new elite in the western Highlands and Islands, 1800–1860', in Devine (ed.), *Improvement and Enlightenment* (Edinburgh, 1989), pp.108–142

——, (ed.), *Improvement and Enlightenmant* (Edinburgh, 1989)

——, (ed.), *Irish Immigrants and Scottish Society in the Nineteenth and Twentieth Centuries* (Edinburgh, 1991)

——, *Clanship to Crofters' War: the social transformation of the Scottish Highlands* (Manchester, 1994)

——, and Dickson, D. (eds.), *Ireland and Scotland, 1600–1850* (Edinburgh, 1983)

De Vries, J., *European Urbanisation, 1500–1800* (London, 1984)

Dillon, T., 'The Irish in Leeds, 1851–1861', *Thoresby Society Miscellany* 16, 1974, pp.1–28

Dodsghon, R., *Land and Society in Early Scotland* (Oxford, 1981)

——, 'West Highland chiefdoms, 1500–1745: a study in redistributive exchange', in Mitchison and Roebuck (eds.), *Economy and Society in Scotland and Ireland, 1500–1939* (Edinburgh, 1988), pp.27–37

——, ' "Pretense of Blude" and "Place of Thair Dwelling": the nature of Scottish Clans, 1500–1745', in Houston and Whyte (eds.), *Scottish Society, 1500–1800* (Cambridge, 1989), pp.169–198

Donnachie, I., and Whatley, C. (eds.), *The Manufacture of Scottish History* (Edinburgh, 1992)

Dunlop, J., *The British Fisheries Society, 1786–1893* (Edinburgh, 1978)

Durkacz, V., 'The source of the language problem in Scottish education, 1688–1709', *Scottish Historical Review* LVII, 1978, pp.28–39

——, *The Decline of the Celtic Languages* (Edinburgh, 1983)

Engman, M., Carter, F., Hepburn, C., and Pooley, C. (eds.), *Ethnic Identity in Urban Europe* (Dartmouth, 1992)

Eyre-Todd, G., *History of Glasgow* (Glasgow, 1934)

File, N., and Power, C., *Black Settlers in Britain, 1555–1958* (London, 1981)

Fitzpatrick, D., *Oceans of Consolation: personal accounts of Irish migration to Australia* (Melbourne, 1995)

Flinn, M. *et al* (eds.), *Scottish Population Statistics* (Cambridge, 1977)

——, 'Malthus, emigration and potatoes in the Scottish north-west, 1770–1870', in Cullen and Smout (eds.), *Comparative Aspects of Scottish and Irish Economic and Social History*, pp.47–64

——, *The European Demographic System, 1500–1820* (Cambridge, 1981)

François, E. (ed.), *Immigration et société urbaine en Europe occidentale, XVIe-XXe siècles* (Paris, 1985)

Fraser, W., and Maver, I. (eds.), *Glasgow Volume II: 1830–1912* (Manchester, 1996)

——, and Morris, R.J. (eds.), *People and Society in Scotland Volume II, 1830–1914* (Edinburgh, 1990)

Fraser-Mackintosh, C., 'The Gaelic Census of the Counties of Inverness, Ross and Sutherland', *Celtic Magazine* VI, 1881, pp.438–441

Friedlander, D., and Roshier, R. (eds.), 'A study of internal migration in England and Wales', *Population Studies* 19, 1965, pp.259–279 and 20, 1966, pp.45–59

Friedmann, J., *Cultural Identity and Global Process* (London, 1994)

Gailey, R., 'Settlement and population in Kintyre, 1750–1890', *Scottish Geographical Magazine* 76, 1960, pp.99–107

——, 'Mobility of tenants on a Highland estate in the early nineteenth century', *Scottish Historical Review* XL, 1961, pp.136–145

Gammie, A., *The Churches of Aberdeen* (Aberdeen, 1909)

Gauldie, E., *The Dundee Textile Industry, 1790–1885* (Edinburgh, 1969)

Gibson, A., and Smout, T. C., *Prices, Foods and Wages in Scotland, 1550–1780* (Cambridge, 1995)

Gilbert, A., *Religion and Society in Industrial England: Churches, Chapels and Social Change, 1740–1914* (London, 1976)

Gilley, S., 'English attitudes to the Irish in England, 1798–1900', in Holmes (ed.), *Immigrants and Minorities in British Society* (London, 1978), pp.81–110

Gillies, W., 'A Century of Gaelic Scholarship', in Gillies (ed.), *Gaelic and Scotland: alba agus a'ghàidhlig* (Edinburgh, 1989), pp.3–21

——, *Gaelic and Scotland: alba agus a'ghàidhlig* (Edinburgh, 1989)

Gray, M., *The Highland Economy, 1750–1850* (Edinburgh, 1957)

——, 'Scottish emigration: the social impact of agrarian change in the rural Lowlands, 1775–1875', *Perspectives in American History* 7, 1973, pp.95–174

——, 'North-east agriculture and the labour force, 1790–1875', in MacLaren (ed.), *Social Class in Scotland, Past and Present* (Edinburgh, 1976), pp.86–104

——, *The Fishing Industries of Scotland, 1790–1914: a study in regional adaptation* (Aberdeen, 1978)

——, 'Farm workers in North-East Scotland', in Devine (ed.), *Farm Servants and Labour in Lowland Scotland, 1770–1914* (Edinburgh, 1984), pp.10–28

Grigg, D., 'E.G.Ravenstein and the "laws of migration" ', *Journal of Historical Geography* 3, 1977, pp.41–54

Haldane, A., *The Drove Roads of Scotland* (Edinburgh, 1952)

Harper, M., *Emigration from North-East Scotland* (Aberdeen, 1988)

Henderson, J., *General View of the Agriculture of the County of Sutherland* (London, 1812)

Heron, R., *Scotland Delineated* (Edinburgh, 1797)

Hill, N., *The Story of the Old West Kirk of Greenock* (Greenock, 1898)

Hindley, R., *The Death of the Irish Language* (London, 1991)

Hoerder, D., and Moch, L. (eds.), *European Migrants: new perspectives* (Boston, 1996)

Holmes, C., *Immigrants and Minorities in British Society* (London, 1978)

Houston, R., ' "Frequent Flitting": geographical mobility and social structure in mid-nineteenth century Greenlaw', *Scottish Studies* 27, 1983, pp.31–47

——, 'Geographical mobility in Scotland, 1652–1811: the evidence of testimonials', *Journal of Historical Geography* 11, 1985, pp.379–394

——, and Whyte, I. (eds.), *Scottish Society, 1500–1800* (Cambridge, 1989)

——, and Withers, C., 'Population mobility in Scotland and Europe, 1600–1900: a comparative perspective', *Annales de Demographie Historique* 1990, pp.285–308

Howatson, W., 'The Scottish hairst and seasonal labour,1600–1870', *Scottish Studies* 26, 1982, pp.13–36

Hudson, P. (ed.), *Regions and Industries* (Cambridge, 1989)

Hunter, J., *The Making of the Crofting Community* (Edinburgh, 1975)

——, *A Dance Called America* (Edinburgh, 1994)

——, *Glencoe and the Indians* (Edinburgh, 1996)

Inglis, K., *Churches and the Working Classes in Victorian England* (London, 1963)

Innes, C., *The Black Book of Taymouth* (Edinburgh, 1885)

Jackson, J., *The Irish in Britain* (London, 1963)

Jedrej, C., and Nuttall, M., *White Settlers: the Impact of Rural Repopulation in Scotland* (Luxembourg, 1996)

Johnson, C., 'Secular clergy of the Lowland District, 1732–1829', *The Innes Review* 34, 1983, pp.66–87

——, *Developments in the Roman Catholic Church in Scotland* (Edinburgh, 1983)

Johnson, S., *A Journey to the Western Isles of Scotland* (London, 1775)

Jones, G., 'The Welsh in London in the nineteenth century', *Cambria* 12, 1985, pp.149–169

Jones, H., 'Population patterns and processes from c.1600', in Whittington and Whyte (eds.), *An Historical Geography of Scotland* (London and New York, 1983), pp.93–118

——, 'Evolution of Scottish migration patterns: a social-relations-of-production approach', *Scottish Geographical Magazine* 102, 1986, pp.150–158

Kearns, G., 'Zivilis or Hygaeia: urban public health and the epidemiologic transition', in Lawton (ed.), *The Rise and Fall of Great Cities* (London, 1989), pp.17–38

——, and Withers, C. (eds.), *Urbanising Britain: essays on class and community in the nineteenth century* (Cambridge, 1991)

Kennedy, W., *Annals of Aberdeen* (Aberdeen, 1818)

King, R., Connell, J., and White, P. (eds), *Writing Across Worlds: Literature and Migration* (London, 1995)

Knowles, A., 'Immigrant trajectories through the Rural-Urban Transition in Wales and the United States, 1795–1850', *Annals, Association of American Geographers* 85, 1995, pp.246–266

Kussmaul, A., *Servants in Husbandry in Early Modern England* (Cambridge, 1981)

Kyd, J.(ed.), *Scottish Population Statistics* (Edinburgh, 1952)

Lawton, R. (ed.), *The Census and Social Structure: an interpretative guide to the nineteenth century census for England and Wales* (London, 1978)

——, (ed.), *The Rise and Fall of Great Cities* (London, 1989)

Lees, L., 'Patterns of lower-class life: Irish slum communities in nineteenth-century London', in Thernstrom and Sennett (eds.), *Nineteenth-Century Cities* (London, 1976), pp.342–361

——, *Exiles of Erin: Irish migrants in Victorian London* (Manchester, 1979)

Leneman, L., *Living in Atholl: a social history of the estates, 1685–1785* (Edinburgh, 1986)

——, (ed.), *Perspectives in Scottish Social History* (Aberdeen, 1988)

Levitt, I., and Smout, T. C., *The State of the Scottish Working-Class in 1843* (Edinburgh, 1979)

Lockhart, D., 'Patterns of migration and movement of labour to the planned villages of north-east Scotland', *Scottish Geographical Magazine* 98, 1982, pp.35–49

——, 'Migration to planned villages in Scotland between 1725 and 1850', *Scottish Geographical Magazine* 102, 1986, pp.165–180

Lorimer, G., *The Days of Neil McVicar* (Edinburgh, 1926)

Lovett, A., Whyte, I., and Whyte, K., 'Poisson regression analysis and migration fields: the example of the apprenticeship records of Edinburgh in the seventeenth and eighteenth centuries', *Transactions, Institute of British Geographers* 10, 1985, pp.317–332

Low, J. (ed), *New Statistical Account of Scotland* (Edinburgh, 1831–1845)

Lucassen, J., *Migrant Labour in Europe, 1600–1900: the drift to the North Seas* (Beckenham, 1987)

Macbean, L., *Buchanan, the Sacred Bard of the Scottish Highlands* (London, 1919)

Macdhomhnaill, T., *Murchadh Ruadh Poileasman Gaidhealach air Ghalldachd* (Motherwell, 1983)

Macdonald, D., *Scotland's Shifting Population, 1770–1850* (Glasgow, 1937)

Macdonald, I., 'The beginning of Gaelic preaching in Scotland's cities', *Northern Scotland* 9, 1989, pp.45–52

——, *Glasgow's Gaelic Churches: Highland religion in an urban setting, 1690–1995* (Edinburgh, 1995)

Macdonald, J., *General View of the Agriculture of the Hebrides* (Edinburgh, 1811)

——, 'On the agriculture of the county of Sutherland', *Transactions of the Highland and Agricultural Society of Scotland* XII, 1880, pp.1–90

Macdonald, M., 'History of the Gaelic Society of Inverness', *Transactions of the Gaelic Society of Inverness* XLVII, 1971, pp.1–25

Macdonald, S. (ed.), *Inside European Identities: ethnography in Western Europe* (Oxford, 1993)

——, *Reimagining Culture: historians, identities and the Gaelic renaissance* (Oxford, 1997)

Macdonald, W., 'On the agriculture of Inverness-shire', *Transactions of the Highland and Agricultural Society of Scotland*, IV, 1872, pp.1–65

Macdonell, M., *The Emigrant Experience: songs of Highland emigrants in North America* (Toronto, 1982)

Macdougall, I., *Hoggie's Angels: Tattie Howkers Remember* (East Linton, 1995)

Macgregor, J., *The History of St. Columba Parish* (Glasgow, 1935)

Macinnes, A., 'The impact of the civil wars and interregnum:political disruption and social change within Scottish Gaeldom', in Mitchison and Roebuck (eds.), *Economy and Society in Scotland and Ireland, 1500–1939* (Edinburgh, 1988), pp.58–69

——, 'Crown, Clan and Fine: the 'civilizing' of Scottish Gaeldom, 1587–1638', *Northern Scotland* 13, 1993, pp.31–56

Macinnes, J., *The Evangelical Movement in the Highlands of Scotland* (Aberdeen, 1951)

Macintosh, G., *Biographical Memoir of the late Charles Macintosh* (Glasgow, 1847)

Mackenzie, G., *Letters to the Proprietors of Land in Ross-shire* (Edinburgh, 1803)

——, *A General Survey of the Counties of Ross and Cromarty* (Edinburgh, 1811)

Mackinnon, K., *The Lion's Tongue* (Inverness, 1974)

——, *Gaelic in Scotland, 1971: some sociological and demographic considerations of the Census Report for Gaelic* (Hatfield, 1975)

Maclagan, D., 'Stock rearing in the Highlands, 1720–1820', *Transactions of the Royal Highland and Agricultural Society* 1958, pp.63–71

Maclaren, A. (ed.), *Social Class in Scotland, Past and Present* (Edinburgh, 1976)

Maclean, I., *The Literature of the Celts* (Glasgow, 1926)

Maclean, M., *The People of Glengarry: Highlanders in Transition, 1745–1820* (Montreal and London, 1991)

Macleod, R. (ed.), *The Book of Dunvegan, 1340–1920* (Aberdeen, 1938)

Macpherson, A., 'Migration fields in a traditional Highland community, 1350–1850', *Journal of Historical Geography* 10, 1984, pp.1–14

Macwilliam, A., 'The Glasgow Mission, 1792–1799', *The Innes Review* 4, 1953, pp.84–91

McDonald, M., 'The construction of difference: an anthropological approach to stereotypes', in MacDonald (ed.), *Inside European Identities: ethnography in Western Europe*, pp.219–236

McGregor, D., *The Necessity of Applying the Territorial System to the Gaelic Non-Church Goers of Glasgow* (Glasgow, 1860)

McKay, M., *The Rev Dr John Walker's Report on the Hebrides of 1764 and 1771* (Edinburgh, 1980)

McKerral, A., 'The tacksman and his holding in the south-west Highlands', *Scottish Historical Review* 26, 1947, pp.10–25

McLeod, H., *Class and Religion in the Late Victorian City* (Oxford, 1974)

Mannion, J. (ed), *The Peopling of Newfoundland: essays in historical geography* (St. Johns, 1977)

Mewett, P., 'Occupational pluralism in crofting: the influence of non-croft work on the patterns of crofting agriculture in the Isles of Lewis since about 1850', *Scottish Journal of Sociology* 2, 1977, pp.31–49

Meyer, D. *The Highland Scots of North Carolina* (Raleigh, CA.,1963)

Millar, J., *The Origins of the Distinction of Ranks* (London, 1779)

Mills, D., and Pearce, C., *People and Places in the Victorian Census: a review and bibliography of publications based substantially on the manuscript Census Enumerators' Books, 1841–1911* (Cheltenham, 1989)

Mitchison, R., 'Webster Revisited: a re-examination of the 1755 'census' of Scotland', in Devine (ed.), *Improvement and Enlightenment* (Edinburgh, 1989), pp.62–77

——, and Roebuck, P. (eds.), *Economy and Society in Scotland and Ireland, 1500–1939* (Edinburgh, 1988)

Moch, L., *Moving Europeans: migration in Western Europe since 1650* (Bloomington, Indiana, 1992)

Morris, R.J., 'Urbanisation and Scotland', in Fraser and Morris (eds.), *People and Society in Scotland Volume II, 1830–1914* (Edinburgh, 1990), pp.73–102

——, (ed.), *Class, Power and Social Structure in Nineteenth-Century British Cities* (Leicester, 1991)

Mowat, I., *Easter Ross, 1750–1850* (Edinburgh, 1982)

Munro, R., *Taming the Rough Bounds: Knoydart, 1745–1784* (Coll, 1984)

Murchú, M., *East Perthshire Gaelic: social history, phonology, texts and lexicon* (Dublin, 1989)

Nadel-Klein, J., 'Reweaving the fringe: localism, tradition and representation in British ethnography', *American Ethnologist* 18, 1991, pp.500–517

Nelson, M., and Rogers, J. (eds.), *Urbanisation and the Epidemiologic Transition* (Uppsala, 1989)

Newte, T., *Prospects and Observations on a Tour in England and Scotland* (London, 1791)

Nicholas, S., and Shergold, P., 'Internal migration in England, 1818–1839', *Journal of Historical Geography* 13, 1987, pp.155–168

O'Cuiv, B., *Irish Dialects and Irish-Speaking Districts* (Dublin, 1971)

O'Dowd, A., *Spalpeens and Tatti Hokers: history and folklore of the Irish migratory agricultural worker in Ireland and Britain* (Dublin, 1991)

Omand, D.(ed.), *The Ross and Cromarty Book* (Golspie, 1984)

Ommer, R., 'Highland Scots migration to southwestern Newfoundland: a study of kinship', in Mannion (ed.), *The Peopling of Newfoundland: essays in historical geography* (St. Johns, 1977), pp.212–233

——, 'Primitive accumulation and the Scottish *clann* in the old world and the new', *Journal of Historical Geography* 12, 1986, pp.121–141

Orr, W., *Deer Forests, Landlords and Crofters* (Edinburgh, 1982)

Osborne, R., 'The movements of people in Scotland, 1851–1951', *Scottish Studies* 2, 1958, pp.1–46

O'Tuathaigh, M., 'The Irish in nineteenth-century Britain: problems of integration', in Swift and Gilley (eds.), *The Irish in the Victorian City*, pp.13–28

Pennant, T., *A Tour in Scotland and the Voyages to the Hebrides* (London, 1790)

Perceval-Maxwell, M., *The Scottish Migration to Ulster in the Reign of James I* (London, 1973)

Phillipson, N., and Mitchison, R. (eds.), *Scotland in the Age of Improvement* (Edinburgh, 1970)

Pooley, C., 'Welsh migration to England in the mid-nineteenth century', *Journal of Historical Geography* 9, 1983, pp.364–382

——, and Turnbull, J., 'Long-run migration trends in British rural areas from the eighteenth to the twentieth centuries', *International Journal of Population Geography* 2, 1996, pp.12–31

——, and Whyte, I. (eds.), *Migrants, Emigrants and Immigrants: a social history of migration* (London, 1991)

Prebble, J., *The King's Jaunt: George IV in Scotland, 1822* (London, 1988)

Reid, W., and Hume, J., *Edinburgh Gaelic Chapel, 1769–1969* (Edinburgh, 1969)

Richards, E., *The Leviathan of Wealth* (London, 1973)

——, 'How tame were the Highlanders during the Clearances?', *Scottish Studies* 17, 1973, pp.35–52

——, *A History of the Highland Clearances Volume 1: Agrarian Transformation and the Evictions* (London, 1982)

——, *A History of the Highland Clearances Volume 2: Emigration, Protest, Reasons* (London, 1985)

——, 'Varieties of Scottish emigration in the nineteenth century', *Historical Studies* 21, 1985, pp.470–487

Robertson, I., 'Changing form and function of settlement in south-west Argyll, 1841–1861', *Scottish Geographical Magazine* 83, 1971, pp.29–45

Robertson, J., *General View of the Agriculture of the Southern Districts of the County of Perth* (London, 1794)

Rose, M., *Australia, Britain and Migration, 1915–1940: a study of desperate hopes* (Cambridge, 1995)

Ryder, M., 'Sheep and the Clearances in the Scottish Highlands: a biologist's view', *Agricultural History Review* 16, 1968, pp.155–168

Said, E., *Orientalism* (London, 1978)

Sanderson, M., *Scottish Rural Society in the Sixteenth Century* (Edinburgh, 1982)

Schofield, R., Reher, D., and Bideau, A.(eds.), *The Decline of Mortality in Europe* (London, 1991)

Selkirk, Earl of, *Observations on the Present State of the Highlands of Scotland with a view of the Causes and Probable Consequences of Emigration* (Edinburgh, 1806)

Shaw, F., *The Northern and Western Islands of Scotland: their economy and society in the seventeenth century* (Edinburgh, 1980)

Sime, W., *History of the Church and Parish of St. Cuthbert's or West Kirk of Edinburgh* (Edinburgh, 1829)

Sinclair, J. (ed.), *Statistical Account of Scotland* (Edinburgh, 1791–1799)

——, *Analysis of the Statistical Account of Scotland* (Edinburgh, 1826)

Singer, W., 'On the introduction of sheep farming into the Highlands; and on the plan of husbandry adopted to the soil and climate, and to the general and solid interests of that county', *Transactions of the Highland and Agricultural Society of Scotland* III, 1807, pp.536–597

Sloan, W., 'Religious affiliation and the immigrant experience: Catholic Irish and Protestant Highlanders in Glasgow, 1830–1850', in Devine (ed.), *Irish Immigrants and Scottish Society in the Nineteenth and Twentieth Centuries* (Edinburgh, 1991), pp.67–90

——, 'Employment opportunities and migrant group assimilation: the Highlanders and Irish in Glasgow, 1840–1860', in Cummings and Devine (eds.), *Industry, Business and Society in Scotland since 1700* (Edinburgh, 1993), pp.197–217

Smith, J., *General View of the Agriculture of the County of Argyle* (London, 1805)

Smith, J., 'Class, skill and sectarianism in Glasgow and Liverpool, 1880–1914', in Morris (ed.), *Class, Power and Social Structure in Nineteenth-Century British Cities* (Leicester, 1991), pp.195–234

Smout, T. C., *A History of the Scottish People, 1560–1830* (Glasgow, 1972)

——, 'Aspects of sexual behavour in nineteenth-century Scotland', in Maclaren (ed.), *Social Class in Scotland, Past and Present* (Edinburgh, 1976), pp.36–54

Southall, H., 'The tramping artisan revisits: labour mobility and economic distress in early Victorian England', *Economic History Review* 44, 1991, pp.247–294

Stevenson, D., *Alasdair MacColla and the Highland Problem in the Seventeenth Century* (Edinburgh, 1980)

Stocking, G., *Bones, Bodies, Behaviour: essays on biological anthropology* (Madison, Wisconsin, 1988)

Storrie, M., ' "They Go Much From Home": nineteenth-century Islanders of Gigha, Scotland', *Scottish Economic and Social History* 16, 1996, pp.92–115

Strang, J., *Glasgow and its Clubs* (London, 1856)

Sundin, J., and Soderland, E. (eds.), *Time, Space and Man: essays on macro-demography* (Stockholm, 1979)

Sutherland, A., *A Summer Ramble in the North Highlands* (Edinburgh, 1825)

Swift, R., and Gilley, S. (eds.), *The Irish in the Victorian City* (London, 1985)

Taylor, C., *Partick Past and Present* (Glasgow, 1902)

Thernstrom, S., and Sennett, R. (eds.), *Nineteenth-Century Cities* (London, 1976)

Tidswell, D., 'Mobility from place of birth in early nineteenth-century Scotland', in Dawson, Jones, Small, and Soulsby (eds.), *Scottish Geographical Studies* (St. Andrews, 1993), pp.112–119

Tilly, C., 'Migration in modern European history', in Sundin and Soderland (eds.), *Time, Space and Man: essays on macrodemography*, pp. 156–189

Treble, J., 'The seasonal demand for adult labour in Glasgow, 1890–1914', *Social History* 3, 1978, pp.43–60

Walker, J., *An Economical History of the Hebrides and Highlands of Scotland* (Edinburgh, 1808)

Werly, J., 'The Irish in Manchester, 1832–1849', *Irish Historical Studies* 18, 1973, pp.345–358

Whittington, G., and Whyte, I. (eds.), *An Historical Geography of Scotland* (London and New York, 1983)

Whyte, H., *Noise and Smoky Breath: an illustrated anthology of Glasgow poems, 1900–1983* (Glasgow, 1983)

Whyte, I., *Agriculture and Society in Seventeenth Century Scotland* (Edinburgh, 1979)

——, 'Protoindustrialization in Scotland', in Hudson (ed.), *Regions and Industries*, pp.228–251

——, 'Population mobility in early modern Scotland', in Houston and Whyte (eds.), *Scottish Society, 1500–1800* (Cambridge, 1989), pp.37–58

——, 'Geographical mobility in a seventeenth-century Scottish rural community', *Local Studies* 32, 1984, pp.45–53

——, 'The geographical mobility of women in early modern Scotland', in Leneman (ed.), *Perspectives in Scottish Social History* (Aberdeen, 1988), pp.83–104

——, and Whyte, K., 'Patterns of migration of apprentices into Aberdeen and

Inverness during the eighteenth and early nineteenth centuries', *Scottish Geographical Magazine* 102, 1986, pp.81–91

Williams-Davies, J., 'Merched y Gerddi: a seasonal migration of female labour from rural Wales', *Folk Life* 1979, pp.12–23

Williamson, J., 'The impact of the Irish on British labour markets during the Industrial Revolution', *Journal of Economic History* 46, 1986, pp.693–720

Withers, C., *Gaelic in Scotland, 1698–1981: the geographical history of a language* (Edinburgh, 1984)

——, 'Highland Clubs and Gaelic Chapels: Glasgow's Gaelic community in the eighteenth century', *Scottish Geographical Magazine* 101, 1985, pp.16–27

——, 'Kirk, Club and Culture Change: Gaelic chapels, Highland societies and the urban Gaelic sub-culture in eighteenth-century Scotland', *Social History,* 10, 1985, pp.171–192

——, *Highland Communities in Dundee and Perth* (Dundee, 1986)

——, 'A population observed: Gaelic speakers in Rothesay and the Isle of Bute in 1834', *Scottish Gaelic Studies* XIV, 1986, pp.102–122

——, ' "The long arm of the law"; migration of Highland-born policemen to Glasgow, 1826–1891', *Local Historian* 18, 1988, pp.127–135

——, 'Destitution and migration: labour mobility and relief from famine in Highland Scotland, 1836–1850', *Journal of Historical Geography* 14, 1988, pp.128–150

——, *Gaelic Scotland: the transformation of a culture region* (London, 1988)

——, 'On the geography and social history of Gaelic', in Gillies (ed.), *Gaelic and Scotland* (Edinburgh, 1989), pp.101–130

——, 'Highland migration to Aberdeen, c.1649–1891', *Northern Scotland* 9, 1989, pp.21–44

——, 'Gaelic speaking in urban Lowland Scotland: the evidence of the 1891 Census', *Scottish Gaelic Studies* XVI, 1990, pp.115–148

——, 'Give us Land and Plenty of it: the ideological basis to land and landscape in the Scottish Highlands', *Landscape History* 12, 1990, pp.45–54

——, 'Class, culture and migrant identity: Gaelic Highlanders in urban Scotland', in Kearns and Withers (eds.), *Urbanising Britain: essays on class and community in the nineteenth century,* pp.55–79

——, 'The historical creation of the Scottish Highlands', in Donnachie and Whatley (eds.), *The Manufacture of Scottish History* (Edinburgh, 1992), pp.143–156

——, 'Rural protest in the Highlands of Scotland and in Ireland, 1850–1930', in Connolly, Morris and Houston (eds.), *Conflict, Identity and Economic Development: Ireland and Scotland, 1600–1939,* pp.172–187

——, 'The demographic history of the city, 1831–1911', in Fraser and Maver (eds.), *Glasgow Volume II: 1830–1912* (Manchester, 1996), pp.141–162

——, and Watson, A., 'Stepwise migration and Highland migration to Glasgow, 1852–1898', *Journal of Historical Geography* 17, 1991, pp.35–55

Withrington, D., 'The SSPCK and Highland schools in the mid-eighteenth century', *Scottish Historical Review* XLI, 1962, pp.88–99

Woods, R., and Woodward, J. (eds.), *Urban Disease and Mortality in Nineteenth-Century England* (London, 1984)

Womack, P., *Improvement and Romance: constructing the myth of the Highlands* (London, 1989)

Wrigley, E. (ed.), *Nineteenth-Century Society: essays in the use of quantitative data* (Cambridge, 1972)

——, 'Urban growth and agricultural change: England and the continent in the early-modern period', *Journal of Interdisciplinary History* 15, 1985, pp.683–728

Zelinsky, W., 'The hypothesis of the mobility transition', *Geographical Review* 61, 1971, pp.219–249.

Index